BELITUNG

BELITUNG

The Afterlives of a Shipwreck

Natali Pearson

University of Hawai'i Press

Honolulu

Library of Congress Cataloging-in-Publication Data

Names: Pearson, Natali, author.

Title: Belitung : the afterlives of a shipwreck / Natali Pearson.

Other titles: Afterlives of a shipwreck

Description: Honolulu : University of Hawai'i Press, [2022] | Includes
    bibliographical references and index.

Identifiers: LCCN 2022026770 | ISBN 9780824892944 (hardback) |
    ISBN 9780824894801 (pdf) | ISBN 9780824894818 (epub) |
    ISBN 9780824894825 (kindle edition)

Subjects: LCSH: Belitung (Ship) | Treasure troves—Indonesia—Billiton Island. |
    Shipwrecks—Indonesia—Billiton Island. | Pottery, Chinese—Tang-Five
    dynasties, 618-960. | Underwater archaeology—Indonesia—Java Sea. |
    Excavations (Archaeology)—Indonesia—Billiton Island. | Cultural property—
    Protection—Indonesia—Billiton Island. | Cultural property—Protection—China. |
    Billiton Island (Indonesia)—Antiquities. | Museums—Acquisitions—Moral
    and ethical aspects.

Classification: LCC DS647.B6 P43 2022 | DDC 910.4/520959819—dc23/eng/20220928

LC record available at https://lccn.loc.gov/2022026770

    ISBN 9780824892968 (paperback)

Cover photo: Once centuries of sediment had been washed out, perfectly preserved
Changsha bowls could be seen packed tightly inside large storage jars. Photo by
Michael Flecker, 1999.

For JKP

Distancing

don't

fear

distancing

between

islands

our

ocean

will

always

connect

us

~ Craig Santos Perez

CONTENTS

ILLUSTRATIONS

Figures

Maps

PREFACE

This book was written during the coronavirus pandemic of 2020–2021. Words and phrases like "social distancing," "lockdown," and "flattening the curve" became part of our vernacular. The closure across the world of all but essential services brought into stark relief just what was needed to get by each day: health care, groceries, somewhere safe to sleep, support networks, and the internet.

It quickly became apparent that many people did not have access to these essential services and that the health crisis sweeping the planet was exacerbating already grave inequalities. Within this context, writing the story of a shipwreck felt like both an indulgence and a distraction. But something else also became clear as the pandemic played out: the importance of remembering our shared humanity. The online world came alive as historians and archaeologists shared lessons from the past, reminding us of times when people had been driven apart and when they had come together. We may have been physically isolated, but we were still connected through our technologies and our histories. The pandemic reminded us that we are all connected—that thick, invisible networks cover our planet like vibrant cobwebs, and that disruptions to these webs of connectivity affect supply chains, the sharing of information, and our ability to see our loved ones. Even as we retreated from the world, these networks affected us and connected us. They had their benefits, and also, in our reliance on them, their dangers.

Then I came across "Distancing," a poem by Craig Santos Perez, a native Chamorro from the Pacific island of Guam. In this poem, Perez reminds us of the invisible connections between islands, seemingly separated by the sea. For Perez, however, the ocean is a connective device. These connections, between islands and between people, are enduring. Perez's poem helped bring into focus the story I wanted to tell, of an ancient shipwreck and the networks it spans across time and space.

More than a thousand years since it was wrecked, the *Belitung* continues to cause ripples. It is one of the most significant shipwreck discoveries, and one of the most controversial maritime exhibitions, of recent times. As we grapple with the challenges of today, the story of the *Belitung* reminds us that sites, objects, and people—and, critically, the relationships between them—have the power to shape the stories we tell ourselves. These entanglements ripple into the present, just as our current uncertainty shapes the future. This book seeks to do justice to these complex histories, in the process serving as a reminder that no matter the apparent distance between us, we are all still, somehow, connected.

Natali Pearson
Gadigal Land, Sydney, Australia
July 24, 2021

ACKNOWLEDGMENTS

I am deeply grateful for the support I received while researching and writing this book, which draws on research I conducted for my dissertation at the University of Sydney. *Belitung: The Afterlives of a Shipwreck* brings together Southeast Asia, museums, and the ocean, and I have benefited profoundly from the guidance and mentoring I have received from my peers and colleagues in Sydney, Australia, and beyond.

I am so grateful for the support, energy, and general excellence of my colleagues at the Sydney Southeast Asia Centre—Elisabeth Kramer, Thushara Dibley, Ariane Defreine, and Minh Le. It is my great privilege to work with you all. In particular I wish to thank Michele Ford for the invaluable role she played in bringing this book to life. Under her intensive and values-based mentoring, particularly the rigors of the SSEAC Book Club, writing this book became not only achievable but, dare I say it, fun. The University of Sydney is home to a community of scholars passionate about Indonesia, heritage, and archaeology. Adrian Vickers has been a trusted advisor and colleague throughout, and he deserves the credit for introducing me to this shipwreck in the first place. Thanks also to my supervisors Chiara O'Reilly and Anna Lawrenson in Museum and Heritage Studies for their encouragement and expertise throughout my training and research. For the electrifying members of Perspectives on the Past: Michael Leadbetter, Cheng Nien Yuan, and Jarrah Sastrawan—what a stimulating interdisciplinary community we have created for ourselves. Thank you PoP for always being there. To the blue humanities scholars I've swum with, sometimes literally—especially Astrida Neimanis, Sue Reid, Killian Quigley, and Steve Mentz—thank you for letting me dip my toes into your ideas about ocean justice, bodies of water, multispecies wrecks, and more.

One of the most rewarding aspects of this project has been the opportunity to build relationships with my colleagues in Indonesia. I am particularly grateful for the support and friendship of Zainab Tahir and Nia Naelul Hasanah Ridwan, both at the Ministry of Marine Affairs and Fisheries, and Shinatria Adhityatama at Arkenas. I hope we can continue to work together for many years to come.

I am also grateful to Stephen Murphy, who oversaw the installation and curation of the Tang Shipwreck Collection at the Asian Civilisations Museum and who has been responsive and generous throughout this project. The museum itself has also been a delight to work with, and I would particularly like to thank Denisonde Simbol for facilitating copyright permissions for many of the images used in this book and Kennie Ting for the fabulous energy he has brought to the role. In America, thank you to the staff at the Asia Society Museum, especially Kelly Ma, Marion Kocot, Adriana Proser, and Elaine Merguerian. I am privileged to have been involved with the Asia Society's biennial Arts & Museum Summit since its inception under Melissa Chiu in 2013. Thanks also to Tad Bennicoff at the Smithsonian Institution, who provided archival material with such efficiency.

A number of other people provided me with "missing links"' in my research, including Geoff Wade in Canberra, Richard and Jane Wesley in Hong Kong and Sydney, and Kwa Chong Guan in Singapore. Tansen Sen, thank you for letting me join you and Pierre-Yves Manguin for dinner after the opening of *Secrets of the Sea* in New York—invitations like that don't come every day. Horst Liebner, thank you for sharing your entire Endnote library with me, and for the opportunity to browse your physical library in Makassar. Michael Flecker also played a key role in this story and this book would be poorer without his contributions and detailed comments. Thank you for giving me permission to use your beautiful images in this book and elsewhere.

Thank you to my friendly readers who provided comments on some or all of my draft manuscript: Amanda Respess for her insights into the Changsha bowls; Andrew Chittick for his work on the Chinese ceramics industry; Jean Gelman Taylor for always reminding me to think about the people who made the objects; Craig Forrest for his expertise and approachability on all things maritime and legal; Mark Staniforth for opening doors to Australia's maritime archaeology community; and Jeffrey Mellefont for his passionate interest in Indonesia's maritime histories. Tom Vosmer, I don't know how I convinced you to read the whole thing but I am so grateful that you did! Thank you for your lively anecdotes and for sharing with me your deep expertise on maritime technologies of the western Indian Ocean. Your comments helped animate the *Jewel of Muscat* for me in ways I had not anticipated. I have also benefited from the input of Marieke Bloembergen, John Miksic, and Laurajane Smith, who examined my dissertation in 2018 and provided important feedback that has informed this book. I also wish to express my gratitude to the two anonymous reviewers of this manuscript, whose responses were so considered and constructive.

Thank you Masako Ikeda, acquisitions editor at University of Hawai'i Press, for saying yes! I appreciate your professionalism and steady hand throughout the publishing process. I am also thankful for my mapmaker, cartographer Rhys Davies. I enjoyed the process of working with you to bring these maps to life. Craig Santos Perez, thank you for letting me use your beautiful poem "Distancing" in my book.

I received financial support from the Australian Government, the University of Sydney, the Sydney Southeast Asia Centre, and the Asian Studies Association of Australia. I have benefited deeply from institutional investments in Asian languages and the humanities, and it is my hope that funding cuts to these areas of research will be reversed.

I am grateful to the friends who let me stay with them on my travels: Lou and Ru in Singapore; Alex and Dean, and Karlie and Pete in Canberra; Tammie and Alex in London; and, in Hong Kong, Aasha and Patrik, Paul and Lou, and Vanessa and Richard. I apologize for keeping you up late telling you about my latest fascinating (to me) discovery. To my mum and dad, thank you for always encouraging me in the pursuit of my academic dreams. Mum, I will always remember walking around Borobudur with you on my first visit to Indonesia in 1997.

Last but not least, I have often thought about the author who dedicated his book to his wife and children by saying that, without them, it would have been finished years earlier. I thought that would be my experience too, but it has been the opposite. Without the encouragement, routine, and relief provided by my husband and daughter, I could not have finished this book. My gratitude for your patience, support, and understanding is boundless. Thank you so very much for seeing me through this, and for the sacrifices you have made. I dedicate this book to our daughter, in the hope she will take inspiration from having the privilege to do something you love.

Abbreviations

ACM	Asian Civilisations Museum (Singapore)
ACUA	Advisory Council on Underwater Archaeology
CAMM	Council of American Maritime Museums
ICMM	International Congress of Maritime Museums
ICOM	International Council of Museums
ICOMOS	International Council on Monuments and Sites
ICUCH	International Committee on the Underwater Cultural Heritage
ILA	International Law Association
IMA	Institut du Monde Arabe (Institute of the Arab World, France)
ISEAS	Institute of Southeast Asian Studies, Singapore (renamed ISEAS-Yusof Ishak Institute in 2015)
MuCEM	Musée des Civilisations de l'Europe et de la Méditerranée (Museum of European and Mediterranean Civilisations, France)
NUS	National University of Singapore
NYU	New York University
PanNas BMKT	Panitia Nasional Benda Berharga Asal Muatan Kapal yang Tenggelam (National Shipwreck Committee, Indonesia)
RMS	Royal Merchant Ship
SEAMEO-SPAFA	Southeast Asian Ministers of Education Organisation Project in Archaeology and Fine Arts
SHA	Society for Historical Archaeology
UNCLOS	United Nations Convention on the Law of the Sea
UNESCO	United Nations Educational, Scientific and Cultural Organization

Introduction

In mid-1998, as President Suharto's regime crumbled and Indonesia began the slow business of unwinding decades of authoritarian rule, local fishers revealed a startling discovery: a shipwreck, laden with ceramics, in the Java Sea. This was a ninth-century western Indian Ocean–style vessel, wrecked in waters near Belitung Island with a cargo of more than sixty thousand Tang dynasty ceramics. Subsequent analysis of the vessel's materials and construction techniques suggested it originated in modern-day Oman or Yemen, where its timber planks had been sewn together with twine and sealed with animal fat. The huge quantities of Chinese cargo, probably destined for the Middle Eastern market, testified to a commercial endeavor on a global scale. The vessel and its cargo are unique in the annals of maritime archaeology for what they reveal about early trade networks and the centrality of the ocean within the Silk Road story.

Shipwrecks are anchored in the public imagination, their stories of treasure and tragedy told and retold in museums, cinema, and song. At the same time, they are sites of scholarly inquiry, a means by which maritime archaeologists interrogate the past through a scientific examination of its material remains. Every shipwreck is an accidental time capsule, replete with the sunken stories of those on board, of the personal and commercial objects that went down with the vessel, and of an unfinished journey. But this shipwreck also has a modern tale to tell, about how nation-states appropriate the remnants of the past for their own uses in the present, and of how the transnational qualities of shipwrecks position them as critical considerations in international debates about who owns—and is responsible for—shared heritage.

The Indonesian fishers brought their discovery to the attention of a licensed maritime salvage company based on Belitung Island. As was then required under Indonesian law, the company obtained a permit to recover the objects from the seabed. After years of desalination and conservation, the assemblage was sold by the salvage company to Singapore for US$32 million. There, the objects are on permanent display at the Asian Civilisations Museum, where they attest to the role, however tenuous, of Singapore within this ancient trade and exchange network. But the commercial nature of the salvage contravened the principles of the 2001 United Nations Educational, Scientific and Cultural Organization (UNESCO) Convention on the Protection of the Underwater Cultural Heritage, prompting widespread international condemnation. Major museums around the world have refused to host international traveling exhibitions of the collection, and some maritime archaeologists have declared they would rather see the objects thrown back in the sea than ever go on display. In a retrospective imposition of international norms suggestive of neocolonialism, much of the controversy involved Western institutions leveling their criticism at Indonesia and Singapore.

Transformed from submerged site to permanent museum display, this shipwreck and its commercially salvaged cargo have come to represent some of the most contested and controversial terrains in the display of underwater cultural heritage. The *Belitung* subverts the UNESCO model, which preferences *in situ* preservation as a first option and firmly opposes any form of commercial exploitation.[1] The shipwreck was not managed the way it should have been *and yet* we have a largely intact assemblage of salvaged, conserved, and displayed objects that can be accessed by the public and by scholars. Did the end, in this case, justify the means?

Tracing the afterlives of this vessel helps make sense of this paradox. Its first incarnation was as a seafaring vessel over a thousand years ago, transporting people and objects across vast distances. This voyage was interrupted by the wrecking event, in which ship, cargo, and possibly even lives were lost. So began the first of its afterlives, submerged and hidden beneath the water. Its second afterlife started with the wreck's discovery in the 1990s, in which people, place, and object came into contact at a reef where jars were said to grow. From here, the afterlives of the vessel and its objects began to take different trajectories as they diverged across multiple storylines. These new connections—informed by institutional and nationalistic ownership models—reveal the influences that have shaped the management, preservation, and interpretation of this particular shipwreck, and in turn shed light on the management of underwater cultural heritage more broadly.[2]

Known at various times as the *Batu Hitam* (Black Rock), the *Belitung*, and later, in Singapore, as the *Tang*, the different names given to the wreck are an indication of the diversity of private and public claims at stake. By mapping these turning points, influences, and legacies, this book reveals that the power to attribute meaning to underwater sites and objects is primarily a function of ownership. It is in these insights into the personal and political uses of heritage that the benefits of a critical approach to underwater cultural heritage become apparent. Although the story of this shipwreck poses a threat to established institutional approaches, it also presents new ways of thinking about what protection and preservation mean in an underwater context.

Toward a Critical Heritage Approach

The *Belitung* is one of an estimated three million ancient shipwrecks worldwide, making underwater cultural heritage a rich area of inquiry for maritime archaeologists. Unlike terrestrial heritage, however, underwater cultural heritage usually requires specialist diving equipment and skills to access. Whereas a temple can—theoretically, at least—be visited by anyone, a shipwreck is out of reach by sheer virtue of its inaccessibility. Shipwrecks loom large in the public imagination not despite this inaccessibility, but because of it.

Hidden beneath the waves, shipwrecks are both sites for scholarly research and places for the projection of romantic and treasure-fueled imaginings. At the same time, new technologies are enabling their discovery at an unprecedented rate. Around the world, underwater cultural heritage is under threat of damage and destruction—from environmental degradation, from the devastating effects of fishing trawlers, from opportunistic looters and industrial-scale salvagers. Should we think of these shipwrecks as an archaeological resource, or as an economic one? Should we leave them *in situ* and out of sight, or bring them to the surface at any cost? Are we to reify them, or use them as fodder for popular culture? The binary values ascribed to shipwrecks have contributed to their loss and destruction, not their preservation. The absence of a considered and nuanced approach—a *critical* approach—to how underwater cultural heritage is valued has real consequences for how such heritage is managed.

How should the mysteries of the deep be defined, and by and for whom? Instead of thinking about shipwrecks as sites of scientific inquiry or as inspiration for a blockbuster movie, are there other ways in which we can understand "value" as it relates to shipwrecks? What changes, for example, if we think of shipwrecks as embedded within a social landscape or as part of a network of connections stretching across time and space? This book calls for a new approach to underwater cultural heritage, one that responds to these increasingly common dilemmas and accounts for the major developments that have occurred in heritage studies in recent decades. Such developments have seen a shift in the understanding of value in a heritage context from something that is inherent to something that is ascribed. Heritage is not a given—it is constructed by local, national, and international actors. It is not about sites that need to be protected or objects that need to be conserved.[3] Rather, heritage is a process of cultural production, "framed by particular discourses, which engages in negotiations over the meaning and values of the past in terms of present day needs and aspirations."[4]

Heritage has long shaped, and been shaped by, power. What constitutes heritage—how it is defined, managed, and interpreted—has been determined by nationalism, colonialism, cultural elitism, and Eurocentrism. The UNESCO model, which seeks to map, inscribe, and preserve heritage, is central to this authorized heritage discourse.[5] This model is underpinned by what Holtorf describes as the "conservation paradigm," which prioritizes loss aversion without questioning what is being preserved, why, and for whom.[6] Through its world heritage conventions, UNESCO has informed our understanding of what constitutes heritage (and what does not) by favoring certain geographies, typologies, religions, chronologies, and classes.[7] In the process, it has been all too easy to overlook heritage that does not fit this model.

In recent years, scholars have begun to disrupt this discourse by challenging the foundations of privilege upon which it is based. The burgeoning critical heritage studies movement is characterized by interdisciplinarity and inclusiveness, with a focus on heritage that has been marginalized and excluded by traditional scholarly approaches and on the political and economic imperatives that mobilize it.[8] Bloembergen and Eickhoff, for example, have argued that applying a critical lens to the process of heritage formation in colonial and postcolonial Indonesia reveals the vested interests of the state in creating and commodifying archaeological sites such as Borobudur for political and commercial purposes.[9] In privileging contemporary political imperatives rather than solely the colonial past, their assessment aligns with Legêne, Purwanto, and Nordholt's warning against "colonial determinism."[10]

This is not to suggest that critical heritage studies implies a uniform approach. Some critical heritage scholars point to the substantial scholarly value of tracing the complex interactions that inform heritage formation, which frequently point to the influence of former colonial powers.[11] Others emphasize the relationship between heritage and the "critical" issues with which it is increasingly enmeshed, such as poverty and inequality, climate change, sustainability, human rights, democracy, and the future of the state.[12] These different understandings of "critical" can and do sit alongside each other.

This critical lens has been productively applied to terrestrial heritage, enabling a shift beyond the idea of heritage as primarily object- or site-based to include intangible forms of heritage. But underwater cultural heritage has been largely ignored in discussions about the uses of the past. Technological advances might have made underwater sites more accessible, but conceptual and theoretical developments in critical heritage studies have had limited impact on our understanding of the political, social—and cultural—uses of underwater cultural heritage. Instead, the tropes of treasure and tragedy continue to dominate the mysteries of the deep.

This book develops a critical approach to how we define, invoke, and appropriate underwater cultural heritage. It explores the ways that power relations shape, and are shaped by, underwater sites and objects. By extending critical heritage studies from the terrestrial to the underwater, the discussion that follows provides ballast to ongoing debates about the deployment of the past as a method for staking a claim to narratives about the present and the future.[13] In so doing, it contributes to debates about the politics of representation and the role of the nation-state in heritage production, including that which lies underwater. It also allows us to attend to those who have been marginalized in the *Belitung*'s story—the coastal communities who used the wreck as a source of fish; the skilled shipbuilders who worked timber and fiber into an oceangoing vessel; the prolific ceramicists who produced the objects; the well-connected merchants who bought and sold them; the people for whom the cargo was destined—thereby creating space for a more inclusive consideration of underwater cultural heritage. In this regard, it engages with a critical approach on multiple levels.

Ancient ships, and the wrecks they become, travel across generations and geographies. They are not only transnational but pre-national, predating the formation of the very power structures that claim these submerged objects and stories for their own purposes. Such complexities demand a more nuanced approach than the dominant discourse permits—one that disrupts national ownership models and foregrounds not only the archaeological but also the social context of the site and objects. Underwater cultural heritage is, as UNESCO suggests, part of humanity's shared heritage—but it demands a critical approach if its stories are to be told.

The Role of the Museum

The lure of the deep is powerful. Shipwrecks are, as Rodley says, "natural subjects for exhibitions. They come with a built-in narrative. The human history and the drama inherent in the loss of a ship, her crew and passengers, makes these sites natural vehicles for telling compelling stories."[14] But it is only in the last century that museums have had the opportunity to acquire and exhibit objects recovered from submerged sites.

Multiple attempts were made, for example, to recover the *Mary Rose* from the bottom of the Solent following its sinking in 1545. It was not until 1982 that the hull was finally raised, an event so spectacular that it was broadcast live to a worldwide audience of over sixty million people. The famed warship, said to be King Henry VIII's favorite, was meticulously excavated and conserved before going on display at the Mary Rose Museum in Portsmouth's historic naval dock-yard. The exhibit was a finalist at the 2018 European Museum of the Year awards, where it was described as being "close to perfection" and an "exceptional achievement" through its use of ship, people, and objects to tell a compelling story.[15] But this was one of the most expensive and complicated maritime excavations in history. And, although the Mary Rose Museum opened in 1984, the conservation and display were not finalized until 2016 when it reopened after a major renovation. The national heritage authority has indicated there is unlikely to be another excavation of this magnitude in England, instead suggesting that virtual reality will replace material culture as the primary means by which audiences can engage with shipwrecks.

A more recent and equally impressive example is that of China's Nanhai One shipwreck, on display at the purpose-built Maritime Silk Route Museum.[16] This is a Southern Song dynasty (1127–1279) wreck that was discovered in 1987 near Hailing Island. In a remarkable feat of engineering, the entire wreck (including the estimated sixty to eighty thousand objects that make up its cargo) was recovered from the seabed and is being excavated inside the museum behind clear plastic walls and within sight of the viewing public. This spectacular archaeological experience encourages visitors to engage closely with both the objects and the methods of excavation and conservation, and has been lauded by UNESCO. The shipwreck itself is centered within the museum, both literally and figuratively, with rich context added through dioramas, displays, and even a cinema in which footage of the excavation can be viewed.

These examples show the key role that museums can play as interlocutors between those who can access the deep and those who cannot. Museums collect, conserve, and research objects recovered from the ocean, display and interpret them to the public, and make them available for scholars and researchers. They are safekeepers, custodians, "contact zones," where the museum-going public can encounter otherwise-inaccessible objects.[17] This intermediary role is critical but also problematic for museums for three reasons, the first of which relates to objects. While virtual reality creates opportunities for creative storytelling and meaning-making, most museums still rely on material culture—on objects—for their exhibitions and displays. But the international standards articulated by UNESCO preference shipwrecks and their associated relics remaining in the ocean. And, as the case of the *Mary Rose* demonstrates, some governments are losing their appetite for cost- and labor-intensive maritime excavations.[18] At the same time, the activities of opportunistic fishers, commercial salvagers, and illicit looters mean that underwater cultural heritage that has *not* been scientifically excavated is coming to the surface at rates never before seen.[19] Looking forward, these competing models will exacerbate the already existing tensions between a museum's role as an educator and its ethical responsibilities to display objects with established provenance.[20]

The second issue relates to people, specifically the museum-going public. The prevalence—and glamorization—of narratives about plundering pirates and sunken treasure in many shipwreck exhibitions indicates that museums are struggling to marry education and entertainment when it comes to exhibiting underwater cultural heritage. As Rodley cautions, the temptation to feed "an uncritical, naïve public appetite for shipwrecks, pirates and tragedy" without also providing an opportunity to learn about issues relating to the provenance of the objects on display "does a disservice to the public's understanding of the importance of archaeology."[21] So is education, as it relates to underwater cultural heritage, about conveying quantitative information—the details of the ship, its passengers and cargo, and the circumstances of its sinking—or the historical context of maritime trade and war? Is it about teaching audiences (to quote one visitor) that "many people died on this ship"?[22] Or is it about encouraging critical reflection on broader questions, such as the moral implications of salvaging objects from an underwater grave? At stake here is whether it is possible for an exhibition to be both affectively and critically engaging, or whether the immersive visitor experience is disrupted by the incursion of these broader ethical considerations.

The third issue is that of the museum itself. Intermediaries are not neutral, and neither are museums. As trusted public institutions designed to inculcate social values, museums possess significant potential to act as agents of diplomacy, advocacy, and justice.[23] The funding model of most public museums has placed them in a position whereby they are subject to both the strategic priorities of their funding bodies and scrutiny by the taxpaying public, while at the same time needing to generate their own revenue—often through blockbuster exhibitions, ambitious expansion projects, or by becoming venues for hire—to cover the shortfall. In an increasingly crowded cultural sector, they run the risk of being reduced to an "edutainment" role, generating "content" to attract "audiences."[24] Despite the friction created by these competing priorities, museums continue to be advocates for cultural heritage, in the process becoming implicated in international debates about the relationship between heritage, diplomacy, global governance, and the nation-state.[25]

In responding to these challenges, Rodley places the onus on museums to be "more thoughtful and deliberate consumers" that embrace their potential "as safe venues for exploring ethical issues these sites embody."[26] Here, Rodley draws on the idea of the museum as a safe place for unsafe ideas.[27] Others have resisted the notion that museums are safe, let alone neutral, arguing that their white walls belie the power structures behind them.[28] Many museums bear the weight of their history as colonial collecting institutions, and remain unable or unwilling to interrogate the unprovenanced objects in their collections.[29] However, recent controversies over historical statues have drawn attention to the need to decolonize the museum, including through repatriation and restitution. These debates have spilled beyond the museum walls and into the public discourse, indicating both the influence and the necessity of these cultural institutions. As a result, museums are now undergoing a process of transformation as spaces that both embrace and challenge their audiences, as well as institutions that project into society.

Despite this complexity, or perhaps because of it, museums remain trusted institutions, and, in an increasingly divided world, one of the few public spaces where people can encounter alternative views and engage in debate about critical issues. They are also safekeeping places with an eye to the future. In a world of deepfakes and hate speech, such spaces are vital. The decisions they make about how and what to display—and about what is left out—implicate them in global conversations about truth, justice, sustainability, and equality. As such, they bear a heavy responsibility not only to their funding bodies or to the objects in their collections, but to the diverse individuals and communities they serve. These elements must be essential considerations in our understanding of museums as interlocutors between the ocean and the land.

The role of interlocutor places museums at the forefront of debates about provenance and the production and commodification of heritage. What emerges is a need for museums to occupy a much-needed middle ground regarding the exploitation, ownership, and interpretation of contested heritage. These issues coalesced in the controversy surrounding the exhibition of world's best-known shipwreck. *Titanic: The Artifact Exhibition* opened at the National Maritime Museum in Greenwich, London, in October 1994. On display were objects recovered by a private corporation from this famous—and famously inaccessible, due to its depth some 12,500 feet (3,800 meters) below the surface—wreck. The exhibition epitomized the "shipwreck as romantic tragedy" theme and was the first iteration of what would become a decades-long, and hugely popular, touring exhibition. But as one of the world's principal maritime museums, the museum was bound by ethical guidelines and standards that prohibited the exhibition of commercially salvaged underwater material. Its actions were widely criticized by maritime archaeologists, with many finding it hard to reconcile the museum's ethical commitments with its display of objects that had been salvaged for profit.[30] There was a sense that, in doing so, the museum had lent legitimacy to the objects and, by association, the methods by which they had been recovered.[31]

The exhibition thus became much more than the story of how the world's largest ship sank on its maiden voyage: it came to symbolize the tension between a museum's need to attract audiences and its ethical responsibilities to protect and preserve underwater cultural heritage. At the heart of this tension was the question of value—how it was ascribed, how it was prioritized, and how the conflict between archaeological, economic, and cultural values was managed. Maritime archaeologist Jeremy Green describes this as a "museological dilemma," whereby museums are "interested in 'block-buster' exhibitions and getting people through the door" while at the same time trying to avoid being associated with "material that has been recovered by treasure-hunters (in a non-archaeological manner)."[32]

This dilemma is framed on one side by revenue, and on the other by ethics, premised on the notion that the role of a museum in protecting and preserving underwater cultural heritage is to exhibit only those objects that have been excavated using established archaeological principles. To do otherwise would be to legitimize and encourage commercial salvage and, by extension, treasure hunting. These principles are spelled out in the 2001 UNESCO Convention, and are embedded in the codes, policies, and charters of professional associations and their members.[33] Although the wording differs, these documents are united in their opposition to the commercial exploitation of heritage objects and to the display of such objects, which they argue lends legitimacy to the means by which they have been recovered. Inherent in these standards is the notion of shared heritage, and the responsibility of all states to protect and preserve this shared heritage.[34]

For museums, the choice is stark: display the objects and condone commercial salvage—and by implication treasure hunting—or demonstrate a commitment to protecting and preserving underwater cultural heritage by declining to display the objects. But this dichotomy is false. The real dilemma lies in the choice between two ideologies that go to the very core of what it means to be a museum: their ethical responsibilities to establish provenance, and their educational responsibilities to the public. For, while the International Council of Museums (ICOM) Code of Ethics precludes the display of objects of "questionable origin," it also allows museums to make exceptions for unprovenanced objects that "may have such an inherently outstanding contribution to knowledge that it would be in the public interest to preserve it."[35] When it comes to exhibiting underwater cultural heritage, then, the real museological dilemma is not whether or not to exhibit, but how to do so ethically. It is this question that the *Belitung* has compelled museums to confront.

Materiality as an Analytical Lens

Central to an ethical exhibition of underwater cultural heritage is what Harrison describes as a dialogic approach to heritage.[36] In this model, heritage is understood as emerging from relationships between people, place, practices, and objects. It places material culture on an equal footing with other actors, thereby acknowledging the way in which heritage can affect certain actions or interactions. As they are disturbed, recovered, traded, and displayed, sites and objects become imbued with new values and are appropriated for new purposes by a diverse range of actors. But sites and objects are also actors within this network of social connections, and are shaping just as much as they are being shaped.

To operationalize this dialogic approach to heritage, I build on a concept developed by Cherry, who suggests that monuments can be "re-modelled, re-used, re-sited, re-made, cast aside, destroyed or abandoned to accommodate changing political and social climates."[37] They survive "through re-invention and transformations," accruing and accumulating afterlives as they are materially altered, represented, replicated, and interpreted. Through these afterlives, monuments—and objects—become mobile, and more readily appropriated. Cherry's ideas about the afterlife of material culture resonate with calls for museums to emphasize the "biography" of objects as a way of untangling their histories and meanings.[38] Similar ideas about not viewing material culture in isolation from the networks that have created and used it have also emerged in the field of archaeology.[39] There is, increasingly, a need to acknowledge "the way human and object histories inform each other."[40] Humans are involved not only in the production, exchange, and consumption of objects but also in their recovery, commodification, and interpretation. Such histories and interventions are inseparable from the object itself. As they are removed, replicated, or displayed, the stories of objects are no longer solely entwined with those of the monument or sites from which they originate—they become imbued with new histories of their own.[41]

Such entanglements become yet more complex when the heritage in question is a shipwreck. This is because most ships, being fundamentally transnational in nature, are often not wrecked in their "region of origin or among the people of whose cultural patrimony they properly belong."[42] Untangling the issue of ownership is complicated by the question of how "origin" is understood—whether it is where the vessel was constructed, where the cargo came from, where the vessel sank, or indeed some other understanding. Since its discovery and recovery, the transnational nature of the *Belitung*—constructed, possibly, in Oman or Yemen, carrying a mostly Chinese cargo, and lost in Indonesian waters—has seen aspects of its story appropriated by various nation-states for different purposes. But the political entities of the past are unlikely to correspond with the modern nation-states that have inherited their territory—or their material legacy—thus confounding who might lay claim to an ancient wreck and on what grounds. As Tan explains:

> Considering that the concept of the nation-state is a relatively recent invention, claims to shipwrecks based on their location in "territorial" waters [are] rather insufficient, especially since some of these shipwrecks predate the nation-state. Much of modern Southeast Asia's boundaries, in fact, are a product of European colonization and thus seems inadequate as a basis to lay claim to ancient shipwrecks.[43]

A dialogic approach, which foregrounds the social connections of the ship and its objects, has profound implications for how shipwrecks are characterized in both the popular and the scholarly imagination. Positioning material culture within a network of connections that goes beyond modern understandings of ownership allows us to tease out the broader social, political, cultural, and even environmental value of shipwrecks. This, in turn, makes it possible to account for the many ways underwater heritage sites and objects change and are changed depending on where they are, who they are with, and how and why they are being used.

The biography of an object can be understood in multiple parts: its creation, and all that entails; the process by which it enters the museum, including the circumstances by which it came to be in the public domain or in a private collection; and, finally, the relationship between the object and those who encounter it. At each stage, an object can retain a vestige of its previous incarnation: a coral encrustation attesting to time spent underwater, the memory of being touched in an exhibition, a controversy of titanic proportions. From the moment the first object was discovered in the waters around Belitung Island, it was no longer possible to talk about the site or the objects without accounting for the diversity of their experiences. These entanglements have indelibly informed the biography of the objects in question. Moreover, with the passing of time, these entanglements have become increasingly complex. The salvaged objects have traveled around the world for research, conservation, and marketing; some have done so legally, and others have not. Some objects looted from the site have been reunited with the assemblage, while others remain separated. Unknown numbers of objects are in private collections, having been stolen from the site and sold. The hull has been destroyed by looters, but a reimagined version of it lives on in a replica vessel, the *Jewel of Muscat*, constructed in Oman and sailed to Singapore to celebrate the anniversary of bilateral ties.

In this book, I suggest that a judicious and carefully executed decision by a museum to exhibit commercially salvaged underwater cultural heritage can contribute to the protection and preservation of this heritage. This suggestion is not made lightly. I recognize that it could be seen by some as condoning commercial salvage and, by implication, treasure hunting. But it is not the display of problematic underwater cultural heritage per se that legitimizes the exploitation of underwater cultural heritage—it is the failure to encourage critical reflection about the ethical issues associated with the recovery and display of objects from submerged sites. An understanding of the entangled afterlives of these objects is, I propose, central to this critical reflection.

Many museums are still coming to terms with how to manage and display difficult heritage, including commercially salvaged underwater cultural heritage, in a way that ensures they can meet both their educational and their ethical responsibilities. This involves consideration not only of where the objects came from, but how they came to be in the museum and the changes that take place within the museum context. To do this, museums must risk being brave.[44] Establishing the biographies of objects recovered from the deep allows museums to move beyond the common tropes of treasure and tragedy and to instead display these objects in a way that encourages critical reflection about issues relating to the protection and preservation of underwater cultural heritage. Accounting for the diversity of a shipwreck's afterlives by situating it within broad networks that straddle time and space allows for new perspectives, alternative interpretations, and greater public engagement and access. As agents for social action and change, museums are fundamentally implicated in this process.[45]

Outline of the Book

The following chapters untangle the multiple threads of the *Belitung's* story, demonstrating how establishing the biography of the wreck and its objects can be used to develop a critical approach to underwater cultural heritage. Chapter 1 begins by examining its original incarnation as a seafaring vessel engaged in trade across the Indian Ocean and into Southeast Asia and China. This vessel is significant because it sailed the Maritime Silk Road, offering unprecedented insights into the exchange of ideas, goods, and people. This was a connected world. Built in a western Indian Ocean style, the vessel traveled across that ocean and through Southeast Asian waters to collect its precious cargo of Chinese ceramics and other objects. This chapter also examines the objects themselves, contextualizing them within a broader commercial enterprise. Finally, it considers the people of the *Belitung*, both at sea and on land. The vessel, its crew, and its cargo shed new light

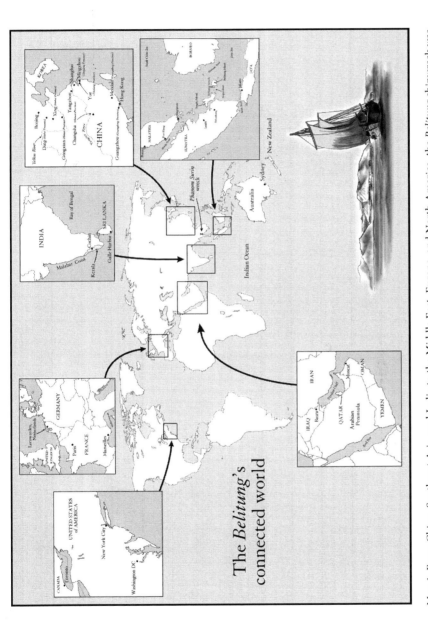

Map 1. From China, Southeast Asia, and India to the Middle East, Europe, and North America, the *Belitung* shipwreck was, and remains, part of a connected world. This map traces where the vessel may have been built and traveled to, where its cargo was made and may have been intended for, the ports it may have visited, and the museums in which its objects were to be, or have been, displayed. It also depicts key locations from the *Jewel of Muscat*'s story.

on production and manufacturing networks within China and the logistics of how orders were placed and filled across the Indian Ocean.

Chapter 2 traces the first afterlife of the *Belitung* from the moment of its wrecking off the east coast of Sumatra in the early 800s to the point of its discovery in the 1990s. Precisely why the *Belitung* sank is unknown. Seafarers planned their trade around the annual monsoon cycle, and it may be that the *Belitung* simply began its outgoing journey too late to avoid dangerous monsoonal storms. The presence of reefs near the wreck site may also provide some explanation. However, scholars remain divided on why the ship was so far south, and there is unlikely to ever be a definitive answer as to why the ship sank where it did. From a practical and legal perspective, the wreck sits in what would become Indonesian territory. The chapter outlines Indonesia's complex political and regulatory environment, including the evolution of legislation that permitted the commercial recovery of valuable objects from shipwrecks such as the *Bakau* and the *Intan*, but also required that a percentage of the realized commercial value of the salvaged objects be given to the Indonesian government. It concludes by orienting the reader to Belitung Island in the late 1990s at the moment when the wreck was discovered.

Chapter 3 then examines the process by which the *Belitung* was salvaged between 1998 and 1999 and subsequently sold. Having been out of sight and effectively out of mind for some eleven hundred years, it was at this point that the site, the ship, and its objects again began to accumulate histories, meaning, and significance through the events and, just as importantly, the people they encountered. The chapter reveals the political maneuvering and legislative ambiguities that led to the fate of the *Belitung* cargo being forever tied to that of the *Intan* shipwreck, salvaged in 1997. It sheds light on the objects' post-discovery afterlives—traveling to New Zealand for conservation, to Germany for appraisal, to China and the United Kingdom for marketing—thus reinforcing the notion that these objects move in time and space, and have histories and biographies of their own. As successful purchaser of the objects, Singapore has played a key role in shaping the story of the *Belitung*, including retrospectively as it positions itself as central to Southeast Asian maritime histories. In telling these entangled stories, this chapter necessarily focuses on the effect of political deliberations and equivocations on the display and interpretation of the objects in museums. The chapter concludes with Singapore in possession of the objects, poised to make a decision on their future display.

Chapter 4 examines the competing claims made about the *Belitung*. It does so by examining the major international travelling exhibition, *Shipwrecked: Tang Treasures and Monsoon Winds*, which precipitated international controversy. It interrogates the reasons for, and consequences of, the decision by the Smithsonian Institution to cancel its planned exhibition of *Shipwrecked* just months before it was due to open in response to criticism from individual archaeologists, mobilized though professional associations, about the commercial nature of the salvage. The Smithsonian Institution announced that not only was it canceling the exhibition but also that it intended to re-excavate the wreck site to reveal context that was initially lost or ignored. This decision betrayed considerable arrogance and a fundamental lack of understanding about the Southeast Asian context, including the fact that Indonesian archaeologists had already revisited and surveyed the site in 2010. Criticism about the salvage company, specifically its failure to recover the hull, also demonstrated a lack of understanding about the terms under which Indonesia had issued the salvage permit in 1998. Contrary to popular opinion, the salvage company had not left the hull *in situ* because it had no market value: in fact, they had been required to do so by the terms of their permit. The chapter then identifies how different nations—most notably Oman, through the *Jewel of Muscat* project—sought to claim a piece of the *Belitung*'s story for their own, effectively marginalizing the origin claims of other countries.

Chapter 5 charts how Singapore was able to overcome the controversy and ensure the collection continued to be exhibited.[46] The first step, just months after the Smithsonian cancellation was announced, was to mount a small, temporary exhibition in January 2012 that allowed visitors to touch some of the objects. In November 2015 thousands of the objects were installed in a permanent exhibition in a public museum, and smaller traveling exhibitions continue to be shown internationally. Although each iteration has been different, these exhibitions have effectively legitimized the objects as museum exhibits, with the cumulative effect of embedding the objects within a museological context. Each iteration has underscored Singapore's efforts to give historical credence to a position that is crucial to that country's self-image as "a global maritime entrepôt, and the lodestone on which Southeast Asia turns."[47] In so doing, Singapore has perpetrated its own form of neocolonialism within Southeast Asia.

The book concludes by identifying the benefits and challenges of bringing a critical heritage studies approach to the *Belitung* and to the study of underwater cultural heritage more broadly. Contextualizing the lives and afterlives of this shipwreck within a critical heritage framework reveals not only the multiplicity of its encounters with people, places, and ideologies, but also the consequences of these encounters. By recognizing the affective nature of the shipwreck both as imagined site and as tangible heritage, and the agency of the relics it carried, it becomes possible to acknowledge the romance of the shipwreck while also providing alternative, and more sustainable, ways for heritage consumers to engage with underwater sites and objects. In so doing, this book disrupts the received wisdom of the museological dilemma by reappraising what is understood by protection and preservation of underwater cultural heritage in a museum context. Instead of limiting what museums can exhibit to virtual reality or objects that have been painstakingly excavated, this book dares to ask whether protection and preservation in an underwater context might, in fact, mean revealing the stories of the deep to the public in all their conflicted, controversial glory.

CHAPTER ONE

Created

The *Belitung* shipwreck has come to symbolize contested heritage, taking its place alongside other controversial exhibitions that reflect the complex terrain that museums increasingly negotiate. Although the clamor has diminished over time, the *Belitung* is still regularly cited by UNESCO as the exemplar of the problems associated with commercial salvage. For-profit operations are no better than treasure hunting, contends UNESCO, for the way in which they prioritize economic rather than historical and archaeological value. Vital context is lost in the rush to monetize a shipwreck, and future research opportunities are destroyed as assemblages are dispersed on the open market. For a museum to display such material is, therefore, to condone the method by which it was recovered.

Long before it became shorthand for controversy, however, the *Belitung* was a vessel transporting people and objects across the ocean. This was the first incarnation of the *Belitung*, and it is here that the story of this shipwreck begins. Much of our knowledge of this first life is tentative. But there is one thing about which we can be certain: when this ship first sailed, sometime in the second quarter of the ninth century, it was not known as the *Belitung*. Throughout this chapter—and, indeed, the rest of this book—it is important to keep in mind that the names we use to describe this vessel reflect our contemporary geocultural context. Calling this vessel the *Belitung*, as I have chosen to, rather than the *Tang*, as it is officially known, positions Southeast Asia, specifically Indonesia, within broader narratives about the Maritime Ceramic Route. This is an intentional choice, designed to acknowledge and even problematize the Sino-centric discourse associated with the Maritime Ceramic Route (and its terrestrial equivalent, the Silk Road) and its modern successor, China's Belt and Road Initiative.[1]

This question of nomenclature brings us to a bigger issue: How does one determine the identity of an ancient ship? Should we look to where the vessel was constructed, or where the timber grew? Is the shape of the hull a more useful guide, or perhaps the anchor? Or should we be attending to the attribution of the artifacts it carried—in which case, does the domestic assemblage determine the affiliation of a ship?[2] Or should we look to the cargo as a useful indicator of, if not affiliation, then ownership? Although definitive answers remain elusive, the act of asking these questions in itself reveals the multiple identities that coexist within a single vessel.[3] The plurality of these identities is further complicated by the transnational nature of seafaring, characterized as it is by fluidity and mobility, and the futility of attempting to apply modern perspectives, in which the nation-state dominates, to the ancient past. To tell the story of the *Belitung*, therefore, is to begin not in China where its cargo originated, or even in Southeast Asia where it was found. The story is far more complicated than that.

There are multiple threads to consider in piecing it together. The first is that of the vessel itself: an engineering marvel capable of traversing the ocean's waves, harnessing the monsoon winds, and transporting staggering quantities of goods. Then, of course, there are the objects themselves, the material manifestations of ancient, global conversations about form and function. There are also the people: not just those who traveled on board—its diverse crew and, possibly, passengers— but those involved in building the vessel, commissioning the objects, and the many other, often unacknowledged, activities required to put this cargo-carrying vessel to sea. Together, these components—the vessel, its objects, and its people—constitute what we now call the *Belitung* shipwreck. What becomes apparent, in attempting to untangle these threads, is the diversity of endeavors that coalesced to bring about this particular vessel, and how these contributed to the creation of a window into the past that is both accidental and entirely unique.

The Vessel

It is not easy to determine with precision the identity, so to speak, of a ninth-century timber vessel that has lain submerged in saltwater for some twelve hundred years. Analysis of the *Belitung*'s remains indicated its planks had been fastened together not with wooden dowels or iron fastenings (as were common in the boatbuilding traditions of Southeast Asia and China, respectively), but with cordage sewn over thick wadding both inside and outside the hull.[4] The *Belitung* had been, quite literally, stitched together, making it the first sewn-plank vessel to be discovered in the greater Indian Ocean. Certain elements of the vessel's form—such as the structure of the joinery of the through-beams to the planking, and the stitching of these beams to the hull—are identical to western Indian Ocean traditions seen on contemporary Omani fishing craft, suggesting continuity in boatbuilding traditions over many centuries.[5] Parallels could also be seen between the *Belitung*'s stitching and hull form, and those depicted in the iconic thirteenth-century painting of an Arab ship in the *Maqamat al-Hariri* (Arabic literary tales). Considered together with this ethnographic and iconographic evidence, the vessel's construction techniques suggested the *Belitung* was either built in the western Indian Ocean, or by shipwrights based elsewhere but trained in these sewn-plank boatbuilding techniques.[6] But matters were complicated by the presence on board of a peculiar style of anchor: an iron grapnel with a wooden shank.[7] Similar anchors have been found off the coast of Vietnam, but never in the western Indian Ocean.[8] Ascribing a definitive origin to the vessel was, therefore, not straightforward.

To further pinpoint the likely origin of the *Belitung,* researchers turned to the vessel's timbers. Although it is possible to identify and map timber species by geographical distribution, analysis of ancient samples can prove frustratingly elusive.[9] This is because timber was then, as it is now, a commonly traded commodity. The tropical hardwood teak (*Tectona grandis*), for example, is native to India, Myanmar, Laos, and Thailand, but its superb qualities as a shipbuilding material meant that it was also used widely in the Arabian world.[10] Furthermore, the accuracy of modern timber identification relies on the availability of existing anatomical charts, making it difficult to distinguish between similar timbers that have not already been commercially exploited and charted.[11] Shipwrecked timbers pose additional challenges due to the disintegration of waterlogged samples.[12]

Many of the *Belitung*'s timbers were so degraded that there was almost no cellulose remaining in the cell walls. This made sectioning and comparative identification very difficult.[13] Initial analysis of these samples extended to the genus level only. All but one genus identified were Indian in origin. Yet the interconnectedness of the ancient world resisted the drawing of definitive conclusions that the vessel was made in India.[14] Fresh analysis of the timbers was later conducted by a shipwreck specialist, using a different method for sectioning the samples. This new analysis reversed the results entirely. Instead, it suggested, all but one of the samples originated from *outside* India.[15] Two—*Afzelia africana* (African mahogany) and *Afzelia bipindensis*—were native to Africa, and, in the case of the latter, to Africa only.[16] Another, probably *Juniper procera* (African juniper), was native to Africa and parts of the Arabian peninsula. The only timber sample of Indian origin—and the only one that both the initial and the later analysis could agree on—was the teak.[17] But it was still not possible to state with absolute confidence where the vessel came from. Indeed, this new analysis has recently been disputed by some scholars, who consider the timber sample identifications unreliable at the species level.[18] Another necessary consideration was *how* the different timbers had been used. Had the best quality timber been saved for the structural elements, suggesting scarcity, or had it been also been used on the nonstructural elements, hinting at abundance? According to the new analysis, the best and "most useful" shipbuilding timbers had been reserved for the ship's key structural elements, while lower-quality timbers had been used for the nonstructural elements.[19]

Such details—about which timber was used where—can appear overly technical. But an understanding of boatbuilding timbers and technologies provides critical insights into a vessel's origins, as well as into cargo sizes, distances traveled, seaworthiness, and speed.[20] In this case, knowledge about ship structure and the qualities of different timbers added weight to the conclusion that the *Belitung* was constructed in the western Indian Ocean, possibly on the Arabian peninsula where boatbuilding timbers were scarce, rather than by experienced sewn-plank shipwrights based in India, for example.[21] As one maritime archaeologist explained, "Indian woods were imported into Arab countries for shipbuilding, but it is highly unlikely that an African timber would be sent to India where there is such a plenitude of excellent shipbuilding timbers."[22] Despite this second analysis, their identification remains controversial—so controversial, in fact, that scholars cannot rule out the possibility that the vessel was constructed somewhere on the east coast of India, or perhaps even in Myanmar or Sumatra.[23]

Timber was not the only material used to construct the vessel. Some of the double wadding, used inside and outside the hull and over which the stitches were sewn, was observed to be paperbark (*Melaleuca* spp.), while some of the cordage appeared to be hibiscus (*Hibiscus* spp.).[24] Significantly, both paperbark and hibiscus are indigenous to Southeast Asia.[25] Coir, from coconuts, and common across the Indian Ocean, was also noted.[26] The presence of Southeast Asian botanicals offers precious insights into—and possibilities for—the vessel's seafaring life, as well as into the lives of those who traveled on it. One possible scenario is that this wadding and cordage was original, and that the ship had not been re-sewn at all, offering the tantalizing possibility that the ship had a much stronger Southeast Asian connection than initially appreciated. Another scenario is that, having sailed east across the Indian Ocean, some of the *Belitung*'s original coir stitching and wadding was replaced in Southeast Asia using local materials.[27] Re-stitching was a time-consuming and laborious process that would have seen the crew come ashore for weeks, if not months. As their vessel was pulled apart and sewn back together, we are left to wonder about those who worked on this ship—both at sea and on land—and their experiences and encounters.

For the most part, the assessment that the *Belitung* was constructed in the western Indian Ocean, in either Arabia or the Persian Gulf, and re-stitched in Southeast Asia remains widely accepted. Oman's support for the construction of a contemporary replica of the *Belitung* in 2010 added weight to the narrative that this was an Arabian ship. But archaeologists have been compelled to revisit this assessment following the discovery of another medieval sewn-plank vessel in Thailand in 2013.[28] Dubbed the *Phanom Surin* after the landowners in whose field it lay, this eighth- or ninth-century vessel is much bigger than the *Belitung*, but shares with it a surprising number of structural similarities. These include not only the stitching but also the use of double wadding, the bluntness of the keelson, and a near-identical planking pattern. As with the *Belitung*, the construction techniques used on the *Phanom Surin* suggested that this was a vessel from the western Indian Ocean. But analysis of timbers, conducted by three different laboratories, yielded confounding results. While successive analyses of the *Belitung* had returned markedly different outcomes, analysts agreed that the *Phanom Surin* was made entirely from Southeast Asian timbers. Even the cordage, from sugar palm, was Southeast Asian.

How can we explain this combination of structural features hailing from the western Indian Ocean and materials sourced entirely in Southeast Asia? Does it mean the *Phanom Surin* had been built in Southeast Asia by a community of shipbuilders trained in western Indian Ocean boatbuilding traditions? Or do these sewn-plank vessels testify to an autochthonous Southeast Asian shipbuilding tradition otherwise missing from the archaeological record? And what are the implications for our understanding of the *Belitung*, with which the *Phanom Surin* shares so many commonalities? These are tantalizing questions for which we do not—and may never—have the answers. Revisiting the *Belitung*'s wreck site to collect additional timber samples for further analysis is not an option: the site was destroyed by looters after the official salvage ended in 1999. For now, scholars can only await further analysis of the *Phanom Surin* to help make sense of these seemingly irreconcilable facts—or hope that another first-millennium sewn-plank vessel will be found in Southeast Asia.

Setting aside the challenge of ascertaining where the *Belitung* was constructed, scholars can agree that to build a ship was to embark on a project of almost bewildering complexity, ambition, and enterprise. It required skills, knowledge, raw materials, and time, and the efforts of many people. A millennium later, experts working to recreate the *Belitung* noted the labor- and resource-intensive nature of the process.[29] Ships were, to use one oft-quoted observation, "the most complex artefact routinely produced prior to the Industrial Revolution."[30] Sourcing the raw materials would have required not only tree-fellers but also labor to transport the timber to the construction yard. Work then began on constructing the vessel: making the rope, shaping the timber, stitching the planks. There was no single design blueprint; instead, designs and technologies evolved in response to myriad factors including the availability of resources, local conditions, cultural influences, and the purpose for which a particular vessel was to be used. Plans for conceptualizing and constructing a vessel might be written down, but more likely, such knowledge was held in the mind of a master boatbuilder in a profound example of intangible cultural heritage. Those plans were then implemented by carpenters, shipwrights, dockworkers, and other skilled and unskilled workers. Once at sea, the *Belitung* continued to implicate people from all walks of life: pilots and navigators, the captain and crew, merchants, and perhaps even (as the presence of a bronze cymbal in the wreckage suggests) musicians.

The primary influence on the *Belitung*'s departure date would have been the weather.[31] Sailing routes are governed by wind patterns, the reliability and predictability of which enable seafarers to plan voyages with a degree of confidence. Travel between the network of ports that connected the Indian Ocean with the South China Sea was reliant on these seasonally reversing monsoonal winds, which affected the flow of the ocean's surface currents. Warm, humid winds—the southwest summer monsoon—blow from April to August. This weather pattern reverses itself from November onward, when cold, dry winds—the northeast winter monsoon—blow in the opposite direction.[32] The rhythm of the monsoon meant that outward and return journeys had to be carefully planned, because a holdup of just a few weeks could result in the journey being delayed by a full year. The monsoon's cycles determined the rhythm of life for travelers and traders, who could use those months before the wind turned to repair their vessel. Missing from the historical record is the affect of the ship—the feelings, sounds, and smells it generated. What noises did the sails make as they filled with wind? Did the ship's planks creak and its stitches swell? How did the crew prepare their food? Did they sing from boredom, or utter prayers of devotion, or shout to the sky? Did the stench of the materials used to render the ship watertight fade over time?[33] When did the crew stop noticing the smell of the salt air? Did they expect to return? What was it *like*?

Interrogating where the *Belitung* came from and how this assessment was made—and locating this within broader contemporary narratives around who owns and is responsible for underwater cultural heritage—is critical to attempts to sketch the lives and afterlives of the *Belitung*. Doing so reveals the difficulties of determining with confidence the precise origins of this vessel. Without conclusive evidence available, many scholars continue to work with the premise that this was a Middle Eastern, probably Arabian, vessel—although, as work continues on the *Phanom Surin*, it has become increasingly difficult to rule out the possibility that the *Belitung* was a Persian, Indian, or even Southeast Asian vessel. Such attempts to determine the origin of the vessel are just one part of this story, however; there is also the issue of what, and whom, the *Belitung* was carrying.

The Objects

Had the *Belitung* gone down with little or no cargo on board, it would have likely attracted little interest beyond scholarly circles. While the vessel—with its stitched hull, diversity of timbers, and similarities to the *Phanom Surin*—raised fascinating questions for specialists about Indian Ocean boatbuilding traditions in the first millennia, it was its cargo that attracted and sustained widespread international attention. The objects on board the *Belitung* were numerous, fragile, and beautiful, and spoke to an ancient exchange of ideas and commodities across the globe. There was gold and silver. There were strings of coins, bronze mirrors with cosmological decorations, and thousands of lead ingots.[34] There was star anise (*Illicium verum*) that had survived a thousand years underwater, aromatic resin for caulking the boat, and Southeast Asian amber.[35]

Of the estimated seventy thousand objects transported by the *Belitung*, the overwhelming majority were Tang dynasty (618–907) ceramics, making this the largest and most intact assemblage of ninth-century Chinese ceramics ever found in a single location.[36] Approximately sixty-five thousand of these ceramics were bowls from the kilns of Changsha, located on a tributary of the Yangtze River in the south-central Chinese province of Hunan.[37] Measuring about 14 cm in diameter and about 5 cm in height, these underglaze-decorated stoneware bowls fit snugly into the palm of a hand. It is not hard to imagine three or four stacked on a shelf somewhere, ready for use. One of these bowls was inscribed with a date equivalent to July 16, 826 CE, likely the date the bowl was manufactured and possibly also the year it was shipped.[38] As one archaeologist observed:

> It is highly unlikely that this was a normal trading voyage of the ninth century. This is probably a unique cargo. It probably wasn't 60,000 [*sic*] Chinese bowls every year. This may have been a "once in twenty years" kind of voyage, if that.[39]

This was not some small private trade—these were commercial quantities that had been ordered and assembled for export.[40] The cargo also contained smaller quantities of more precious ceramics, numbering in the hundreds rather than the thousands. They included highly unusual green-splashed ware from the kilns of Gongxian, exquisite white porcelain from the Xing and Ding kilns of northern China, and jade-like green wares from Yue.[41]

It is common for shipwreck cargoes to be characterized by multi-duplicate ceramics, and the presence of such an enormous number of Changsha bowls within the *Belitung*'s cargo provides valuable opportunities for comparisons within,

Figure 1. Considerable quantities of star anise were found at the wreck site, along with other organic materials including resin, amber, nuts, and seeds. Photo by Michael Flecker, 1999.

rather than across, typologies. The bowls feature a polychrome underglaze, with iron and copper pigments conjuring colors of ochre and green. Because the chemistry of glazes can react unpredictably to the firing process (which, for stoneware, was relatively high), the consistency of these polychromatic colors is evidence of the technical mastery of those who produced these bowls. Most share a similar decorative scheme. First, they were coated with a layer of plain slip, a common technique in ceramic production to increase consistency and strength. The four sides of the bowl's rim were then dipped in a dark brown wash. This framed a free-form design painted in the center of the bowl.[42]

Some motifs appear frequently, such as mountains, landscapes, and animals, with individual variations across these common designs providing glimpses of the people who painted them. While some designs are refined, others show evidence of haste or carelessness in the thickness of the brushstroke or the drippings of the paint. Some designs appear less often: Buddhist stupas and swastikas, banners or steles, a poem in Chinese characters,[43] a sea monster. One particularly special bowl bears a Chinese inscription meaning "tea bowl," providing early textual evidence of the cultural significance of this beverage.[44] Another depicts the profile of a curly-haired man with a large nose, perhaps the face of a foreigner from Central or West Asia. Groundbreaking new research has also confirmed the presence of both Arabic and Persian inscriptions on the bowls. These inscriptions, viewed through the lens of Chinese art history, were initially presumed to be clouds and other nature motifs. However, brushstroke analysis has revealed the presence of calligraphic elements across thousands of bowls in consistent combinations. These calligrams, inscriptions, and examples of "pseudo script" were popular features of ceramics in the Abbasid empire (750–1258), which had its capital in Baghdad, and were intended to evoke wonder and sharpen focus by confounding the eyes.[45] In them, Allah is present but hidden in misty mountains and clouds of vapor. Religious studies scholar Daniel James Waller describes these pseudo scripts as "ostentatious displays of non-writing."[46] Their presence implies that the bowls were destined for the Middle East, and that those decorating the bowls were familiar with this market.

National Geographic described the Changsha bowls as "the Tang equivalent of Fiestaware"—simple, functional, and mass-produced. Others have likened the cargo, with its inexpensive multi-duplicates, to "a kind of ancient Ikea."[47] Although these assessments convey a sense of the commercial nature of the cargo, they undersell its significance. The dominance of ceramics, and the Changsha bowls in particular, testifies to the existence of mass production techniques in China in the ninth century, and to the desirability of these ceramics outside of China.[48] This was far more than a floating Ikea. Instead the Changsha bowls were a form of "mass-market luxury" that had consumer appeal—and could be afforded—beyond small elite circles.[49]

The ceramics also offer valuable insights into the impact of maritime trade on the network of relationships that ordered, produced, and transported these objects.[50] The market was not in China: archaeological data indicate that these bowls held very little domestic appeal.[51] The implication is that these bowls were made to order—and, therefore, that someone had not only placed the order but that arrangements had been made to transport it. In his analysis of the transformation of the Chinese ceramic industry in the ninth century, scholar Andrew Chittick points to the presence of a large Arab and Persian diaspora in Yangzhou, a bustling port city located in the Yangtze River delta and connected to the kilns of Changsha through a network of rivers. Large communities of Middle Easterners—and others, including Malays, Indians, and Chams—had lived and worked in Chinese port cities from at least the seventh century.[52] In 760, a massacre of the foreign population in Yangzhou, motivated by the city's reputed "lust for wealth," resulted in the deaths of several thousand Arabs and Persians.[53] These diasporic populations recovered surprisingly quickly, and by the early ninth century were again flourishing.[54] They were perfectly positioned to commission orders of the volume seen on the *Belitung*. Attuned to the desires of the Middle Eastern market yet based in China where they could observe production, they played a pivotal role in what Chittick calls the "economic logic" that propelled innovations in the Changsha kilns during the Tang dynasty.

Orders had to be sufficiently large for merchants to justify the investment of time and resources, and the risks, associated with maritime trade. To maximize economic returns, they had to make the seasonal reversal of the winds work for, rather than against, them. Ships arrived with the southwest monsoon (from April until August) and departed, with their cargo, on the northeast monsoon (from November until March). This meant that orders were placed and filled within months rather than years. Commissioned trade ceramics were made to order, and only produced if a vessel was already waiting in port. These factors placed tremendous pressure on the kilns, which had to be capable of rapidly increasing the scale and speed of their production. Skilled craftspeople, probably centered on households, constituted the core pool of labor. They worked the kilns year-round, and had the technical knowledge and skills to throw the bowls, prepare the glazes, and maintain correct and consistent temperatures in the kiln. These kiln households knew their value, which they marked with a brand on the ceramics they produced. But there were a range of activities that required less expertise: sourcing raw materials such as clay and firewood, applying the slip, and loading and unloading the kilns. To enable the kiln households to scale up production at short notice, proposes Chittick, they turned to the agricultural sector, which could provide a large pool of labor in the quiet period between April, when the rice was sown, and October, when it was harvested. This availability coincided almost exactly with the arrival and departure dates of the vessels for which the ceramics were destined.

Once fired, the bowls were transported by river and then by sea. To do so safely, they were coiled helically inside tall stoneware jars from Guangdong in the south, which may have already been used and reused by that stage.[55] Up to 130 bowls

Figure 2. An already-broken storage jar reveals Changsha bowls coiled helically inside. More than one hundred bowls could be stored in this way, yielding valuable insights into the sophisticated nature of ceramic production and transportation in Tang dynasty China. Photo by Michael Flecker, courtesy of the Asian Civilisations Museum, 1999.

could be stored in this way.[56] Others were stacked and tied with string or rope. The bowls were probably padded with a type of "organic bubble wrap," such as mung beans or rice straw.[57] These sophisticated packing techniques were designed to prevent damage during the sea journey, but were also to prove instrumental in protecting the bowls from the impact of the wrecking event and the centuries underwater that followed.

The Belitung was also carrying ceramics from the Gongxian kilns (Henan province) on the north-central plains. These kilns had a reputation for producing playful and experimental ceramics, as attested to by around 160 green-splashed wares, including a number of tube cups.[58] These unusual cups have a tube attached to the side that connects to a hole at the bottom, hidden by an animal figure such as a fish or a turtle. The tube functioned as a straw, presumably for the mouth, although some observers have suggested that these are "nose-drinking cups" as described by Song dynasty poet Fan Chengda.[59] Used for wine in the winter and water in the summer, the nose-drinking experience was, says this famed poet, so pleasurable it made you speechless.[60] Meanwhile, a saucer bearing a finely molded dragon medallion decoration was of particular interest to ceramic experts. Such molding had previously been dated to the Northern Song period (960–1127), immediately after the Tang dynasty. Its discovery in the Belitung's cargo upset this accepted chronology, forcing the dating of such molded decorations to be moved back by one hundred years.[61]

Gongxian also produced the three blue-and-white stoneware saucers that formed part of the Belitung's cargo. Each featured a distinctive cobalt lozenge design.[62] These saucers were innovative in both design and use of materials, and remain the first and only intact vessels of high-fired underglaze stoneware painted in cobalt blue to be discovered and salvaged.[63] They epitomize the long-distance conversations, and confluence of materials and ideas, that was taking place across the globe in the ninth century. This was a story of circular desire and innovation between China and the Middle East, facilitated by connections across land and sea. In Basra (Iraq), potters had attempted to copy the fine white vessels produced by the northern Chinese kilns of Xing and Ding. Without the pure white clay of northern China, or the ability to fire their kilns at the high temperatures needed to produce porcelain, the Basra potters were compelled to coat their creations with an opaque white glaze. They added designs in cobalt, in the process forging a new path for Middle Eastern ceramics. Chinese potters then responded with their own version of these Middle Eastern blue-and-whites, using their own clay and firing techniques and importing cobalt from the Middle East. The three blue-and-white vessels found on the Belitung can thus be understood as a response to Middle

Eastern ceramics that in turn had responded to Chinese ceramics. Scholars have described this as a "call-and-response" scenario involving materials, technologies, and styles that resulted in the creation of new, experimental hybrids.[64]

The Gongxian kilns were also responsible for the creation of perhaps the most spectacular object found on the *Belitung*: a 104-cm-tall, green-splashed ewer, featuring an incised lozenge motif reminiscent of designs that were popular in the Middle East in the ninth century.[65] Described by one expert as "an unprecedented ceramic tour de force," the ewer's height, delicacy, and elegance represent a remarkable achievement in ceramic production, confirming not only Gongxian's reputation as a center of experimentation but also the technical skills of its craftspeople in creating such an object.[66] Curiously, this ewer depicts rivets around the handle, typically used to affix plates of metal. Being ceramic, however, such rivets were unnecessary. Their inclusion is therefore entirely decorative, testifying to the strong relationship between Chinese ceramics and metalware whereby cheaper ceramic materials were used to copy the grander and more expensive materials of silver, gold, and bronze. However, some scholars have cautioned against the assumption that this stylistic influence was purely one-directional. Ceramics expert Regina Krahl has suggested that by the end of the eighth century, gold and silver makers were in fact looking to ceramics makers for inspiration rather than the other way around.[67]

As Krahl explains, this reversal can be connected to the apogee, and subsequent decline, of the Tang dynasty from 750 onward. Military (over-)commitments affected the court's finances, which in turn had a serious impact on previously extravagant funeral practices. Ostentatious displays of wealth were no longer considered appropriate. By the end of the eighth century, the expensive furnishing of tombs had dramatically decreased, and opulent burials full of ceramic figures all but ceased. This had serious consequences for ceramics manufacturers, whose livelihoods depended on the provision of burial goods. Demand had previously been driven by imperial patrons and funerary practices.[68] Manufacturers now had to look for alternative markets for their products. They turned to producing ceramics for the living rather than the dead. Competition among kilns was fierce, leading to rapid innovations and improvements in quality. Their efforts to create new markets were boosted by the new fashion of ritual tea drinking. This newly acquired standing of ceramics changed the way craftspeople saw each other. Potters no longer need to copy gold and silversmiths, and certain ceramics might have even been appreciated more highly than precious metalware.[69]

This may well have been the case for the small quantity of fine white ceramics from the northern kilns of Xing and Ding (both south of Beijing in Hebei

Figure 3. The magnificent green-splashed ewer stands more than a meter tall, and is distinguished by its flared foot, incised lozenge motif, and delicate strap handle. Considered a masterpiece of technical craftsmanship and creative experimentation, it is alleged to have been looted from the site before being returned for a fee. Ewer, Gongxian Kiln, Henan Province, China, Tang dynasty, around 830s. Stoneware. Credit: Asian Civilisations Museum, Tang Shipwreck Collection. Photo by John Tsantes and Robert Harrell, Arthur M. Sackler Gallery, 2005.

province) and the green-glazed stoneware from the southern kilns of Yue (Zhejiang province) on the *Belitung*.[70] Whereas many of the other objects in the cargo appear to have been made for the international market, these objects were highly valued in China itself. Likened to the purity of snow and the beauty of jade, respectively, these vessels were extremely desired by Chinese connoisseurs and may in fact have well been more valuable than silver or gold.[71] They were also desirable to foreign buyers, with examples found throughout Southeast Asia and the Middle East.[72] Approximately three hundred pieces of the white ware were found on the *Belitung*, pure in color and refined in form. The green wares, of which around two hundred were found, were equally exquisite. Sometimes known as celadon, they included round and square dishes, jars, basins, and incense burners. Both Xing/Ding and Yue wares were coveted for tea, with one famed poet and tea connoisseur expressing a personal preference for the way the green glaze of the latter enhanced the color of his tea. Others preferred the neutral background provided by the white ware, which allowed the reddish hues of the beverage to come through.[73] The green wares from Yue constituted some of the relatively few southern Chinese ceramics on the *Belitung*. Also from southern China were around fifteen hundred green stone wares from Guangdong province. Most of these were "massive, sturdy, functional containers for storage and transport."[74] However, some, from the kilns of either Chaozhou or Meixian, were echoes of the Yue prototypes. Thickly potted and coarser grained, and with a translucent, crackled glaze, they fared better underwater than did the finer Yue wares.[75]

The *Belitung*'s ceramic cargo originates from at least six kiln sites across five provinces stretching from the south to the north of China. But although they dominated the cargo, they were not the only objects being transported. More than thirty gold and silver objects, "almost certainly" produced in Yangzhou, were on board.[76] There were cups and dishes, both round and square, of solid gold, including a pair with a unique design of broad leaves and matching swastikas (an auspicious symbol in Buddhist art).[77] The uniqueness of this design, and its rarity in Tang dynasty China, suggests these were specially made for overseas export.[78] There were four silver bowls, one with a rare design of a seated rhinoceros (believed to appear at times of good governance).[79] There was a wine flask of gilt silver with a pivoting handle, the only known example from the Tang dynasty.[80]

Also aboard were fourteen finely crafted silver boxes for medicine, cosmetics, or incense, including one large box with four smaller ones contained therein.[81] The silver boxes featured designs of flowers or clouds with vines, birds, and animals, and were shaped like fans, leaves, or lobed ovals. There were two platters and a

Figure 4. This oversized gold cup is the only one of its kind to have been found outside of China. It features musicians and a dancer on its eight sides, and a thumb rest decorated with the faces of two bearded men. More than sixty gold and gilded silver objects were recovered from the wreck site. Octagonal cup with musicians and a dancer, China, around 830s. Gold, height 9 cm. Credit: Asian Civilisations Museum, Tang Shipwreck Collection. Photo by John Tsantes and Robert Harrell, Arthur M. Sackler Gallery, 2005.

golden bracelet with an engraved floral design. One of the most outstanding objects was an oversized solid gold cup, octagonal in shape and decorated with dancers and musicians with curly hair and long, billowing clothing. The musicians hold wind, string, and percussion instruments and may have been enslaved entertainers. The thumb rest on the cup's ring handle features the faces of two bearded men, possibly from Central Asia.[82] The value of the gold on this cup alone was equivalent to ten years' salary for a low-ranking Chinese official.[83]

These gold and silver items were exquisite in their detailing and constituted some of the most significant discoveries of Tang gold and silver ever made, either within or outside China. With their images of "exotic animals and entertainer slaves," these objects had a social function.[84] They spoke of "tying knots, forging links and connections, wishing long life, pairing friends and couples, and exchanging tributary offerings."[85] These objects linked the *Belitung* to the highest echelons of society, possibly even the imperial court, and have prompted endless speculation as to why they were being taken out of China. Some scholars have pointed to the recurrence of pairs of ducks (a symbol of marital bliss) on a number of the objects as a sign they were wedding gifts, possibly destined for the Sailendra rulers in Java.[86] So rare are these gold and silver objects, however, that others have speculated they were a "hoard of smuggled goods for private sale."[87] The lack of certainty further complicates notions of ownership when it comes to ancient vessels and the many networks they moved within. The octagonal cup, of which no other example has been found outside of China, remains a particular source of intrigue for many scholars.[88] Indeed, such is the gleam of some of these objects that it is difficult to believe they have been submerged at all.

There was other non-ceramic cargo on board, including twenty-nine Chinese bronze mirrors, one of which dated from the Han era (206 BCE–220 CE), and was thus already an antique at the time the ship sailed.[89] The largest bronze mirror salvaged from the wreck was inscribed with a date equivalent to 759 CE. There were several hundred Chinese bronze coins, of the same type but in different sizes. The first batch was minted from 621 CE, and the second batch from 758 CE, most likely prior to 845 CE. There were two kilograms of gold leaf, which became permanently separated from the rest of the cargo after the wreck was salvaged.[90] The *Belitung* was also carrying the largest amount of Tang silver bullion found to date; some eighteen ingots with a purity of 99.5 percent.[91] These are the earliest examples of Chinese silver bullion being used for foreign trade.[92] Thousands of lead ingots made up what has been described as "paying ballast," used to stabilize the ship and for trade.[93] These, too, were later separated from the assemblage, with only several dozen recovered and two thousand left on the seabed.[94]

The *Belitung*'s cargo was key in determining the date the ship had sailed. Techniques included correlating the dates found on coins, mirrors, and the bowl with the results of radiocarbon analysis on the star anise, resin, and a piece of timber from beneath the keelson.[95] The bowl inscribed with a date of 826 CE correlated to the highest-probability radiocarbon results, and the wreck has been confidently dated to the second quarter of the ninth century. This dates the *Belitung*'s journey to the second half of the Tang dynasty, which was, by that time, in decline.

There is one commodity noticeable for its absence: silk. Despite being one of China's "premier exports," not a single piece of silk was found in the *Belitung*'s wreckage.[96] This may have been because none was on board. Space on the vessel was limited and silk was, after all, a far easier commodity to transport on camel or horseback than heavy, breakable ceramics. Or perhaps silk was present on the *Belitung* but did not survive the ravages of the underwater environment.[97] Either way, the absence of silk on a vessel that is so frequently and specifically used to invoke the Silk Road/Ceramic Route narrative is an important reminder of the limitations of focusing on a single commodity, be it silk or ceramics, in any consideration of the ancient trade and exchange networks across the Indian Ocean.

The People

Building the *Belitung* required a skilled and unskilled labor force, capable of crafting a seaworthy vessel from a variety of local and imported raw materials. To sail this vessel required an equally competent team of sailors, navigators, carpenters, sail-makers, and others with the skills to survive at sea. As with so many aspects of the *Belitung*'s story, information about the people who traveled on this vessel is limited. We cannot assume that the same people crewed the vessel for the entirety of the voyage. Instead, this was probably a changing cohort with people boarding and disembarking according to their skill sets, personal circumstances, and other considerations to which we will never be privy. It is also reasonable to assume that this was a heavily gendered environment from which women were excluded—although this is, again, something we cannot know for certain. We also cannot rule out that some of the crew may have been indentured labor.

It is, however, possible to gain glimpses of the identity of the ship's inhabitants by looking at the personal objects they carried with them. Very few of the items recovered from the *Belitung* were from the Middle East: three turquoise-glazed earthenware vessels, consisting of two amphorae and a jar; and a tiny blue glass bottle small enough to fill with medicine or cosmetics and slip into a pocket. A bronze scale bar, hook, and weights, all from Southeast Asia, testify to merchants and measurement. Other objects provide only broken glimpses of the past: a bronze handle, perhaps belonging to a sword; a wooden handle, possibly from a parasol or fly-whisk; a shaped wooden stick, possibly for repairing fishing nets; fragments of gold bracelets; part of a lacquer dish. A single gold coin and an Indonesian bronze mirror are equally elusive.[98]

These personal objects constitute what maritime archaeologist George Bass describes as a ship's "domestic assemblage," being neither commercial cargo nor navigational equipment required to sail the vessel. The domestic assemblage, he proposes, is key to revealing the affiliation of a ship. Whereas commercial cargo is "transitory," the domestic assemblage is both a "more permanent and a more accurate reflection of the origins of the captain, the crew, and the ship."[99] The *Belitung*'s domestic assemblage included objects from China, Southeast Asia, and the Middle East, and provides clues as to what life was like on board. An ink stone engraved with an insect "almost certainly" belonged to a literate Chinese merchant, who may have been a passenger rather than a crew member.[100] A bird-shaped stoneware whistle and a dog figurine, probably used as a paperweight, were the only animal figurines found, suggesting they were personal keepsakes rather than objects of trade.[101] A bone die (the earliest one ever found on a shipwreck) and four ivory game pieces in the shape of acorns hint at long days at sea and the use of games to pass the time. A bronze needle, meanwhile, suggests work: it was probably used for repairs, including of the sails, of which no trace remains. The absence of devotional items doesn't necessarily imply an absence of religion. Rather, religion may have been practiced through forms of observance like recitation and prayer, which are better suited to life at sea than a shrine.[102]

The size of the vessel suggests that no more than ten to twenty people would have traveled on board at any one time. The *Belitung* was not a large vessel—no more than sixty-five to seventy-two feet in length and with a maximum width of between twenty-one and twenty-six feet—and yet it carried approximately seventy thousand objects, weighing approximately twenty-five metric tons (27.5 US tons) in cargo, the majority of which were ceramic bowls.[103] The crew and any passengers would have lived, worked, cooked, washed, toileted, and slept on the deck, perched above the cargo's bulk on light, removable planks or slats of some sort.[104] A wooden rolling pin and a stone mortar and pestle were used to prepare food, and large stoneware vats were used to carry fresh water. Lead weights for a fishing net indicate the crew sourced protein from the ocean. Their diet was supplemented by nuts and seeds, a handful of which were found in the wreckage. Animals such as goats may have also traveled on board, providing milk and meat.[105] A stoneware grater in the shape of a fish is both practical and whimsical.[106] The *Belitung* also carried several earthenware kettles, a stoneware lantern, and a candlestick.[107] Large bronze tweezers may have done double duty as a surgical tool to pluck splinters from calloused hands and a cooking tool to remove bones from fish.[108]

The crew used lead sounding weights to measure the depth of the ocean, but there is no material evidence as to how they navigated the ocean. Long before the development of modern navigational equipment, seafarers charted their voyages across the globe with great skill, creativity, and ingenuity. Although there is some textual evidence of Arab navigation techniques, detailed technical information from the ninth century is limited. The *Jewel of Muscat* journey in 2010, which echoed parts of the *Belitung*'s approximate voyage, provided an opportunity to experiment with traditional Arab navigational techniques, specifically star-altitude measurement.[109] By measuring the height of certain stars from the horizon, the navigator could determine the vessel's latitude—how far north or south it was from the equator. The higher the star sat in the sky, the less precise the measurement.

The Pole Star, which sits close to both the North Celestial Pole and the horizon in the Indian Ocean, was the "foundational" star, while other stars were also measured, sometimes in relation to each other.[110] To do this, seafarers used specialized tools. One such tool consisted of a small plank with a piece of string through its middle. The string was knotted at various intervals to indicate certain latitudes, and was customizable to a user's finger measurements. Another required no rope, only wood, and had its origin in ancient practices that required nothing more than the human hand. Seafarers would determine their position by holding up their hand, "placing the bottom edge on the horizon and aligning the Pole Star with the tip of the appropriate fingers." Latitude was measured by the width of a finger, with each finger corresponding to a predetermined measure. Individual variations in hand size and arm length saw this practice replaced over time in favor of standardized wood instruments. Eric Staples' account of the star-altitude measurement experiments conducted on the *Jewel of Muscat* as it traveled from Oman to Singapore offers a compelling insight into the challenges of navigating without modern equipment—particularly once the vessel reached Sri Lanka, from where the Pole Star was no longer visible—and of the value of a master navigator with knowledge of the route.[111]

The journey involved months at sea. Long-distance ocean voyages were "physically tough and dangerous," meaning that "attrition of the crew must have been a factor."[112] Given the length and complexity of the *Belitung*'s voyage, it is likely that crew members were replaced along the way. New crew members would have brought with them specialized local knowledge about the weather, geographical features and landmarks, and threats such as pirates or hidden reefs. Some may have even acted as skilled navigators along certain sectors.[113] It is likely, therefore, that this was a diverse crew: multiracial, multilingual, multireligious, and assembled from everywhere.[114] We can only guess at how they communicated across language differences or how disputes were managed. It is also vital to acknowledge those on land. Archaeological data suggest the vessel may have been re-stitched at some point, an activity that would have involved a lengthy stopover. Significant effort would have been required to load and arrange the many thousands of objects that made up the cargo. Street vendors and dockworkers would have provided supplies at ports along the way. Acknowledging the labor of these people, even as we know so little about them, is an important aspect of the *Belitung*'s story.

In attempting to develop a clearer picture of the *Belitung*'s life, it is the people who remain most elusive. The vessel's domestic assemblage includes Middle Eastern, Southeast Asian, and Chinese objects. The distance traveled suggests hardship—disease, lack of access to fresh water or food, unrest—but in the end the only hardship we have proof of is that the vessel was, ultimately, wrecked. No traces of human remains were found on the wreckage, and we have no way of knowing whether there were any survivors. While the vessel and its cargo speak loudly across the centuries, the voices of those who contributed their labor to the *Belitung*'s story are clamorous in their absence. In telling the story of the *Belitung*, it is important to be aware of these gaps and silences.

Conclusion

As with so much of our knowledge about the *Belitung*'s first life, efforts to determine the identity of the vessel, the objects, and the people raise as many questions as they answer. How were the heavy ceramics transported from kiln site to the water, for example? What was the role of intermediaries in facilitating the movement of objects from the interior to the coast, and of purchasing agents in tracking and tallying the trade within and beyond China? Was the vessel loaded at one port, or multiple ports? Were the objects destined for more than one market? Was there a direct maritime route between China and the Middle East, or did the journey rely on intermediaries? And who bore the cost of the loss? Despite this lack of certainty, efforts to understand the *Belitung*'s first life as a seafaring vessel are essential because they compel us to center people, labor, resources, geography, and weather, among other aspects, in our considerations.

We do know that this vessel, its people, and its cargo were part of a connected world. The *Belitung* sailed in the ninth century, at a time when maritime technologies and activities were already well advanced. Across Africa, the Middle East, India, and Southeast Asia, maritime ports formed nodes in an Indian Ocean network that connected coast with hinterland, east with west, boatbuilders with imperial courts.[115] The *Belitung* exemplifies the scale of these early maritime connections, bringing together different communities of sailors, merchants, traders, builders, craftspeople, and travelers. These connections enabled the formation of relationships between consumers, traders, and producers, and constituted an essential part of the global supply chain by connecting the Abbasid empire in the west with the Tang dynasty in the east, through the kingdoms of Southeast Asia.

The legacies of these relationships are constituted today through the concept of the Silk Road and the Maritime Ceramic Route, which are in turn mobilized by the geopolitical imperatives of the Belt and Road Initiative. But focusing solely on trade and commodities (particularly single commodities of silk and ceramic) elides the true polyvocality of the *Belitung*, which implicated not only a diversity of objects but also people and ideas. Untangling its first life has allowed us to move beyond these commodity-, trade-, and nation-focused approaches in which there is just one historically attributed identity, to a better understanding of its multiple identities based on the vessel itself, its people, the domestic assemblage and commercial cargo, and the networks they comprise. The wrecking of the *Belitung* interrupted these networks. But, as the following chapter explores, it also created opportunities for entirely new ones.

CHAPTER TWO

Wrecked

Like all wrecks, the *Belitung* was a ship that failed. The raw materials and boat-building knowledge that went into its construction, the seafaring brilliance of those on board, the endless hours spent making and loading the thousands of objects that made up its cargo, the investment of financial and human capital required to transport people and objects across the ocean: all this and more was lost when the ship foundered. The consequences of its interrupted voyage were devastating not only for the crew but also for others who had a stake in the vessel's safe passage: the merchants, financiers, producers, and consumers of the commercial and luxury goods it was carrying. Never reaching their destination, those objects were lost to their makers as well as to those who anticipated their arrival.

But the ship's failure created a new, albeit unintended, story. As it slipped beneath the surface, its trajectory changed from that of a seafaring vessel to that of an underwater cultural heritage site. Terrestrial sites, such as ruined temples, remain part of a social landscape. But the life and afterlife of a shipwreck is distinct and segmented, defined as it is by an interrupted voyage. The *Belitung* was no longer part of a social landscape of early ninth-century travel and trade. Hidden underwater for centuries, it became part of another world—shaped by currents, corroded by salt, colonized by coral and other sea life. Tracing this transformation helps clarify the unique circumstances by which the *Belitung* has subverted international and institutional ideals about the management of underwater cultural heritage.

The *Belitung* is one of millions of such vessels, wrecked by misadventure or deliberately scuttled to avoid capture or to create artificial reefs. The question of how to manage these wrecks is, however, relatively new. So conditioned are we to see them as "treasure" that discussion about regulatory frameworks and management practices seems tedious and unnecessary. But the legislative context plays a key role in determining the fate of shipwrecks; as this chapter shows, it is an essential consideration in efforts to establish the many influences on the *Belitung*'s afterlife. Had the *Belitung* wrecked elsewhere—somewhere too deep to ever be chanced upon, for example, or in a different maritime zone—its fate would have been entirely different. As it was, being wrecked in shallow waters in the Indonesian archipelago set the *Belitung* on course to become one of the most contested and controversial shipwrecks in the world.

The Black Rock

We do not know what caused the wrecking of the *Belitung* approximately two nautical miles from the shore of Belitung Island (Pulau Belitung), in the tropical waters that connect the South China and the Java Seas. It is reasonable, however, to assume that the vessel struck the nearby reef, perhaps at night or during a storm, before drifting to its watery grave just fifty-six feet below the surface. Nestled tightly in the ship's hull, most of its well-packed cargo of ceramics survived the initial impact with the reef and then the seabed. The relatively low breakage level— estimated to be around 20 percent—tells us it was not a particularly violent or rapid descent.[1] Determining whether any crew or passengers survived is less straightforward. No human remains have ever been found at the site, and it is possible—although not likely, given the distance—that survivors could have swum to shore.

Had they done so, they may have noticed certain geological features on the island, specifically an abundance of dark, high-gloss objects similar in appearance to obsidian or pitchstone. These were tektites: "small, pebble-like glassy objects of Earth material that have been melted by meteorite impact, splashed up into our atmosphere, and fallen to Earth again under gravity."[2] These space-splashed objects are found throughout Southeast Asia, with those from Belitung Island known as "Billitonites," after "Billiton," as Belitung Island is also known. When discovered a millennium later, the wreck was initially dubbed the *Batu Hitam*, or Black Rock, in recognition of the presence of these glossy, grooved objects on the island. The name did not last, however, and the wreck soon became known as the *Belitung*. The different names by which this vessel has been known—*Batu Hitam, Belitung*, and, later, *Tang*—has contributed to a degree of confusion, with some scholars who are less familiar with the wreck occasionally referring to the *Batu Hitam* and the *Belitung* as if they were different wrecks.[3] The use of different names reminds us that certain qualities of the wreck—*where* it was found, *what* it was carrying—have been foregrounded (and other qualities therefore minimized) as ownership of the wreck has changed.

Belitung Island is a somewhat unexpected place for a vessel of possible Middle Eastern origin, and carrying ceramics from the Tang dynasty, to be wrecked. The island itself is small, and triangulated by the much larger islands of Sumatra to the west (via the Gaspar Strait and the nearby island of Bangka), Borneo to the

east (via the Karimata Strait), and Java to the south (via the Java Sea). The principal trading routes connecting the Indian Ocean and the South China Sea in the
ninth century took vessels through the Melaka Strait, far to the north between
Sumatra and the Malay peninsula. The fact that the *Belitung* wreck was found
well southeast of this traditional route has led to intense speculation about what
the ship was doing in these waters at all. One theory is that the vessel was attempting to navigate through the Melaka Strait when it was blown off course and
wrecked. But this explanation is difficult to sustain because of the distance—
around 450-odd nautical miles—between the Karimata and Melaka Straits.
Alternatively, the vessel may have been in the area intentionally, raising several
tantalizing possibilities for scholars of ninth-century global trade.

Some, for example, have interpreted the wreck's southerly location as evidence
of a direct maritime route between China and the Middle East, as distinct from a
linked network that relied on intermediaries such as the Sumatran-based Sriwijayan maritime kingdom (c. seventh–thirteenth centuries).[4] One theory suggests
that the *Belitung* was returning to the Middle East via the more southerly Sunda
Strait (between Sumatra and Java), and not the Melaka Strait, when it sank. This
challenges the idea that the Melaka Strait was the principal sea route between
India and China in the ninth century. Scholar Stephen Haw conjectures that the
Melaka Strait did not open up as an established sea route until after the ninth
century; Haw argues that, at the time of the *Belitung*'s voyage, when Sriwijaya was
the preeminent trading polity in the archipelago, the principal sea route skirted
close to the Sriwijayan capital in southern Sumatra and then continued south to
the nearby Sunda Strait.[5] According to Haw's interpretation of historical data, the
Belitung was not off course at all, but traveling a well-established route that followed the east coast of Sumatra in a southerly direction before continuing its journey westward through the Sunda Strait. However, the Sunda Strait theory is not
widely accepted in the scholarly community, with others interpreting the wreck's
location as indicative of the presence of warehousing facilities at a nearby entrepôt,
or trading hub.

Advocates of this theory, such as archaeologists Qin Dashu, Kunpeng Xiang,
and John Miksic, have suggested that the *Belitung* did not travel to China at all,
but instead loaded its cargo at a Southeast Asian port, probably in Sumatra.[6] Both
Qin and Miksic believe it unlikely that Middle Eastern trade vessels traveled to
China to collect their diverse cargo. Rather, they propose that a wide range of ceramics was assembled by intermediaries in China and transported to a Sriwijayan
entrepôt, where they were collected by Middle Eastern and other traders. Qin
supports this theory by pointing to the many different kiln-sites that produced
the ceramics in the *Belitung*'s cargo.[7] He argues that this diversity of kilns—and

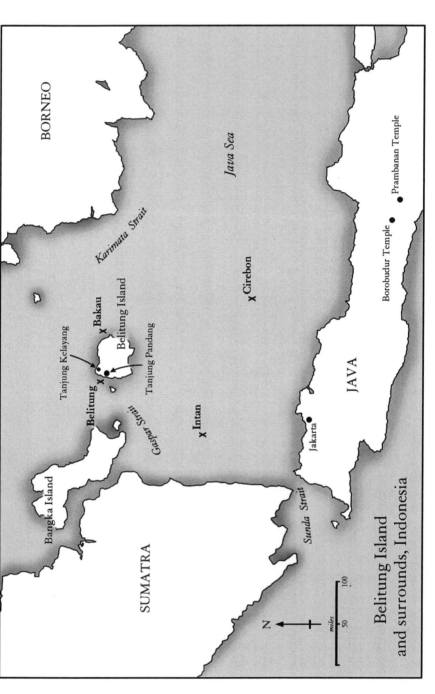

Map 2. Belitung Island, Indonesia, showing the location of the *Belitung*, *Intan*, and *Bakau* shipwrecks, all of which were salvaged by Seabed Explorations in the late 1990s. The island is located between Sumatra, Borneo, and Java.

hence the likely diversity of shipping ports, of which we know little—would have made a multi-stop voyage to China inefficient. The Sriwijayan entrepôt theory explains the vessel's location closer to the Sunda than the Melaka Strait, and, more significantly, effectively re-centers Southeast Asian maritime histories in a story that would otherwise be dominated by China and the Middle East. In this version, Southeast Asian waters were not just the final resting place for a ship engaged in trade between two centers of power but significant destinations in their own right. This theory does not engage with the possibility that the ceramics were assembled at a *single* Chinese port for loading. Nevertheless, the idea that Southeast Asian actors were not only participants in, but central to, global ninth-century maritime trade should not be dismissed.

Many believe that the vessel did, in fact, travel to China, and that it loaded its cargo at just one port rather than making multiple stops. Michael Flecker, who led the second salvage season, considers it "most likely" that the vessel traveled to Guangzhou on China's southern coast, which was a major port of call for Arab traders.[8] According to this theory, coastal vessels collected the Changsha, Xing and Ding, and Gongxian ceramics from the ports of Mingzhou (present-day Ningbo) and Yangzhou in the north of China, and delivered them to Guangzhou for distribution. Hsieh Ming-liang, meanwhile, has used a comparison of ceramics from the *Belitung* with those recovered from terrestrial sites to argue that Yangzhou was the likely port of loading.[9] A number of other scholars concur with this theory, arguing it was more economically efficient for the *Belitung* to travel northward to a port such as Yangzhou in the Yangtze Delta region, perhaps stopping at Guangzhou en route.[10] Both Guangzhou and Yangzhou were home to substantial numbers of foreigners.[11] These different interpretations are not necessarily mutually exclusive. The China Theory, for example, does not exclude the possibility that the ship was also engaged in trade with a Sriwijayan entrepôt, sourcing items such as nutmeg and cloves.[12] Equally, the China Theory could potentially coexist with the Sunda Strait theory.

Setting aside whether the vessel loaded its cargo at a local entrepôt or at one or more ports in China, another variable to consider when determining why the wreck sank where it did is not where it had traveled *from*, but where it was traveling *to*. Whereas the cargo suggests that the vessel's ultimate destination was the Middle East, its next destination after loading could well have been the island of Java, where Tang ceramics have been found near the Prambanan temple complex.[13] Or it may have been trading other valuable commodities, a possibility entertained by the discovery of aromatic Sumatran resin in the ship's cargo.[14] Some scholars have gone so far as to ask whether the ship was traveling to the Middle East at all—perhaps, postulated one, it had instead been "purchased by a Chinese or

Indonesian merchant for dedicated trade between these two regions."[15] In short, scholars remain divided on why the *Belitung* was so far south, where it loaded its cargo, or where it was traveling to, and there is unlikely to ever be a definitive answer to these questions. Currently, the weight of academic opinion is that the *Belitung* was "an Arab ship en route to the Middle East when it sank."[16] Perhaps the most useful assessment is that, in the absence of further information, such considerations can only ever be speculative.[17]

These speculations remind us that the *Belitung* is not just—as shipwrecks are so often described—a time capsule.[18] Before it sank, it was part of a network of lived connections we may never truly understand. This lack of certainty introduces a degree of ambiguity to the question of moral ownership. We know that the wrecking disrupted the intended trajectory of the vessel and its crew and cargo, but we do not know exactly what this intended trajectory was. Who owned the objects when they sank? What debts had been incurred or promises made? What material, economic, and social networks were disrupted by the failure of the vessel? In seeking to determine the *Belitung*'s influences, turning points, and legacies, the wreck raises many more questions than it answers. But there is one certainty: it sank in what would later become the territorial waters of Indonesia, thus affording Indonesia the legal right to decide the future of the wreck and its cargo.

An Ocean Sewn with Islands

With over thirteen thousand islands, Indonesia is not only the first but also the greatest archipelagic state in the world.[19] Renowned Indonesian historian Adrian B. Lapian placed the maritime domain at the heart of Indonesian national and historical consciousness when he described Indonesia not in terrestrial terms but as "an ocean sewn with islands."[20] Its territorial waters extend up to two million square miles, and the length of its coast exceeds fifty-nine thousand miles, making Indonesia second only to Canada in having the longest coastline in the world.[21] This archipelago has been at the crossroads of international exchange for centuries, both as a place of passage and as a destination in and of itself. Maritime networks and ancient seafaring routes passed through these waters and enabled the transoceanic exchange of goods, ideas, languages, and people. Within the archipelago itself, small-scale coastal communities traded both with each other and places beyond. Fishers and salt makers, and the communities to which they belonged, made up a complex network that extended beyond the coast and into the hinterland.[22] The local and foreign seafarers who lived and worked in these waters faced a litany of marine dangers—storms, coral reefs, piracy—and many ships and their crew met their fate here.

Indonesia's underwater cultural heritage is both abundant and diverse.[23] According to commonly quoted data from the year 2000, there are at least 463 shipwrecks in Indonesian waters.[24] Less commonly noted is that these ships date to the period from 1508 to 1878, and that the figure of 463 relates only to shipwrecks that have been positively identified.[25] Of those, ninety-three have been verified and just fourteen explored.[26] Many of these wrecks are located in the western part of the archipelago (which is where Belitung Island is located) along the ancient maritime routes that connect the Indian Ocean to the South China Sea and to the Spice Islands of Maluku in the east.[27] A now-defunct Indonesian underwater archaeology blog put the total number of shipwreck locations at 2,046 while Indonesian and international media sources have cited archival records that suggest that some ten thousand—even up to thirty thousand—Chinese ships sailed to the Indonesian archipelago, never to return.[28] Regardless of what the total number of shipwrecks is, the fact remains that underwater cultural heritage in Indonesia is as plentiful as it is diverse, and as diverse as it is hidden. This heritage includes ancient dhows that traveled to China, East Indiamen carrying tea and spices, and World War II naval vessels. Certainly, many more shipwrecks remain undiscovered, or at least unreported.

These wrecks have the potential to shed light on the rich histories of the archipelago beyond those of the well-known Sriwijayan maritime kingdom or Europeans seeking spices.[29] But the significance of the maritime domain—its histories, and the material legacy of these histories—has long been overlooked in favor of the terrestrial in Indonesia. Questions about how heritage is valued, and by and for whom, have been asked of Indonesia's temples, but not its shipwrecks.[30] This neglect has been compounded by global trends that have seen critical perspectives applied to terrestrial but not underwater sites. While technological developments during the last century have made it easier to access the deep, it is only recently that scholars have begun to examine the ethics, ownership, appropriation, and commercialization of the world's underwater cultural heritage.

Equally, the development of a regulatory framework to protect and preserve underwater cultural heritage has lagged behind that of terrestrial sites, both in Indonesia and internationally. In Indonesia, the legislation that saw the *Belitung* salvaged and sold originates in the unregulated recovery of another notorious shipwreck, the *Geldermalsen*. This was a Dutch East India Trading Company vessel, traveling from China to the Netherlands with a full load of tea, porcelain, and gold when it was wrecked in 1752 near the Riau Islands.[31] The *Geldermalsen*'s salvage in 1985 prompted the introduction of Indonesia's first shipwreck legislation, even as questions remained about whether the *Geldermalsen* was in Indonesian waters.[32] The salvager was Michael Hatcher, who, evoking the treasure-fueled narratives popular in shipwreck exhibitions, described the work of his team as a "race to get what they could before being interrupted by weather, rivals, pirates, or some government."[33]

The *Geldermalsen* salvage was likened to swimming "in a gigantic teapot" because, despite the presence of gold and porcelain, the ship's most precious cargo, at least at the time of its sinking, was in fact tea.[34] This was not a scientific excavation in accordance with established archaeological principles. Describing the discovery of teacups in a crumbled crate, archaeologist George Miller writes:

> The least competent of archaeologists would have recorded which porcelain vessels came from which crates. No attempt was made to save the crates let alone keep track of their contents . . . [Hatcher] recorded almost nothing about the ship and provided almost no conservation for the artifacts.[35]

In 1986, the gold ingots and over 150,000 pieces of porcelain were auctioned by Christie's in Amsterdam. Marketed as "The Nanking Cargo," the auction house actively solicited interest beyond the usual museums and private collectors to "an expanded elite clientele" that included hotels, embassies, department stores, restaurants, and interior designers.[36] The auction raised more than £10 million (US$16 million), and many pieces were sold for ten to fifteen times the catalogue estimate. Concerns grew that these high prices would lead to "a wholesale destruction" of other wrecks.[37] Criticisms were also leveled at the "cynical" profit-making of Hatcher and the Dutch government, with whom Hatcher had signed a contract.[38] Under this arrangement, the Dutch Ministry of Finance received 10 percent of the auction profits. There is no evidence that a parallel arrangement was made with the Indonesian government.[39] Meanwhile, museums—ostensibly the natural home for these objects—were forced to bid on the objects at auction.[40]

The salvage of the *Geldermalsen* was a wake-up call for Indonesia. Hatcher's actions revealed the inadequacy of colonial-era heritage legislation[41] and the vacuum around the legal ownership and management of underwater cultural heritage in Indonesian territorial waters.[42] But the high prices achieved at auction for the *Geldermalsen* cargo also gave the Indonesian government insight into the "eye-opening reality" of the economic value of historic shipwrecks and their cargoes in Indonesian waters.[43]

Frustrated by its inability to prevent the salvage and sale of objects from the *Geldermalsen* or to capitalize on their economic value, the Indonesian government responded by asserting state ownership over wrecks in its territorial waters.[44] Under the terms of a 1989 presidential decree, ships and their cargoes were identified primarily as economic rather than historical resources—resources that belonged to the state. The decree regulated the salvage and utilization of valuable objects (*benda berharga*) from historic shipwrecks in Indonesian waters. A National Shipwreck Committee[45] was formed to issue salvage permits, bringing together representatives from nine different government departments, with fees payable to as many as twenty-two.[46] The new decree was motivated not by protection and preservation, but by ownership and profit.

Over the next twenty years, the National Shipwreck Committee issued more than 180 licenses for survey and salvage activities.[47] The decree also stated that the Indonesian government was entitled to 50 percent of salvaged objects, including representative objects.[48] Salvage companies were permitted to sell the remaining objects. Often this meant that all salvaged objects were sold, with the Indonesian government claiming 50 percent of the gross proceeds of sale, regardless of costs incurred by the salvage company. Provisions to distribute artifacts to local and national museum collections for education and research, to excavate according to established archaeological standards, or to conduct scientific research, were largely ignored. The regulation of commercial management processes in this way had the effect of confirming that underwater objects were marine resources with potential economic value.[49]

The 1989 decree was followed in 1992 by Indonesia's first post-independence cultural heritage law, which asserted its ownership over objects of historical, scientific, and cultural significance. Objects considered to be cultural heritage (*cagar budaya*) were declared state property; if they were not, the finder could exercise ownership rights. This system, in which the state automatically asserted ownership over cultural heritage objects unless it declared otherwise, also applied to underwater objects as stipulated in a number of regulations specifically relating to valuable objects from shipwrecks.

The heritage law sat uneasily alongside the shipwreck decree, creating ambiguity and a situation where the legislation was open to interpretation. Shipwreck objects that had cultural heritage value could not be sold and had to be submitted to the state. To be declared state property, cultural heritage objects had to have certain characteristics, one of which was that they needed to be of great historical, scientific, and cultural value *to Indonesia*.[50] This appeared to suggest that ownership rights were determined by the type of objects found.[51] Furthermore, in a provision that all but guaranteed objects recovered from shipwrecks would never be found to have cultural heritage value, these regulations also allowed for the rest of the recovered objects—that is, those deemed *not* to be of cultural heritage value—to be sold by auction, with half the gross proceeds earmarked for the government and the remaining half allocated to the salvage company. Not only did these provisions reduce the likelihood that an object would be deemed to have cultural heritage value, it also placed further pressure on salvage companies to recoup their costs by generating significant profits. Unsurprisingly, not one of the historic wrecks salvaged under these provisions were found to contain objects of cultural heritage value.

What also remains unclear is whether the Indonesian state could assert ownership over objects that did *not* meet the "great historical, scientific and cultural value for Indonesia" criteria specified in the law. If an object was not considered to meet these criteria, did that mean it could be privately owned—and did that imply that the state had no authority to assert ownership over the objects? And what right, therefore, did it have to assert a claim for 50 percent of the sale price of such objects? When these considerations are applied to the *Belitung*, the implication is that the objects were not considered to be of great historical, scientific, and cultural value for Indonesia—otherwise their sale would not have been legal. But if they were not of great historical, scientific, and cultural value, and therefore not "cultural heritage" objects, what rights did the state have to sell them? Who did have the rights?

More broadly, to what extent could a ship wrecked in Indonesian waters be understood to have historical, scientific, and cultural value to Indonesia—and therefore be subject to Indonesian legislation asserting state ownership over the wreck and its objects—if both the vessel and the cargo came from elsewhere? Was the origin (or intended destination) of these vessels and their cargo the determining factor, or was it their presence in Indonesian waters that yielded historical, scientific, or cultural value for Indonesia? The state-authorized removal and sale of shipwrecks and their cargo also raised important questions about attitudes regarding cultural heritage. Who *did* own the objects and stories from these sites? What were the implications for local communities, scholars, or the wider public when a shipwreck assemblage was split up and sold for profit? And what did all of this mean for Indonesia's museums and other collecting institutions?

Making sense of Indonesia's shipwreck and heritage legislation is difficult. And yet we can trace the presence of the *Belitung* objects in Singapore's Asian Civilisations Museum to these legislative inadequacies, which allowed the Indonesian government to derive financial benefit from the shipwrecks in its waters by allowing for the recovery and dispersal of salvaged objects by commercial operators.[52]

Since the passing of the presidential decree of 1989 and the cultural heritage law of 1992, Indonesia's ambivalence toward the maritime domain and the heritage contained therein has continued to manifest in a complex, contradictory, and ever-changing regulatory framework and ambiguous management practices. These complexities and ambiguities point to fundamental tensions within Indonesia about how its underwater cultural heritage should be valued: as a resource for exploitation, or as a legacy worth protecting and preserving. The Indonesian government's changing attitude toward heritage is seen in the repeated movement of the heritage portfolio between the education and tourism ministries, and also in the different words used to describe underwater objects—as valuable objects (*benda berharga*) or as cultural heritage objects (*cagar budaya*). These unresolved philosophical differences stem from a perception that transnational sites and objects, such as sea-lanes and shipwrecks, are not part of Indonesia's heritage.

After what Flecker describes as "decades of poor outcomes," a decision was made in 2010 to halt the issuing of all new survey and salvage licenses.[53] This decision effectively introduced a temporary moratorium on commercial salvaging activities. The moratorium, made permanent in 2016, placed further pressure on Indonesia's underwater cultural heritage by leaving it exposed to unregulated looting. As Flecker explains:

> With the moratorium in place, once-opportunistic fishermen have become full-time salvors. Some are paid by foreigners to salvage cargoes and to smuggle them out of the country. . . . Now when fishermen are caught, there is no rescue archaeology carried out by licensed salvors, and certainly none by the state. It is unlikely that valuable cargoes would be left unguarded on the seabed, so salvage probably carries on in some other guise until nothing remains.[54]

Opponents of the moratorium, like Flecker, argued that it has made Indonesia's underwater cultural heritage more vulnerable than ever. But many in the international community viewed the cessation of commercial salvage activities as a welcome development, as it brought Indonesia closer to international standards for the protection and preservation of underwater cultural heritage.[55] Indonesia's reputation in international, and particularly institutional, circles had suffered lasting damage from decades of salvaging and selling the shipwrecks in its waters. Criticism of its management of its underwater cultural heritage was characterized by undertones of colonialism, cultural elitism, and Eurocentrism, and found its apogee with the *Belitung* case. As flawed as it was, however, Indonesia's complicated, ambiguous, and problematic regulatory framework created new and unexpected paths for the *Belitung*, whose voyage may have been interrupted, but was far from over.

To fully appreciate the enduring controversy surrounding the *Belitung*, an understanding of these international and institutional perspectives is essential. These perspectives are pervasive in discussions about the state of underwater cultural heritage in Indonesia. Examining them here should not necessarily be interpreted as legitimization of this framework, at least not in the Southeast Asian or, specifically, Indonesian, context. They are characterized by specific expectations about the management of underwater cultural heritage, which many countries, including Indonesia, have not met. Instead, the *Belitung* challenges the notion that the protection and preservation model embodied in international institutional models is responsive enough in situations where resources are limited and underwater cultural heritage is under imminent threat.

Authorizing Heritage

The international community's approach to protecting and preserving underwater cultural heritage prioritizes *in situ* preservation and bans commercial exploitation. This approach is best understood within the context of what Smith calls the "authorized heritage discourse," a top-down approach that is "reliant on the power/knowledge claims of technical and aesthetic experts, and institutionalized in the state cultural agencies."[56] Embedded within this discourse is the idea of heritage as a tool by which nations operationalize state-controlled narratives about the past in order to legitimize the present. Heritage has power because it can be owned, manipulated, and commodified.

Perhaps the ultimate expression of the authorized heritage discourse is the UNESCO World Heritage List, which seeks to identify and inscribe heritage sites—or "properties," to use UNESCO's terminology—of outstanding universal value for the benefit of humanity. The 1972 UNESCO *Convention Concerning the Protection of the World Cultural and Natural Heritage* defines the kinds of natural, cultural, or mixed (natural and cultural) sites that can be considered for inscription. The list of inscribed properties, which number over eleven hundred, includes places such as Yellowstone National Park in the United States (natural site), the Borobudur Temple Compounds in Indonesia (cultural site), and Uluru-Kata Tjuta National Park in central Australia (mixed site). In seeking to define these sites as being of universal value, the 1972 convention laid the basis for a shift toward a broader understanding of heritage as something that is not only about protection and preservation, but—more critically—as something that engages with issues relating to representation of minorities and the politics of identity.

Underpinning the 1972 convention is an understanding of heritage as "a distinctive set of official, state-led practices and ways of engaging with the past."[57] As Harrison explains, this concept emerged "from a long history of thinking in particular ways about the relationship between objects and the past, and about the role of the state in using particular objects to tell particular kinds of stories about its origins."[58] Forrest attributes the success of the convention to its ability to negotiate the "delicate balance" that exists between national sovereignty and international intervention.[59] While heritage has universal value, there was no escaping that heritage sites are located within national borders. And, as Harrison points out, the universal value ascribed to heritage in the 1972 convention sits uncomfortably alongside the idea of heritage as cultural property that could be owned, traded, and trafficked, as embedded in the earlier 1970 UNESCO *Convention on the Means of Prohibiting and Preventing the Illicit Import, Export and Transfer of Ownership of Cultural Property*.[60]

The authorized heritage approach creates unease, even among many heritage experts, because of the conflicts it generates between communities, narratives, sites and objects, and identities. In response to such concerns, the 2003 UNESCO *Convention for the Safeguarding of the Intangible Cultural Heritage* sought to recognize the role of communities in expressing and acting upon what warrants protection, and to do so within the context of valuing the world's cultural diversity, including through the objects related to these expressions of diversity.[61] By centering communities within the safeguarding process, the 2003 UNESCO Convention seeks to redefine how, for whom, and why heritage is protected and preserved.[62] In doing so, it offers an opportunity to move beyond a top-down approach to heritage.

It is instructive to think of how these ideas—about how states and communities use objects to tell stories about the past, about who owns and bears responsibility for protecting and preserving sites (and whether these are in fact two different things), and about the notion of universal heritage for all humankind—apply to underwater cultural heritage. Shipwrecks are essential inclusions in this regard, because they are fundamentally transnational in nature and are often not wrecked in their region of origin or "among the people of whose cultural patrimony they properly belong."[63] This question of origin is further complicated by the question of whether "origin" applies to where the vessel was constructed or where the cargo came from—places that, in the case of the *Belitung*, are different.

Furthermore, the seabed on which these shipwrecks lie is crisscrossed by invisible lines that delineate sovereignty and jurisdiction. This is the domain of the 1982 United Nations *Convention on the Law of the Sea* (UNCLOS), the "constitution for the ocean," which has been widely ratified by members of the international community and provides for states' rights and responsibilities in relation to the management of seabed resources. UNCLOS identifies and distinguishes between different maritime zones, including territorial waters (twelve nautical miles from the baseline, usually the mean low-water mark), the contiguous zone (up to another twelve nautical miles from the outer edge of the territorial waters), the exclusive economic zone (200 nautical miles from the baseline), and the continental shelf.[64] Beyond the limits of national jurisdiction is what UNCLOS terms "the Area," more commonly known as the high seas. In some places, including Southeast Asia, states' maritime zones overlap. They may also be subject to competing territorial claims, such as in the South China Sea. UNCLOS was drafted with navigational, fishing, and other trade- and resource-related rights in mind, and makes only marginal provisions, in Articles 149 and 303, for archaeological and historical objects found at sea.

The development of a dedicated convention on underwater cultural heritage—one that brought together the notion of heritage as both universal and proprietary and considered the complexities of the maritime domain—was long and protracted. The campaign was initiated by maritime archaeologists first in Europe and Australia, then in North America, and only later in Asia, Africa, Latin America, and the Middle East.[65] These cultural heritage professionals, as well as the International Council on Monuments and Sites (ICOMOS) and some member states of UNESCO, wanted a coordinated international response to the removal and destruction of underwater cultural heritage by industrial activities and treasure hunters. Some of this early destruction, such as the case of the *Geldermalsen* in the mid-1980s, had sparked a particularly strong reaction from UNESCO member countries.

The opening of the *Titanic* exhibition in London in 1994 exacerbated concerns that underwater cultural heritage was facing imminent destruction and needed to be morally and legally protected. That year, a draft convention was adopted by the International Law Association and forwarded to UNESCO for consideration. The draft convention sought to ensure that underwater cultural heritage was "treated according to archaeological principles."[66] The International Charter on the Protection and Management of the Underwater Cultural Heritage, which had been prepared by the International Committee on the Underwater Cultural Heritage and adopted in 1996 by ICOMOS, was later added as an annex to provide a standard by which assessments could be made.[67] In 1997, the UNESCO General Conference decided that underwater cultural heritage should be addressed at an international level, and the following year a group of governmental experts met for the first time to begin work on a new convention.

This group of experts were challenged with extending comprehensive protection to underwater cultural heritage wherever it was located—that is, beyond the territorial seas and in all maritime zones, including international waters—and doing so through a system based on cooperation between states. They sought to harmonize the protection of underwater cultural heritage with that of heritage on land, and to provide archaeologists with guidelines on how to manage underwater cultural heritage. Many different voices were involved, and negotiations verged on antagonistic.[68] The committee considered input from experts in cultural heritage law, international law, and the law of the sea, all with different interpretations of the legal framework in which the new convention needed to operate; maritime powers and maritime minnows, the latter frequently with the most at stake; and archaeologists and lawyers, who seemed to understand the concept of rules differently. It also had to deal with the open hostility of influential lobbyists representing auction houses, art galleries, individual collectors, and treasure hunters.[69]

The result was UNESCO's *Convention on the Protection of the Underwater Cultural Heritage* (hereafter the 2001 UNESCO Convention), which was adopted by vote at the 2001 General Assembly.[70] It consisted of a main text of thirty-five articles and an annex of thirty-six rules. The convention's core principles centered on the obligation to protect underwater cultural heritage, the creation of an advanced system of state cooperation, a ban on commercial exploitation, and a preference for preserving underwater cultural heritage *in situ*. It also provided for awareness raising and capacity building for underwater cultural heritage worldwide. The rules contained in the annex constitute the most widely recognized standards in maritime archaeology, and address activities directed at underwater cultural heritage that may, directly or indirectly, "physically disturb or otherwise damage" that heritage.

The 2001 UNESCO Convention came into force in 2009, three months after the twentieth state had ratified it. The slow rate of ratification had some precedent in the slow take-up of the 1970 UNESCO Convention. It was also an indication of the various challenges associated with the implementation of the new convention. Not only did it contain complex provisions requiring new or revised legislation across different areas of law, it also represented a fundamental change to the ethics, behaviors, and attitudes related to underwater cultural heritage.[71] Some countries remained concerned that the convention would obstruct free trade and the activities of commercial vessels. Additionally, civil society (and media) support for the protection of underwater cultural heritage was limited in comparison with, for example, public support for wildlife. Within this context, delays in acceptance were inevitable. Just as underwater cultural heritage has lagged behind terrestrial heritage in terms of awareness, access, and management, it will take time before the principles of the 2001 UNESCO Convention are accepted as "universal" in the same way that the principles of the 1970 UNESCO Convention have been.

The 2001 UNESCO Convention is especially undersubscribed in the Asia Pacific, with just four of the forty-six countries in this region having accepted or ratified it.[72] This constitutes the lowest ratification rate for any UNESCO region.[73] Only one of these that has ratified it, Cambodia, is in Southeast Asia. Other Southeast Asian countries, including Indonesia, the Philippines, and Malaysia, have indicated their interest in signing the Convention, but are yet to do so. For Indonesia, the convention remains a pervasive presence in discussions about the state of underwater cultural heritage.[74] There are justifications for this low ratification rate—legal and resourcing issues, for example, or concerns about the effect of the convention on free trade and movement of commercial fishing vessels. But the slow uptake in the Asia Pacific also reflects the convention's origins in Europe and Australia. In a clear example of authorized heritage in action, representatives from the Asia Pacific were brought in on discussions during the drafting and consultation phase but their voices were not heard.

One of the sticking points for many countries yet to ratify the 2001 UNESCO Convention is the difficulty in implementing its core principles, particularly relating to *in situ* preservation. This is

> a perfectionist policy for shipwrecks full of unique artefacts lost in the waters of developed countries that are willing to commit public funds to carry out archaeological excavations, inclusive of the time-consuming and costly tasks of conservation and long-term storage of large numbers of artefacts, documentation, dissemination, and display . . . [it is] all well and good in countries where the wreck-site can be constantly protected from deliberate or accidental interference, or where civic awareness is sufficiently high to render policing unnecessary. In developing countries, where finding the next meal takes priority over cultural sensibilities, this line of thinking is not only naïve but potentially destructive.[75]

The concept of *in situ* management is underpinned by a recognition of the importance of place as part of the cultural, historical, and archaeological significance of a site. This concept is not new, having been used in international charters and conventions since 1931.[76] As advocates of *in situ* preservation emphasize, it is the first, but not only, option. If a wreck is threatened by fishing trawlers, for example, the convention allows for it to be excavated and preserved *ex situ* as an alternative to *in situ* preservation.[77] The decision to manage a wreck *ex situ* must also be "backed up with strong arguments and a detailed description of planned execution."[78] If an archaeological excavation is indeed necessary to protect a site and its artefacts, then the 2001 UNESCO Convention sanctions such a project.

The conflict between supporters and opponents of the 2001 UNESCO Convention regarding the *in situ* principle brings into stark relief the different approaches to terrestrial heritage and underwater heritage. On land, it is commonplace for commercial archaeologists to be paid a salary to conduct archaeological excavations, compile a report, and confer recovered materials to whomever is the site's designated custodian (typically the government). At sea, however, such approaches continue to be elusive. There also remains the question of whether opposition to *in situ* shipwreck management is a smokescreen for an issue of perhaps even greater concern for commercial shipwreck salvagers, namely the 2001 UNESCO Convention's ban on commercial exploitation and the impact this would have on commercial operators' ability to cover their costs through the sale of salvaged objects.[79]

While disagreement continues on the best way of managing underwater cultural heritage, it is critical to acknowledge the significant power imbalances inherent in institutional models of managing heritage and the consequences these power imbalances have both on the ground (or, more accurately, in the water) and on heritage discourse more generally. Many countries struggle to preserve shipwrecks, whether *in situ* or *ex situ*. Both of these management approaches are prohibitively resource intensive for *many* countries, not just those of the Asia Pacific. We have seen how the full archaeological excavation and preservation of the *Mary Rose* took three decades, prompting British heritage authorities to swear off major excavations in the future because of the resources involved. For this and other reasons, underwater cultural heritage is a low priority around the world, not just in developing countries.

The Reef Where Jars Grow

At the same time as UNESCO was finalizing its deliberations, Indonesia was experiencing its most profound political transformation in decades, with widespread protests, economic uncertainty, and, in May 1998, the resignation of President Suharto. His demise signaled the end of three decades of authoritarian rule and the start of the major political, administrative, and social changes of *Reformasi* (the reform era).[80] This was a period marked by greater democratization, the rise of civil society, and growing demands for regional autonomy.

Developments after Suharto's resignation exacerbated an already complex situation for underwater cultural heritage. In particular, the culture portfolio underwent a series of changes in how it was administered. The changes related to debates regarding whether culture's role was educative, or whether it should be more closely associated with the economic opportunities arising out of tourism. This played out in the repeated transferal of the culture portfolio between different ministries.[81] A dedicated marine affairs ministry was created in 1999 under President Abdurrahman Wahid, resulting in a change of leadership in the National Shipwreck Committee.[82] The greater political freedoms of the *Reformasi* era also gave rise to increased heritage awareness and the emergence of heritage advocacy groups within government and civil society.

There were legislative changes as well. In 2000 a new presidential decree was introduced that clearly defined Indonesia's maritime jurisdiction as it related to shipwrecks in its waters. However, this was complicated by decentralization, which led to new jurisdictions over Indonesia's sea territory. National authorities were no longer solely responsible for all shipwreck surveys and salvages in Indonesian waters—by 2000, these responsibilities had been devolved to the regencies and municipalities (up to four nautical miles from shore) and the provinces (four to twelve miles from shore). The central government, meanwhile, maintained jurisdiction over shipwrecks twelve miles or further from shore. These divisions gave rise to conflicts between the different local, regional, and national bodies, with confusion about who was responsible for what.[83] Within this new division of responsibilities, it was also unclear how artifacts or the proceeds of any sales would be shared.[84] This lack of clarity was a continuation of the legislative ambiguity that had existed during the Suharto era, but there were now many more layers of government involved. It was within this fluid regulatory and political environment that the wreck of the *Belitung* was discovered and salvaged by Seabed Explorations in 1998 and 1999.

Tilman Walterfang, founder, owner, and director of Seabed Explorations, was born in Germany, and studied mechanical engineering before finding employment as the manager of a German concrete factory. His mid-career move into maritime exploration and salvage work was prompted by information he received in 1993 from one of his Indonesian factory staff about "some maritime discoveries."[85] Ceramic bowls had been found in the "translucent, reef-strewn waters" of the staff member's native island of Belitung; treasure, he said, lay under the waves. The regular and inadvertent discovery of ceramics in the waters around Belitung and nearby Bangka Island was a lucrative side business for many local fishers, as had been the case in the aftermath of the *Geldermalsen* several years earlier. His interest piqued, Walterfang visited Indonesia in 1995 and participated in a number of diving expeditions.[86] These expeditions yielded samples from two ancient shipwrecks, which he brought back to Germany to solicit interest from universities and museums.[87]

Having established that there were indeed potentially lucrative ceramics in the waters around Bangka and Belitung Islands, Walterfang resigned from his job and relocated to Indonesia in 1997.[88] There he established his maritime exploration and salvage company and set about exploring the surrounding seas more systematically. Base camp was a small bungalow on the northern part of Belitung Island, near a local fishing village at Tanjung Kelayang. He paid local fishers and divers to report back to him on any objects they came across in the course of their daily activities. More active searches were also undertaken, in a fishing boat named, optimistically, the *Kencana* (Gold).

The first wreck salvaged by Seabed Explorations was the tenth-century *Intan* (Diamond) wreck, in 1997. The *Intan* was the oldest Southeast Asian wreck to be found with a complete cargo. The salvage revealed a highly diverse load of significant historical value to Indonesia because of the evidence it provided of Indonesian seafaring traditions.[89] The wreck lay southwest of Belitung Island, close to the east coast of Sumatra, at a depth of eighty-eight feet. Flecker, who had been employed to oversee the salvage, described the location, with its clear water, slow currents, and plentiful marine life, as "a diver's delight . . . it is hard to imagine a more pleasant working environment."[90] German diver Fred Dobberphul, who would later go on to oversee the first season of the *Belitung* salvage, was employed as Flecker's assistant.

Indonesia required Seabed Explorations, as a foreign commercial entity, to partner with a local Indonesian company in order to obtain a salvage license for the *Intan*. This was a costly exercise: the government charged around US$20,000 for a survey license, and up to US$40,000 for a salvage license. It was Flecker who provided the local connections, which he had fostered in 1996 while working on the thirteenth-century *Java Sea Wreck*.[91] A local company had been established at that time, PT Sulong Segarajaya, with an Indonesian partner and other investors.[92] Flecker was thus well placed to facilitate a partnership between Seabed Explorations and PT Sulong Segarajaya for the *Intan* salvage. A great diversity of archaeologically significant objects were recovered from the *Intan*, including ceramics from China and elsewhere, coins, thousands of ingots (including tin, lead, and silver), and organics including ivory, deer antlers, tiger bones and teeth, an elephant's tooth, human bones and a polished molar, resin, and astonishingly still-fragrant candlenuts.[93]

Following the salvage of the *Intan* in 1997, Seabed Explorations began investigating a wreck found in 1998 by fishers northeast of Belitung Island. Known as the *Bakau* (for the small island near the wreck's location) or *Maranei* wreck, this Ming dynasty (1368–1644) vessel was of Chinese construction and dated from the early fifteenth century, making it contemporaneous with the voyages of Chinese admiral Zheng He through Southeast Asia.[94] The type and diversity of the *Bakau*'s cargo—including coins and ceramics from Thailand, China, and Vietnam—has drawn parallels with a fourteenth-century wreck, the *Turiang*, found in Malaysia, which is thought to be no more than half a century older than the *Bakau*.[95]

The *Bakau* had been looted by fishers prior to the commencement of Seabed Excavations' salvage operation.[96] One of the Seabed Explorations team described their work on the site as "not particularly profitable."[97] When Seabed Explorations became aware of the *Belitung* wreck later in 1998, they shifted their focus away from the *Bakau*. Seabed Explorations did not completely abandon the site, however, and eventually returned to finish the salvage. In May 1999, Flecker—already on-site for his work on the second season of the *Belitung* salvage—dived the *Bakau* wreck for five days. By that stage there was very little left other than the ship's hull and oversized storage jars filled with sediment, "which had obviously been too heavy for earlier salvors to lift."[98] The looting of the *Bakau*, and possibly the distraction of the *Belitung*, meant that only about sixteen hundred objects were retrieved from the *Bakau* wreck. These were desalinated and sorted at Seabed Explorations' base camp, and later conserved in New Zealand.

At this time, in the late 1990s, rumors were circulating on Belitung Island of a "reef in which jars are growing."[99] Local fishing families had been aware of the wreck for some time, perhaps even years. There is disagreement about when—and with whom—these fishing families first shared information about the wreck's coordinates, with implications for who could salvage, and ultimately profit from, the site.[100] What is clear, however, is that Seabed Explorations became aware of the wreck in August 1998 when a fisherman presented a member of the team with

a cup of the Tang period which had a high food [foot] with iridescent, transparent green glaze, at the inner side of the cup was a plastically modelled fish, there was a gap at the bottom of the cup with a connection in form of a straw [sic], which was applied to the outer side of the food cup.[101]

The description of this object is consistent with the green-splashed stoneware tube cups that were found in the *Belitung* cargo. Several days later, the Seabed Explorations employee was approached by two fishers who "intended to offer us the site."[102] The fishers also had with them a Changsha ewer and bowl.

The fishers considered their knowledge of the wreck site to be their property, to be shared as they wished. On August 20, 1998, the Seabed Explorations employee phoned Walterfang, who was in Germany securing funding for the company's projects. Together, they decided to call the head of the salvage department away from his work on the *Bakau* to examine the Tang discovery.[103] Seabed Explorations' Indonesian partner registered the wreck coordinates with the National Shipwreck Committee in anticipation of the complicated licensing process. The Seabed Explorations employee continues:

On the next day, our fishermen—as it was agreed—came to the director of our salvation department—they had diving equipment, a satellite navigation system/GPS for performing an exact location of the discovery was available, too [sic]. After a two-and-a-half hours trip with the Pongpong [local boat] along the Western coast of the Belitung island we reached our des-

Figure 5. Local fishers are frequently the first to know of a wreck's presence. Having long been aware of a "reef where jars grow," fishers on Belitung Island disclosed its location to Seabed Explorations, leading to the official discovery of the *Belitung* shipwreck in 1998. Photo by Michael Flecker, 1999.

tination with sight to the coast of the island. [. . .] In the meantime, the director of our salvation department prepared himself for diving and our discussions resulted first of all in examining the measurements of the shipwreck and in initially taking out individual discoveries for inspection. When the head of the salvation department came back to the surface, he shook his head, beaming all over his face and said: "I have never seen such an enormous amount." Now we were only interested in securing the site. [. . .] Our director now had the difficult task to secure the site as quickly as possible. This was to be done in the Indonesian Government [*sic*] and be carried out within a ten-miles-radius. He also had the task to find the necessary financing. Finally, he succeeded in doing this. [. . .] We agreed on bringing our salvation ship immediately on the next day to the site, with guards of the Indonesian navy for preventing plundering, which had after all already taken place earlier.[104]

These excerpts convey the sense of excitement and urgency experienced by members of the Seabed Explorations team. They also note efforts to quickly secure the site from looting, although it does not indicate whether the threat of looting was from opportunistic locals or from other salvage companies.

Already in possession of a survey license, and with the wreck coordinates at hand, Seabed Explorations was now ready to immediately apply for a salvage license. However, a team of French divers was also active on the island, and the ten local fishing families who lived closest to the *Belitung* wreck site could not agree on who should be allowed to salvage it.[105] Four representatives of the ten families were already working with Walterfang, and they advocated for sharing the information with Seabed Explorations. This decision, about with whom to share the knowledge, was to determine the future of the objects. At the same time, the fishing families' ability to shape the future of these objects extended only as far as having a say in who would salvage the objects, despite the fact that it could reasonably be argued that this wreck and its cargo were part of their heritage, and potentially also their livelihoods.

Seabed Explorations had an Indonesian business partner and was in possession of an unlimited nationwide survey license and the wreck's coordinates. Having just completed the *Bakau* survey, they were fully operational, with finance, ships, and divers. However, due to the dispute with the other dive team, the Indonesian government imposed two additional requirements to secure the salvage license: agreement with the fishers, and payment of a bond, totaling IDR$100 million. Seabed Explorations managed to meet these requirements and was issued the salvage license on August 24, 1998.

It may not be possible to ever determine which dive team was the first to find out about the fishermen's maritime discoveries, or whether illicit payments were made to secure the salvage license, as some have alleged.[106] However, it was Seabed Explorations that was ultimately successful in obtaining the salvage license. This would have major consequences for the objects: as Seabed Explorations was still in possession of the *Intan* assemblage, it was in a position to negotiate with the government to ensure the *Belitung* assemblage was not divided in half as per Indonesian requirements. Whether this outcome would have been achieved had the objects been salvaged by another company is impossible to determine. What is certain is that, by August 1998, there was knowledge of the wreck within the community and also among competing dive teams. There was also knowledge of the high prices shipwreck ceramics could command. At that time, Indonesia had no way of managing shipwreck cargoes other than through their licensed salvage. Had a salvage permit not been issued, the objects would have been recovered illegally and dispersed on the black market for antiquities.

What also stands out in this period is the recognition that these objects could benefit the local community through the generation of employment opportuni-

Figure 6. Broken and intact ceramics strewn across the seabed at the shipwreck site. Photo by Michael Flecker, 1999.

ties associated with the salvage work. In the longer term, local fishing families may have reasonably expected that the discovery of a significant shipwreck would have benefits for tourism on the island, perhaps through the creation of a dedicated museum in which to display the objects.[107] There may also have been hopes of generating income through tourism, a possibility that is strengthened by the fact that the salvage permit, when it was issued, required the *Belitung*'s hull to be left *in situ* with "the hope that the hull would become a tourist attraction for scuba divers."[108] Such cultural tourism opportunities draw attention to the economic potential of shipwrecks besides their salvage and sale, but must be accompanied by appropriate investments in protecting and managing the site.

Conclusion

The wrecking of the *Belitung* signified the end of the vessel's life and the beginning of its many afterlives. Submerged under the water for over a thousand years, it became part of a hidden marine ecosystem. But its proximity to the tektite-strewn island of Belitung, and the fishing communities who lived there, shaped its fate. When it was finally discovered, that discovery took place within a political and regulatory context that facilitated the wreck's resurfacing rather than one in which the wreck would be managed *in situ* by being reburied with sand or covered with artificial seagrass. Indonesia's management approach automatically set the *Belitung* on a new course that would see it confront the 2001 UNESCO Convention and its powerful supporters.

Although it had not sailed contemporaneously with the *Geldermalsen*, the *Bakau*, or the *Intan*, these other shipwrecks influenced the *Belitung* in very specific ways: by drawing attention to the bounty European auction houses placed on Chinese ceramics; by attracting international divers to Belitung Island; and, as the following chapter demonstrates, by serving as a bartering tool by which Seabed Explorations was able to negotiate an unprecedented deal to keep the *Belitung* assemblage intact. Understanding these early influences is essential in establishing the biographies of the wreck and the objects it carried.

As curator John Guy has observed, sometimes "an event occurs which dramatically enlarges the boundaries of our knowledge and raises our understanding of the realities of the past. The discovery of the *Belitung* shipwreck is one such event."[109] Indonesia's complicated, ambiguous, and problematic regulatory framework created new and unexpected trajectories for the vessel and the objects it carried. In the process, the *Belitung* has become the ultimate example of the tensions that are created when authorized heritage discourses are imposed on underwater cultural heritage with little regard for local context. Such tensions arose not just because of the historical significance of the *Belitung* in its original incarnation as a seafaring vessel engaged in trade across and beyond the Indian Ocean, but also because of its post-discovery afterlives. Having been discovered by the fishing families and effectively handed over to Seabed Explorations in 1998, the salvage and sale of the *Belitung*, to which I turn in the following chapter, set the scene for these diverse afterlives to begin in earnest.

CHAPTER THREE

Provenanced

The *Belitung* brought together objects, technologies, and people from the ninth century, their stories discrete and contained for over a thousand years. But from the moment the wreck was discovered and the first object removed, these stories began to travel outward from the wreck site and into the world once more. Laying bare the details of the *Belitung*'s salvage, as this chapter seeks to do, is an important step in understanding the afterlives of this wreck. Having been hidden beneath the water for centuries, the salvaged objects were poised to accrue new meanings and histories. Their trajectory was not linear but instead reflected the multiple factors—and the high stakes—at play. Salvaged, separated, and sometimes even stolen, the objects were no longer part of a single archaeological assemblage. Their stories, however, remain entangled well beyond the Indonesian waters in which they were found.

In the polarized debates that characterize discussions about shipwreck management, the Indonesian model of the late 1990s defies easy categorization. This was certainly not "maritime archaeology" in the way UNESCO or other international institutions understood it, nor was it illegal in the way that looting was. Indonesia's approach to the shipwrecks in its waters from 1989 until 2010 can be best described as legalized salvage for profit. Under this system, the survey and recovery of "valuable objects from the cargo of sunken ships" was accommodated under the permit system administered by Indonesia's National Shipwreck Committee.[1] The way in which this policy intersected with Indonesia's heritage legislation, with its scope for interpretation and flexibility on how salvaged objects were managed, was complex, ambiguous, and even contradictory. Yet, despite its limitations (which, contrary to expectation, actually produced a positive outcome for the *Belitung* cargo by ensuring it was able to be kept together), the salvage was fundamentally legal. Whether or not it was ethical is, of course, another matter. These legal and moral aspects are essential considerations in light of the ensuing (and enduring) criticisms of the salvage process.

Examining the salvage process for both its failures and its positive outcomes does not imply justification for, or support of, treasure hunting, or even commercial salvage itself. Rather, it reveals that commercial salvage was the least destructive option available at the time, and the only way in which this specific shipwreck could be secured from the immediate and devastating threat of looting. Many of the allegations that this was no better than a treasure hunt do, in fact, hold water. But, as this chapter shows, there were many other components to the story. The conclusions arising from this "deep dive" on the circumstances of the *Belitung* salvage pertain to this particular shipwreck and also to the management of shipwrecks more generally, as they demonstrate that context—archaeological, certainly, but also social, political, and institutional—matters.

Salvaging the *Belitung*

The salvage of the *Belitung* began in late August 1998, just three months after President Suharto's resignation. The monsoon season was imminent. Looting posed a major threat. There was widespread knowledge of the wreck both on Belitung Island and also within government circles, which—coupled with perceptions of a bounty on Chinese ceramics recovered from the ocean—threatened the safety of both the objects and the Seabed Explorations team. According to Walterfang, the head of Seabed Explorations, the government's National Shipwreck Committee pushed for the salvage to commence immediately and be finalized within two weeks.[2] The brevity of the salvage was an indication that the government envisaged this as a recovery operation—a "first aid rescue operation," as Walterfang has described it—not an archaeological excavation.[3] As a result, many compromises were made.

Although he was not required to do so under the terms of the salvage permit, Walterfang has said that he attempted to hire an archaeologist. This would have added legitimacy to the project in the eyes of the international and institutional community. However, he had difficulty in doing so "because of the volatile political situation in Indonesia at the time."[4] Instead, Walterfang hired someone with whom he had already worked: German diver Fred Dobberphul, who had assisted Flecker with the *Intan* salvage the year before.[5] Although the 2001 UNESCO Convention had not yet been introduced, the lack of a qualified professional archaeologist on the salvage team was not consistent with the provisions outlined in the draft convention or the associated charter. Nevertheless, Seabed Explorations managed to assemble a team quickly, enabling it to pivot from the *Bakau* to the *Belitung* wreck. A core team of five, most of who were based at Tanjung Kelayang, was supported by up to thirty-six staff. Many were locals, suggesting that the hopes held by the fishing families for a flow of financial resources back into the community had been realized.[6]

Sixteen divers worked in shifts from the salvage ship *Kencana* under the supervision of Dobberphul in his capacity as the head of the salvage department.[7] A grid was laid over the wreck site and records were made of the objects found in each grid square. Up to five thousand ceramic pieces were recovered each day and transported back to land on a vessel named *Dangdut Queen*. Many of the objects were in a superb state. The Changsha bowls, in particular, were in excellent condition, their glaze shining "as brightly as the day they were fired."[8] So beautifully preserved were these bowls that one eminent curator later confessed that his initial belief, upon seeing them for the first time, had been that they were fakes.[9] Once ashore, three or four people classified the objects according to quality, pattern, and type.[10] Higher-grade objects were preserved under lock and key in a separate room at base camp. No computers or other electronic devices were used to catalogue the salvaged objects, and no records from this period have ever been published. Important information relating to the stowage and stratification—an archaeological term that relates to the layering of sediment, debris, and objects over an extended period of time—of the cargo was lost or not recorded at all.[11]

The team was overwhelmed by the quantity of objects coming out of the ocean.[12] Many shipwrecks, the *Belitung* included, reach a state of equilibrium after a certain period of time underwater.[13] Bringing objects out of the sea, thus exposing them to light and oxygen, leads to rapid deterioration. The main challenge for the team therefore lay in how to store the thousands of objects being recovered each day. These objects required immediate desalination—removal of soluble salts through immersion in fresh water—to slow the rate of deterioration. Initially, plastic bowls were brought in from Tanjung Pandang, but these proved to be vastly inadequate. Obtaining these and other necessary equipment to store and desalinate the salvaged objects caused "unspeakable trouble" for the team, and sometimes it was days or even weeks before much-needed materials became available.[14] The solution was to build a large concrete basin near base camp. This too became insufficient to accommodate the ever-increasing numbers of ceramics being recovered from the seabed, and so another pit was excavated, lined with plastic foil, and filled with fresh water. Bamboo frames were built over the desalination pits, acting as a makeshift roof. An electric water pump and long hoses were used to change the water regularly. The large pools were nevertheless affected by excessive algae growth, and mosquito-borne diseases, including dengue and malaria, were rife.[15]

The team worked under significant pressure with extremely limited resources. These pressures created tension on-site. An anonymous report written in 2002 by a former employee of Seabed Explorations outlines how a visiting conservator "really got on our nerves" by providing advice on how to minimize corrosion of the metal objects "without doing anything by [*sic*] himself."[16] Of even greater

Figure 7. Once centuries of sediment had been washed out, perfectly preserved Changsha bowls could be seen packed tightly
inside large storage jars. These special packing techniques contributed to the superb condition of many of the bowls. Photo by
Michael Flecker, 1999.

concern were the mistakes made by junior personnel. One female employee, a
student, mixed up Ming dynasty objects from the *Bakau* wreck with Tang dynasty objects from the *Belitung* wreck. Another student "caused a wall with
plates and bowls to fall down at the site under water. He intended to search for
bowls at the lowest point of this wall, when he draw [*sic*] out one of these bowls, the
whole wall broke down."[17] Meanwhile, the National Shipwreck Committee continued to exert pressure on Seabed Explorations to work quickly. According to Wal-

terfang, "After six weeks of operation we received another deadline to finish it within two weeks."[18] By October, the incoming northwest monsoon forced the conclusion of the first salvage season. In just two months, an astonishing forty thousand objects had been recovered. This comprised most of the ceramic cargo, including the three blue-and-white dishes, as well as the majority of the gold objects.[19] But the team was beset by problems and overwhelmed by the number of objects for which it was now responsible. Security and safety—of both the objects and the staff—became an issue, especially following the discovery of gold.

The shipwreck site itself was also under threat. During the monsoon-enforced break, Indonesian police and navy personnel were stationed over the site, but despite their presence, looting occurred, often at night.[20] Dangerous conditions caused by blustery onshore winds were not enough to deter the looters. Objects that were too heavy or large to lift were smashed so that the divers could access the smaller objects within. Fortunately, however, they had neither airlift nor water dredges, else the destruction would have been even more pronounced.[21]

Meanwhile, work continued on land, with the team sorting, documenting, and desalinating the thousands of objects. A female student spent the monsoon months sorting through approximately four cubic meters of broken ceramic pieces, known as sherds, but became increasingly concerned not only for the security of the objects, which were being targeted at night by thieves, but also for her own safety. She was ethnic Chinese—at a time in Indonesia when to be ethnic Chinese was to be potentially discriminated against or even violently attacked—and responsible for a large quantity of potentially valuable objects.[22] In December 1998, she contacted Walterfang, who was then in Germany, to express her concerns. His requests to the Indonesian police and navy for additional security went unmet. Describing her as, by then, "very emotional," Walterfang says that she decided to conceal the objects in question by covering them with a truckload of sand—information that has, until now, been missing from the historical record.[23] Many people in the team were unhappy about her actions. Walterfang responded by requesting immediate assistance from an Indonesian colleague, who removed the objects from the sand and stored them inside Walterfang's bungalow. They filled seventy-nine fishing baskets.

Nevertheless, rumors spread that Seabed Explorations had left sherds buried on the beach and in the water, and that they did so with the intention of reducing transportation and conservation costs and increasing the value of the objects that were recovered. In a 2010 survey of the site, Indonesian archaeologists found sherds spread out in a radius of approximately twenty square meters, or 215 square feet, from which they concluded that the ceramic fragments had been "removed by the company then thrown back into the sea."[24] They suggested this decision had been made because Seabed Explorations had considered the sherds to be "non-commercial."[25] Seabed Explorations strenuously denies these allegations, pointing instead to the unauthorized actions of the student as well as the "massive wild looting activities" that took place at the wreck site.[26]

By April 1999, with the monsoon over, the salvage could recommence. Walterfang had revised his operations and was, in his own words, "better prepared."[27] Dobberphul was replaced by Flecker, an Australian who had trained as an engineer and had some twenty years of experience in maritime explorations and commercial salvage work in Southeast Asia. Flecker's role was to oversee the salvage and record the site, including the ship's hull.

Twelve divers lived and worked on board the dive ship, which did not return to shore until the salvage operation was complete about two months later. Each diver made two long dives per day, after which they would mark where they had been working on a whiteboard. Flecker made a point of logging the location of one-off objects, but the multi-duplicate ceramics were placed in baskets with a grid label and transferred by boat each evening to be logged on shore. This system was more streamlined than the first season, but still made it difficult for Flecker to oversee the entire operation.[28]

In addition to supervising the recovery of objects, he sought to survey and document what little remained of the hull, which had been dislodged in the first season, before the monsoon.[29] Access to the hull was impeded by coral and concretions—dense, hard rock-like lumps, usually consisting of iron, sand, and sea life—but key components were able to be recorded, including on video.[30] He also surveyed the grapnel-type iron-and-wood anchor, which had suffered some damage but was generally in good condition.[31] Wood-eating *teredo navalis*, the "naval shipworms," were present, threatening the vessel's timber structures.[32] The shipworms had quickly destroyed exposed timbers during the first season, and steps were taken to ensure this was not repeated in the second season.[33] So accurate were Flecker's observations of the hull that they match those of the more recently discovered *Phanom Surin* shipwreck in almost every respect.[34]

By June 1999, the salvage operation had ended. The terms of Seabed Explorations' salvage permit required the hull to be left *in situ*, with the government intending to develop it into a local diving attraction.[35] This had the potential to create long-term economic benefits for the local community, far more so than the short-term employment opportunities associated with the salvage. However, the site was not protected post-salvage, let alone developed. The day after Seabed Explorations concluded its second and final season, up to fifty diving boats were seen above the wreck site, with divers using long iron rods to break apart the hull re-

Figure 8. The shipwreck site revealed neat stacks of Changsha bowls. Over two seasons (August–October 1998, April–June 1999), approximately sixty thousand objects were salvaged from waters off Belitung Island. The overwhelming majority of these—some 57,500 pieces— came from the kilns of Changsha. Photo by Michael Flecker, 1999.

mains in the search for gold.[36] If any ceramics remained, they would have been dislodged and broken by these destructive activities.[37] The whereabouts of the anchor, which was concreted to the hull, are unknown.[38] Having already authorized the salvage and sale of the objects, Indonesia's subsequent failure to preserve what remained of the ship itself was a lost opportunity to preserve a significant piece of maritime heritage, or to capitalize on the economic benefits, through underwater tourism, that it may have provided.

Criticisms of the Salvage

The failure to protect and preserve the wreck *in situ* was one of the major criticisms made by the international maritime archaeology community of the *Belitung* salvage.[39] In particular, Seabed Explorations was heavily criticized for recovering the cargo but leaving the hull and anchor in the water.[40] Many in the international community viewed this as proof that objects with archaeological value were deprioritized at the expense of those with economic value.[41] Maritime archaeology values context. A sunken vessel and its cargo must be considered as a single assemblage: they should not be separated either physically or intellectually. Instead of the government allowing the objects to be separated from the hull, critics argued, why not simply deny Seabed Explorations a salvage permit altogether? But this is an idealistic argument that ignores the spatial and temporal context of the *Belitung*. In this location, at this time—and with the precedent established by the sale of objects from the *Geldermalsen* cargo—the *in situ* preservation of the *Belitung* was simply not possible. There was widespread awareness of the shipwreck's existence among (and beyond) the island's community, and of the presence of Chinese ceramics. Denying a salvage permit would have condemned the site to destruction and the objects to dispersal through the antique shops of Jakarta.[42] In addition to the threat posed by looting, *in situ* preservation also exposed the wreck, like so many others in Southeast Asia's crowded waters, to the threats posed by commercial fishing trawlers, which drag their nets across the seabed and cause indiscriminate damage and destruction to underwater sites and objects.[43] Decades later, the theft of objects from shipwrecks—including the industrial-scale, scrap metal–focused operations that have seen naval vessels from World War II stolen from the Java Sea in their entirety—continues in Indonesian waters, with authorities either powerless or unwilling to prevent it.[44]

The second major criticism of the *Belitung* salvage related to the use of a commercial salvage company to recover the objects instead of the excavation being government-led.[45] This again demonstrates a fundamental lack of understanding of the Indonesian context in the late 1990s. Maritime archaeology in Indonesia was in its infancy at this time. There were simply not the resources to conduct a full archaeological excavation in accordance with the provisions articulated in the draft convention and charter. Aside from capacity limitations, there is also the question of whether there was the political will to conduct a government-led excavation. It is naïve to suggest there was any possibility, amid the political turmoil and anti-Chinese sentiment of 1998, that significant resources be allocated to recovering a shipwreck carrying Chinese cargo. This returns us to a recurring theme of the *Belitung*'s story, namely the question of what constitutes Indonesian, and Indonesia's, underwater cultural heritage, and how the answer to this question determines the way in which such heritage is valued and managed.

The third criticism of the *Belitung* salvage, inextricably connected to Indonesia's failure to preserve the site *in situ* and the decision to mandate commercial salvage within its shipwreck management policies, relates to the absence of established archaeological processes.[46] This criticism is justified. Even though the second salvage season was an improvement on the frenetic "triage" approach of the first season, there is no doubt that essential information was lost and some objects were damaged or stolen. The most stunning ceramic of the entire assemblage, the oversized ewer, is alleged to have been looted from the site before being later returned for a finder's fee.[47] Stories of the sherds being thrown overboard or buried in the sand have become salutary tales within undergraduate maritime archaeology courses, emblematic of just how flawed the *Belitung* salvage process was; others, such as the story of the accidental mingling of objects from the Ming and the Tang periods, are less commonly known but equally troubling. Records of which object came from which grid have never been made available, making artifact distribution, a key data point for maritime archaeologists, all but impossible to determine.[48]

These failures were a direct result of the commodification of underwater objects by Indonesia's regulatory framework, in which they were positioned as economic resources to be mined rather than as archaeological and historical resources to be valued. And, while it is easy to apportion blame to Seabed Explorations, it is important to situate the failings of the *Belitung* salvage within the context of Indonesia's inconsistent and poorly implemented approach to underwater heritage. Provisions to employ archaeological principles and retain objects were never enforced. A salvage company could choose to document the site, but was not compelled to. Salvage companies were required to pay large deposits and fees, which were supposed to ensure compliance with rules and regulations by acting as a type of bond, but instead had the effect of privileging companies that were able to make a high initial investment rather than those committed to ensuring archaeological standards were met. The consequence of this problematic regulatory, political, and social environment was the loss of archaeological data. As early as 1995, Indonesian legal scholars had identified problems with ownership rights and management of cultural heritage objects found within Indonesian waters.[49] But despite the increasing groundswell within the international community to strengthen mechanisms for the protection and preservation of underwater cultural heritage, Indonesia had done little to move toward an archaeological, rather than an economic, valuation of the objects in its waters.

Yet—in a sign of the ambiguity and complexity of the *Belitung* and its afterlives—it was this same regulatory context that led to the assemblage remaining (mostly) together rather than being dispersed. This is because it created an environment that was malleable enough for Seabed Explorations to successfully negotiate with the government for full ownership rights to the *Belitung* objects—rather than the 50 percent Indonesia was legally entitled to—by completing a deal on the objects it had recovered from the *Intan*. These negotiations did not take place, however, until the *Belitung* objects had been conserved and the full potential of the collection as an intact assemblage had been apprehended.

Wrestling for Control

By the end of the second salvage season in June 1999, Seabed Explorations had recovered around sixty thousand objects. Although gold and silver had been found, the ceramics were the real treasure. This was the largest and most intact collection of Tang dynasty ceramics ever found in a single location: masses of utilitarian bowls from the kilns of Changsha, a clutch of experimental green-splashed ware from Gongxian, and a rare assemblage of exquisite snow- and jade-like ceramics from Xing, Ding, and Yue. Seabed Explorations exported most of the objects to New Zealand, where it had established a conservation facility, adapting an aircraft hangar to house the objects, with basins miles in length and banks of shelves up to fifteen feet high.[50] "Far away from the media, far away from the world and tourists," this was, finally, an opportunity to pause and take stock of what had been pulled from the ocean.[51]

Many objects were permanently separated from the assemblage at this point.[52] One of Walterfang's former employees sent about twenty Changsha bowls to contacts in Japan, ostensibly to gauge interest in the collection, but these objects were never returned.[53] An additional forty objects turned up in the marketing material for a German auction house, appearing alongside photos of the conservation facility as if to signal their legitimacy.[54] Walterfang denied any involvement, instead reporting the theft and attempted sale of the objects to German police. The objects were subsequently confiscated, their fate unknown.[55] Most significantly, some seven thousand objects, including more than two kilograms of gold leaf, remained in Indonesia in a government warehouse.[56] These seven thousand objects were used as bargaining chips several years later when Seabed Explorations and the government entered into negotiations over ownership rights to the *Belitung* assemblage.

Notwithstanding the dispersal of more than 10 percent of the sixty-thousand-odd objects recovered, the move to New Zealand allowed Seabed Explorations to gain full control of the remainder. The desalination process, already begun in Indonesia, continued. Conservation and restoration of the objects, overseen by German conservator Andreas Rettel, was time-consuming and costly.[57] Conservation of the silver flask alone took four years and cost $350,000.[58] Some objects, including a partially gilded silver plate and a bronze mirror, were also x-rayed to reveal hidden or distorted images, providing conservators with a clearer idea of the impact of corrosion.[59]

As the slow conservation work continued, Seabed Explorations was occupied with securing ownership rights to *all* of the objects. There was a growing appreciation that the *Belitung* assemblage was too significant to be split in half as required by the Indonesian legislation—to realize its full historic, and indeed economic, potential, it needed to be kept intact. Securing legal title would therefore allow Seabed Explorations to sell the objects together rather than auctioning off individual pieces. The Indonesian government was entitled to either 50 percent of the objects recovered by Seabed Explorations—not only from the *Belitung*, but also the other wrecks it had salvaged, including the *Intan* and the *Bakau*—or 50 percent of the gross proceeds of the sale of those objects. Walterfang had been in discussions with the National Shipwreck Committee for years about the *Intan* objects, recovered in 1997, and had what he describes as "justified" (albeit unspecified) claims arising from administrative mismanagement in the final days of the Suharto regime.[60]

With the objects in New Zealand for the legitimate—but also convenient— purpose of conservation, Walterfang was well positioned to negotiate. He proposed two options. The first was that the *Intan* objects be sold on the market, with Indonesia receiving a 50 percent share of the net profit after return of costs to Seabed Explorations' investors. These costs were high, making this option less attractive for Indonesia. The second option was for Seabed Explorations to relinquish the *Intan* cargo in its entirety, plus a one-off payment (at a price to be determined by the Indonesian government). In return, Seabed Explorations would receive proper title documentation to the cargoes of the *Belitung* and the *Bakau*, and the seven thousand objects that remained in government storage in Indonesia would be returned.

Indonesia's National Shipwreck Committee appointed three representatives to engage in the negotiations. Following an inspection visit to the conservation facility in New Zealand, they elected for the second option. By September 2003, an agreement had been reached that Seabed Explorations would give Indonesia US$2.5 million, the *Intan* cargo, and publication rights to a 750-page research report on the *Belitung*.[61] Seabed Explorations also offered to include one hundred objects from the *Belitung* once the seven thousand *Belitung* objects still in Indonesia's possession were returned. For reasons unknown, these one hundred objects had not been included in the final tally of the assemblage, and instead seem to have been part of a personal collection held by Walterfang. Additionally, Seabed Explorations committed to the development of a multimillion-dollar cultural resource center in Bali, complete with a conservation facility, and the provision of conservation training to Indonesian students.[62]

It is possible that the Indonesian negotiators were not aware of the potential economic value of the *Belitung* cargo when they agreed to this arrangement. Rumors attribute Indonesia's willingness to agree to the terms of this deal to the deliberate withholding, by Seabed Explorations, of certain objects from Indonesian inspection, making it difficult for the Indonesian side to ascertain the full value of the *Belitung* cargo.[63] Others suggest that "several high-ranking officials in the Defence Ministry and the Navy" received unofficial payments from Seabed Explorations to secure the deal.[64] Walterfang denies these allegations, claiming that Indonesia's interest was "all about the payment of US$2.5 million, the return of the *Intan* cargo, and about closing the books" on problems created by previous administrations.[65] But as Flecker has noted, the *Intan* was significant in terms of Indonesia's maritime histories. It may have been for this reason, more than any other, that Indonesia agreed to the deal: it was both Indonesian and Indonesia's.[66] The *Belitung*, by comparison, was a Middle Eastern vessel carrying almost-exclusively Chinese objects, while the *Bakau* was a vessel of Chinese construction; their connections to Indonesian histories were seen as tenuous at best.

Seabed Explorations was granted full title to the *Belitung* cargo in November 2004.[67] However, Walterfang claims that Indonesia failed to honor its side of the bargain. President Yudhoyono's new administration (2004–2014) sought to stonewall the deal. Walterfang was asked to "refrain" from requesting the return of the seven thousand objects, and it was at this point the agreement between Indonesia and Seabed Explorations collapsed.[68] The seven thousand objects were never returned to Seabed Explorations, and thus the offer to give one hundred objects to Indonesia was never fulfilled. A decade later, many thousands of the *Belitung* objects remained in storage at a warehouse in Cileungsi, West Java, waiting to be re-inventoried following the restructuring of the National Shipwreck Committee.[69] By 2017, thirty-nine ceramic vessels were in the collection of the National Museum in Jakarta. The gold leaf, or what was left of it, was also on display (although the wall panel incorrectly attributed it to the *Intan* rather than the *Belitung*) and there were also a significant number of objects in the collection of Jakarta's Marine Heritage Gallery.[70] Needless to say, Seabed Explorations never built the maritime museum in Bali or trained Indonesian students in conservation.[71] The details of the deal were not widely known at the time, and there is still confusion in some of the literature about the commitments and compromises that were made by both sides.[72] This is the first time that these details have been published, representing an important corrective to common misunderstandings that Seabed Explorations failed to pay Indonesia half of the *Belitung*'s eventual sale price.

The deal had undoubtedly been to Seabed Explorations' advantage, and would have been even more so had the seven thousand objects been returned. At the same time, however, the potential benefits for Indonesia should be acknowledged, even if they were never realized. Indonesia did not sell the *Intan* cargo. Instead, at least 664 ceramic objects and up to three thousand stone, glass, and metal objects from the *Intan* cargo had been placed in the care of the Museum of Fine Arts and

Ceramics in Jakarta by 2016.[73] This display constitutes the largest surviving assemblage of shipwreck artifacts in an Indonesian museum, a fact that is often overlooked in the polemics about underwater cultural heritage in Indonesia. Unfortunately, the *Intan* objects have been neglected, and their desultory display in Jakarta stands in stark contrast to the magnificence of the *Belitung* exhibition in Singapore. This raises difficult yet increasingly pressing questions about the ethics of insisting that cultural heritage remains in the country in which it is found if that country has neither the desire nor the resources to care for it.

The deal reveals the extent to which the Indonesian regulatory framework could be manipulated and, furthermore, that the consequences of manipulation could be both negative and positive. Regardless of the initial motives of Seabed Explorations or the Indonesian government in negotiating the *Intan/Belitung* deal, the consequence was that not one but three (including the *Bakau*) shipwreck assemblages were kept intact. Furthermore, one remained in Indonesia, the nation in whose territorial waters the objects had been found. This outcome is in stark contrast to the alternative—which is that the collections be split up—had they been managed in strict accordance with the regulatory framework then in place.

Marketing the Assemblage

With full legal title in place, Seabed Explorations was finally in a position to determine the future of the assemblage. Potential purchasers, particularly art dealers and international auction houses, had been circling since the wreck's discovery in 1998. Their interest was in the unique and rare objects—the gold, the oversized green-splashed ewer, the Yue and Xing ceramics—rather than the more ubiquitous and utilitarian Changsha bowls. One auction house, for example, offered to hold a worldwide roadshow followed by a week-long auction in New York. The range of interest within the private, and later also the public, sector is indicative of the ways in which the objects could be used to support diverse narratives and purposes. This "cherry picking" approach, which preferred individual objects rather than the entire assemblage, betrays fundamentally different understandings of value as it applies to a shipwreck. Whereas the dealers and auction houses were interested in individual pieces, maritime archaeologists were clear that the value lay in the whole—and, more importantly, that this value was not economic but archaeological.

Walterfang undoubtedly courted the auction houses, in a move designed, he says, to placate his investors.[74] He remains adamant, however, that he always did so with the expectation that the *Belitung* objects would be sold as a single collection. The decision to keep the assemblage intact was evidence, he says, of his commitment to the objects' archaeological and historical significance, reflecting the fact that this collection, but also the collections from the *Intan* and the *Bakau*, had been "conserved with a view towards installing them in well-appointed museums."[75]

Seabed Explorations' decision to preserve the *Belitung* collection intact prevented the disappearance of objects into private collections, and has had long-term benefits for scholars and researchers. However, there was also significant economic benefit to be gained from keeping the collection together. Walterfang may have marketed himself as a marine explorer, but he was also a businessman: he knew that by prioritizing the *archaeological* value derived from keeping the objects together, he could also realize greater *economic* value. Whereas other auctioned shipwreck cargoes—such as the *Geldermalsen* and the *Intan*—were notable for their diversity, the *Belitung* cargo was, as we know, distinguished by the unusually high concentration of Changsha-ware ceramics. Flooding the international market with tens of thousands of these ceramics would have undermined the potential for the collection as a whole to achieve a high sale price.[76] Christie's estimated the mass-produced Changsha bowls would fetch around US$3 each at auction, while Sotheby's estimated that they were unlikely to bring more than "five pounds apiece" (close to US$7).[77] For approximately 50,000 bowls, this amounts to an upper-estimate of £250,000 (US$340,500). Even accounting for the higher prices that could be achieved for items such as the ewer and the gold cup, this is still a long way from the sale price of US$32 million that was eventually achieved.

Cognizant of the benefits of selling the assemblage intact, Seabed Explorations took steps to develop a publicity and marketing campaign. This included the development of two publications commissioned and financed by Walterfang: *The Tang Dynasty Shipwreck*, and the more detailed *The Belitung Wreck: Sunken Treasures from Tang China*, a significant section of which is in catalog form. These publications were part of broader efforts by Seabed Explorations to showcase the objects to the international market, which also included inviting experts to observe the objects undergoing conservation and sending select objects to curators at leading museums.[78] When Chinese ceramic specialist Geng Baochang from Beijing's Palace Museum visited New Zealand, he is reported to have broken into song before saying that the objects were national treasures that had to go back to China.[79] In contrast to Indonesia's apparent apathy toward the ancient shipwrecks in its waters, Geng expressed a confident assertion of historical ownership. This claim was based on the origin of the *objects*, and overlooked other considerations such as the origin of the vessel, where it had sunk, or the question of the cargo's destination. This perspective, that the objects were China's because it is there that they had been produced, demonstrates the multiple bases on which a claim of moral ownership or historical connection could be made.

A "Natural" Home for the Collection?

Despite these efforts, by 2004 Seabed Explorations still had not secured a purchaser. The salvaged objects had been out of the water for six years, and the cost of conserving, housing, and securing them was rising. Walterfang was under pressure to pay back his investors, and also had obligations to Indonesia, due in August of that year, arising from the *Intan/Belitung* deal. Although some parties, including the Qatari government and the National Palace Museum in Taipei, had expressed interest in the objects, there were only two serious contenders: the Shanghai Museum in China and the Singapore Tourism Board.

China's interest in the objects was easy to explain. These were Chinese objects and, as Geng's reaction had shown, there was a sense that they belonged in China. The reasons for Singapore's interest were less obvious. There was no direct link with the vessel or the objects, and it was not clear whether the vessel had even traveled as far as Singapore. The city-state's interest in the objects stemmed from their capacity to generate tourism income within Singapore's cultural sector.[80] This emphasis was reflected in the fact that it was the Singapore Tourism Board, not the National Heritage Board, that was involved in the discussions. Quite simply, the collection had the potential to drive economic growth; its connection to the country's history was secondary. Acquiring this unique collection of objects would contribute to Singapore's efforts to cement its position as a "global city" within Southeast Asia, "not just for the arts, but for all aspects of economics and trade."[81] Museums, and the objects within them, were part of this competitive strategy, serving as important vehicles for "transmitting an official version of the past that translates easily into the Singapore it needs for the future."[82]

But Singapore's cultural sector was facing significant challenges. As politician George Yeo explained, there was just not "enough money to build museums or galleries, let alone acquire things."[83] Although Singapore's resort island of Sentosa had been home to a public maritime museum overseen by the Port of Singapore Authority since 1975, dwindling visitor numbers and a slated major redevelopment under the Sentosa Masterplan had seen its doors close in 2001.[84] A corporate restructure of the Sentosa Development Corporation (a statutory body under Singapore's Ministry of Trade and Industry) meant that the redevelopment of a public maritime museum never eventuated. Instead, the focus shifted to the development of Resorts World Sentosa, Singapore's first ever "integrated" (casino-based) resort, which opened in 2010.

Yeo first became aware of the *Belitung* objects in 2002 or 2003 when he was approached by Seabed Explorations' freelance marketing agent. Yeo recalls that the agent "made two arguments that arrested my attention. One, he said that this is a very important wreck, and that it should not be broken up. And two, Singapore is a natural home for the collection."[85] Yeo, who was Minister for Trade and Industry at the time, framed his interest in the objects within the context of early international trade:

> I reflected that this [Tang Shipwreck] is about trade, in an earlier era of globalisation. In fact it was a glorious era, of the Tang, of the Abbasid, of the Srivijaya, or of the Nalanda. So I asked to see him. He dropped by with pictures, I leafed through them, and I said "Okay how much?" He gave me some fantastic number. I said I didn't have the money.[86]

This "fantastic number" was US$48 million.[87] With a failed maritime museum on Sentosa and limited funds, Yeo set the proposal aside as unachievable. Thus, despite Singapore's initial interest, negotiations stalled.

The Shanghai Museum remained engaged. By mid-2004, discussions were well advanced, its offer increasing incrementally from week to week. But Seabed Explorations was facing financial ruin and Walterfang had become increasingly concerned by the slow pace of negotiations. As more time passed, Walterfang was "urged by many people including well known art historians to just sell single artefacts into the art market."[88] Cognizant of his rapidly approaching financial deadline with Indonesia, Walterfang entered into a two-month period of exclusive negotiations with the Singapore Tourism Board in July 2004.[89]

The Singapore Tourism Board may have been in a stronger negotiating position than Walterfang realized at the time: legal documents from this period suggest that it had inside knowledge of the company's precarious financial situation. In these documents, Seabed Explorations alleges that one of its former employees made a series of unauthorized and inaccurate disclosures including that, unless the company was able to conclude a sale "urgently," the objects were likely to be publicly auctioned.[90] Furthermore, claimed Seabed Explorations, the Singapore Tourism Board had also been told that the company would accept US$32 million for the objects—a figure that was much lower than the original asking price.

Worse still, the Shanghai Museum had by now agreed to pay the full US$48 million, with US$32 million from the museum and an additional US$16 million to be contributed by a Chinese donor from New York. But, having entered into exclusive negotiations with Singapore, Seabed Explorations was unable to engage with the Shanghai Museum. Seabed Explorations was therefore "compelled" to option the objects to the Singapore Tourism Board, which it agreed to in August 2004.[91] To tide them over, Singapore, through the Ministry of Trade and Industry, lent Seabed Explorations US$1 million secured against the core items of the collection.[92] This gave Singapore exhibition rights to the objects and the option to purchase them within six months.[93] Historian Rachel Leow describes this "maelstrom of legal wrangling" as the hidden current that swirled beneath the *Belitung* story.[94]

Having secured rights to the objects, the Sentosa Development Corporation (through its wholly owned subsidiary Sentosa Leisure Management Group) and the Singapore Tourism Board conducted direct consultations with the Indonesian government and scrutinized the details of the project as part of their due diligence process. To generate interest from donors and philanthropists, it held a number of private viewings featuring representative and significant objects. One of these viewings was at the Goodwood Park Hotel, owned by the Khoo Teck Puat family, in January 2005.[95] Singapore had been able to outmaneuver other interested purchasers with its well-timed negotiations, but it also benefited from a surprisingly well-timed donation from the family of the late Singaporean banker and hotelier Khoo Teck Puat, who had died in February 2004. Two of his daughters, who had been in the news throughout 2004 for failing to disclose their father's stake in a number of listed companies of which they were directors, were in search of a "worthy cause to support."[96] "Out of the blue"—and just as Singapore's six-month option period was due to expire in early 2005—it was announced that the Khoo Teck Puat Foundation would make a major contribution toward the collection's purchase.[97] The donation is understood to have equated to half of the purchase price, with the Singapore Tourism Board providing the other half from its reserves.[98] Without this contribution, Singapore would not have had the funds to purchase the *Belitung* cargo. The sisters, for their part, were fined for failing to discharge their duties as directors—but escaped jail time.[99]

Yeo described the purchase price of US$32 million as "a reasonable bargain," and suggested that Sentosa might house the collection temporarily until a more suitable venue was available.[100] The Sentosa Development Corporation finalized the purchase of the *Belitung* objects in February 2005.[101] One of the first steps it subsequently took was to rename the assemblage the "Tang Shipwreck Collection."[102] The name change downplayed Indonesia within the narrative and instead centered the wreck within a Chinese maritime past to which Singapore could more easily lay claim.[103] The Maritime Heritage Foundation was established to manage the collection and create a new public maritime museum, to be known as the Singapore Maritime Silk Route Museum.[104] The foundation was also charged with object acquisition, including from shipwrecks, suggesting the *Belitung* objects were just the beginning of a new and improved maritime collection for Singapore.

The Maritime Heritage Foundation's board included representatives from the Sentosa Development Corporation and the Singapore Tourism Board, and it was funded by local and international philanthropists as well as private corporations that "support the preserving of, learning about and sharing of the world's rich maritime and cultural history."[105] As such, it brought together the public and the private, the commercial and the recreational, the educative and the entertaining. From the beginning, it was under pressure to make decisions about the management and development of its newly acquired maritime collection. Despite there being no public maritime museum in which to display the objects, it seemed that a "natural home for the collection" had indeed been found.

But the story did not end there. Although he was no longer formally tied to the shipwreck, Walterfang's involvement did not cease with the sale of the objects to Singapore. On December 22, 2005, police raided his Belitung bungalow amid allegations he had stolen some of the recovered objects. The police left after two days with 168 boxes and baskets, including the 79 baskets of previously buried sherds and all samples from Seabed Explorations' survey operations. The contents of these boxes and baskets were given to the local museum in January 2006.[106] The investigation was eventually dropped, with Walterfang dismissing the allegations as "cheap revenge" on the part of his opponents.[107] Over a decade later, in 2017, he again made the news for selling his personal collection of 162 pieces of Tang dynasty "cultural relics" to the new Tongguanyao Museum in Changsha, China. The acquisition, for which the museum paid Walterfang US$1.485 million, was described in the Chinese media as an opportunity for the objects to return to the kilns in Changsha for the first time—an expensive, much-delayed, and never-intended homecoming.[108]

Alternative Realities

Although we know that Singapore secured the *Belitung* cargo, it is illuminating to imagine a scenario in which it was purchased by one of the other interested parties, such as Qatar or China. The viability of these alternatives demonstrates the potential for the *Belitung* objects to represent different national interests and convey diverse meanings and stories. Qatar, for example, has invested heavily in its museum and cultural sector in recent years as a way of repositioning the nation "as a regional, if not a global, player."[109] This includes targeted purchasing of objects to fill its museums. While Qatar was ultimately not successful in purchasing the *Belitung* cargo, its interest in shipwreck assemblages did not diminish: it subsequently purchased a part of the *Cirebon* shipwreck assemblage, recovered from Indonesian waters in 2006, which accorded with its plans to open a pearl museum.[110]

The Shanghai Museum also failed in its efforts to purchase the objects. But interest from China in the material remains of ancient voyages remains strong. Objects from the *Belitung* continue to appear in exhibitions in Chinese museums, including at the China Maritime Museum in Shanghai and the Tongguanyao Museum.[111] The objects owned by the latter institution came from Walterfang's collection, but the provenance of the objects displayed at the China Maritime Museum is not known. China has also invested heavily in excavating shipwrecks in its own waters, as seen by the ambitious Maritime Silk Route Museum on Hailing Island, home to the entire hull and cargo of the *Nanhai One* wreck.[112]

The costly *Nanhai One* excavation testifies to China's use of its archaeological resources to advance its Belt and Road Initiative. In a 2017 speech, Chinese president Xi Jinping emphasized the historic roots of these modern initiatives—and put objects and display at the heart of this vision—when he mentioned the *Belitung* shipwreck in his opening remarks at the Belt and Road Forum:

> Over 2,000 years ago, our ancestors, trekking across vast steppes and deserts, opened the transcontinental passage connecting Asia, Europe and Africa, known today as the Silk Road. Our ancestors, navigating rough seas, created sea routes linking the East with the West, namely, the maritime Silk Road. These ancient silk routes opened windows of friendly engagement among nations, adding a splendid chapter to the history of human progress. The thousand-year-old "gilt bronze silkworm" displayed at China's Shaanxi History Museum and the *Belitung* shipwreck discovered in Indonesia, bear witness to this exciting period of history.[113]

Lacking China's confidence and Singapore's fortune, Indonesia was never a contender in the negotiations for the *Belitung*'s cargo. Maritime archaeologist Jeremy Green urged Indonesia to "wake up to [. . .] reality" and think about the heritage it could have retained had it not sold the survey and salvage rights.[114] To do this, Green argued, "wealthy sponsors" should have funded a scientific excavation conducted by Indonesian maritime archaeologists.[115] While Indonesia "would not have got half, or whatever its percentage of the sale was, it would benefit from having a permanent exhibition collection that would generate recurring income, with added long-term benefits for the public in knowledge and understanding."[116] What is of most interest in this assessment is the priority Green gives to the objects staying in Indonesia as part of a permanent exhibition, even at the expense of the collection remaining intact. His assessment also overlooks the fact that as a result of the *Belitung* salvage, Indonesia retained the entirety of the *Intan* cargo, widely considered to be of great significance for Indonesian maritime histories and yet facing a dismal future in its current display.

Conclusion

Doing a "deep dive" on the circumstances surrounding the salvage of the *Belitung* provides valuable insights into a key, yet often overlooked, aspect of this shipwreck's story: how the objects themselves were resurfaced. These are historical objects: ninth-century cargo, gifts, trading goods, and personal items. They also exist in the contemporary world, as conserved objects on display to the public. Yet the context and the detail of their provenance—how *these* objects came to be in *that* museum—has until now been largely missing.

Despite provenance being such an essential part of the objects' biography—or perhaps because of it—this part of the *Belitung*'s story has been overshadowed by rumors, allegations (and counter-allegations), and criticisms. Closely examining this "turning point" in the lives of these objects enables us to better understand the influences that informed their post-salvage afterlives. It is instructive to consider what might have been achieved if the *Belitung* salvage had been conducted in line with institutional ideals—if, for example, solid data on artifact distribution had been collected and retained. Such information might assist in answering some of the remaining questions about the *Belitung*: about where it was going and where it had been, or about how it was wrecked.

But these are hypotheticals. Instead, the salvage and sale of the *Belitung* forces us into murky ethical waters, not only in terms of process but also in terms of outcomes. This part of the *Belitung*'s story reveals both the tensions and the possibilities that arise when domestic legislative frameworks that assert ownership over underwater cultural heritage rub up against international ideals about managing heritage that is—by its very nature—fluid, mobile, and transnational. As this chapter has shown, the finger-pointing and blame that characterizes discussions about the *Belitung* within certain institutional and disciplinary circles is, to a degree, valid. At the same time, and as this chapter has also shown, the Seabed Explorations team was working in extraordinary times, and the outcomes they achieved were indeed extraordinary: the recovery and conservation of thousands of archaeologically and historically significant objects, with implications for our understanding of maritime trade and knowledge exchange in the ninth century.

However, although it is important to acknowledge the "great divide" that exists between maritime archaeologists and those who do not adhere to archaeological principles espoused by UNESCO, it is equally important not to dwell on this dichotomy.[117] Focusing on the negative aspects of the salvage, as the international maritime archaeological community has—on the lost opportunities and the stories that could not be told—is entirely reasonable. But good archaeological practice does not take place in a void. It is important to contextualize the criticisms of the salvage—and there were many—with reference to the local circumstances in which it took place. Attending only to the failures runs the risk of denying the stories that *can* be told. The sixty thousand objects, recovered legally and for profit, have effectively become "orphaned" underwater cultural heritage: how they were recovered is not their fault, so to speak.[118] An ethical assessment of the *Belitung* salvage demands examination of the circumstances by which the objects came to be out of the water. Equally, and more urgently, it also necessitates asking what to do with them now they are here. It was this question that Singapore, having invested significant financial and cultural capital in the objects, now had to address.

CHAPTER FOUR

Contested

The nature of the *Belitung*, with its multiple identities incorporating many cultures, meant it could be used by different nations to tell different stories—not only about the past, but, more crucially, about each nation's vision of the future. By 2005, tens of thousands of objects had been salvaged, conserved, and sold to a statutory authority of Singapore's Ministry of Trade and Industry. Even though many objects had, by this point, been separated from the assemblage, this was still the largest collection of Tang dynasty ceramics ever recovered from a single site. Renamed the Tang Shipwreck Collection, the objects conferred an ancient pedigree on Singapore's role as a modern, global trade center and positioned the city-state as inheritor and guardian of an ancient legacy. The change of name downplayed Indonesia within the narrative and instead centered the wreck within a Chinese maritime past—the so-called silk route of the sea—to which Singapore could more easily lay claim. Indonesia's erasure from the story established a pattern that would recur in heated debates.

The sheer quantity of the objects posed logistical challenges. Over the next six years, the Singapore Development Corporation wrestled with how and where to display them, distancing itself from early commitments to a new public maritime museum and instead focusing its energies on developing a major international exhibition. Singapore's changing ambitions for these objects elucidated broader themes relating to public and private interests in its cultural and tourism sectors. Finally, in early 2011, the objects made their debut on the world stage through a major international exhibition, *Shipwrecked: Tang Treasures and Monsoon Winds*. As the product of a collaboration between tourism, heritage, and museum authorities in Singapore and America, *Shipwrecked* had been conceived of as a long-term traveling exhibition. But these ambitious plans collapsed following the last-minute withdrawal of support from the Smithsonian Institution, Singapore's curatorial partner in America. The case became a critical moment for museums in terms of how, or even whether, to exhibit "unscientifically excavated and unprovenanced artefacts" from the ocean, exposing rifts within the Smithsonian Institution and revealing profoundly different understandings about the role of a public museum.[1]

In the meantime, an experimental archaeological reconstruction of the *Belitung*, called the *Jewel of Muscat*, had been built in Oman to celebrate that country's bilateral relationship with Singapore. Sailing from Oman to Singapore in 2010, the vessel eventually found a home in the new, privately funded Maritime Experiential Museum on Sentosa Island, in the process becoming permanently estranged from the objects to which it was indelibly connected through its association with the *Belitung*. The objects were genuine artifacts, but the *Jewel of Muscat* was different: it was a genuine replica.[2] As such, it disrupted the quasi-linear trajectory of the objects, instead suggesting even greater complexity and plurality in their afterlives than might otherwise have been conceivable.

The Tang Shipwreck Collection

Singapore's new Tang Shipwreck Collection numbered some 53,227 ancient artifacts.[3] Although a handful of these objects were already in Singapore when the purchase was finalized in February 2005, around 10,000 arrived in June, and the remaining 43,000-odd in December. Together they would form the basis of the new Singapore Maritime Silk Route Museum.[4] All but the most valuable objects were placed in temporary storage in the basement of the Hua Song Museum, which was not yet open to the public. The objects, amassed on seventy-foot-long steps leading up to the ceiling, filled the basement.[5] Meanwhile, the most valuable objects— including the gold and silver as well as the three blue-and-white dishes—were stored off-site under armed guard at the National Heritage Board's purpose-built conservation facility in the industrial center of Jurong.[6] The task ahead was enormous.

The Sentosa Development Corporation, which had limited experience with heritage conservation or display, was responsible for this fragile and valuable collection. Heritage consultant Pamelia Lee, who had played a role in negotiations to purchase the objects, was appointed to lead the project.[7] Lee was experienced and well connected: she had previously worked for both the Singapore Tourism Board and the National Heritage Board, and was married to Lee Suan Yew, the brother of Singapore's first prime minister, Lee Kuan Yew.[8] In her new role as head of the *Tang Shipwreck Treasure: Singapore's Maritime Collection Project*, Lee aimed to "tell the story of Singapore's early origins and to be able to tell this story with our neighbors."[9] But the objects' connection with Singapore's "early origins" was, at best, tenuous, and for a long time the project team grappled with the question of how to integrate them into the "Singapore Story"—the "grand narrative of how the nation overcame all odds to progress from third world to first."[10]

The first step in this endeavor was to show the objects to the public. The Sentosa Development Corporation had, when it announced the purchase of the Tang

Shipwreck Collection in 2005, made a commitment to building a new public maritime museum, with details about the location and funding model to be determined.[11] But Lee described the work needed to research and study the objects as "a big, long and mountainous road," and emphasized that Singapore's priority was on "doing research, studying the artefacts and building up a collection, rather than on constructing an iconic museum."[12] By June 2005 Singapore was in a position to mount a small exhibition of around sixty objects. In the absence of a dedicated maritime museum, the Singapore Tourism Board partnered with the Asian Civilisations Museum for the *Tang Treasures from the Sea* exhibition (June 15–July 31, 2005).[13] The museum had only been open at its flagship Empress Place location by the Singapore River since 2003. Under its founding director Kenson Kwok, who served in the role until 2008, the museum had developed a reputation for small, high-quality exhibitions.[14] This was accompanied by a five-fold increase in visitor numbers between 1997 and 2007.[15] Singapore's national museum sector was taking a "quantum leap," and the *Belitung* objects, through the *Tang Treasures* exhibition, were part of that leap.[16]

The purchase of the Tang Shipwreck Collection nevertheless brought renewed attention to the fact that none of Singapore's existing museums were able to provide visitors with "any serious understanding of the role which the seas and maritime industries have played and continue to play in the economic development of the nation."[17] And there remained pressure—not least from the Khoo Teck Puat estate, which had contributed some US$16 million toward the purchase—to find a permanent solution to the management and development of the collection. As the years passed it became apparent that Singapore was having difficulty finding a museological solution that justified the huge investment it had made. Four years after taking delivery of the assemblage, the bulk of the objects were still in storage at the Hua Song Museum (which, by then, had finally opened).[18] In 2009, historian Rachel Leow described the museum basement as "a little like a bomb shelter," due to the enormous quantity of objects that still crowded the space.[19] She noted,

> There's talk of a great Maritime Silk Route Museum to be built in Singapore to house and exhibit these wares. Its story will no doubt vaunt Singapore's central place at the elbow of a great oceanic route that ran parallel to the overland Silk Road. Its objectives will no doubt be to inscribe Singapore into a wider and more ancient world history, and to give historical credence to a position that is crucial to Singapore's self-image today: as a global, maritime entrepôt, and the lodestone on which Southeast Asia turns.[20]

Here, then, was the grand narrative the project team had been looking for: Singapore as a port on the ancient silk route of the sea, connecting the city-state to the *Belitung* objects and, in the process, embedding it at the center of global trade. But as George Yeo—who had played a key role in securing Singapore's purchase of the *Belitung* objects—explained, Singapore "hardly had enough money for the cargo, let alone the museum to house it or the research facility to understand what we have acquired."[21]

Advocates were concerned by the idea that a maritime museum might be built on Sentosa as part of the island's new integrated resort: would such a museum be educational in its focus, or would it be an entertainment venue designed to attract visitors to the casino?[22] Inspired in part by developments in Hong Kong—which saw the Hong Kong Maritime Museum relocate from the south side of Hong Kong Island to a more prominent venue on Victoria Harbour—they proposed that Singapore construct a major maritime museum not on Sentosa Island but at the historic Clifford Street pier area, where thousands of sea passengers and immigrants had disembarked upon arrival in Singapore. This museum, dedicated to the seas and the maritime world's role in Singapore and Asia, "would greatly enhance awareness of this aspect of Singapore's society. A vibrant maritime museum with a firm status as part of the national identity would enhance Singapore culturally."[23] Stephen Davies, founding director of the Hong Kong Maritime Museum, was invited to Singapore to share his insights into the Hong Kong experience, including how to attract public and private sponsorship. But the efforts of these advocates went unheeded and the Clifford Street proposal was never pursued, leaving Davies to question why there was not more support for maritime museums in Southeast Asia, including Singapore.[24]

While these debates raged, the Sentosa Development Corporation continued with its strategy of temporary displays. One short-term solution was to show some of the objects in a hotel owned by the family of Khoo Teck Puat. In 2007, about eighty-eight objects went on display in a dedicated room on the ground floor of Singapore's Goodwood Park Hotel.[25] The pieces, mostly ceramic, were chosen as representative of the entire collection, "with the aim of sharing a part of history with hotel guests and visitors."[26] The display consists of tall glass cases and a number of wall panels in a small, carpeted room adjacent to the hotel café.[27] The objects are technically on loan, but the fact that the room has been named the Tang Treasures Suite—and that it is part of a hotel owned by the donors who made the purchase of the collection possible—suggests that the loan is more permanent than temporary. The display is free and open to the public, but the room can also be hired for private lunches and dinners for up to twelve people, "for those who get a kick out of dining off modern tableware while being surrounded by the historic

Chinese real deal."[28] This display encapsulates the continuous interplay between public and private interests. Such entanglements were inevitable given the commercial nature of the salvage.

In 2009, a small selection of ceramic objects from the *Belitung* went on display as part of a larger exhibition at NUS Museum, the oldest university museum in Singapore. Called *Southeast Asian Ceramics: New Light on Old Pottery* (November 14, 2009–July 25, 2010), it was held on the occasion of the Southeast Asian Ceramic Society's fortieth anniversary. The exhibition featured a selection of ceramics from across Southeast Asia, including from shipwreck assemblages. A number of objects from the Tang Shipwreck Collection were included in this exhibition, where they were identified as originating from the *Belitung* shipwreck rather than from the Tang Shipwreck Collection.[29] The exhibition was accompanied by a detailed catalog that included essays on kilns in China, shipwrecks in the region, and the movement of ceramics in and between Southeast Asia and China.[30] The *Belitung* objects, which numbered no more than a dozen, included a Changsha ewer and bowl, a green-splashed bowl and tube cup from Gongxian. The National University of Singapore also developed an undergraduate module, *Sinbad, Shipwrecks and Singapore*, for its prestigious University Scholars program, which incorporated the *Belitung* into its syllabus.[31]

By 2010, then, the objects in the collection had been displayed in three different exhibitions: the small *Tang Treasures* exhibition at the Asian Civilisations Museum, a long-term exhibition at the Goodwood Park Hotel, and the *Southeast Asian Ceramics* exhibition at the NUS Museum. Each of these had provided the public with an opportunity to see some of the objects, but they were far from the blockbuster exhibition that might have been expected of such a vast and costly assemblage. These temporary solutions had instead fueled questions about the nature of Singapore's maritime histories and how these histories should be represented in its museums. It seemed that, until these debates were resolved, there would be nowhere to display the objects permanently and at scale. But that all changed with the arrival of the *Jewel of Muscat*.

The *Jewel of Muscat*

Once Singapore's purchase had become public, much of the initial interest in the *Belitung* shipwreck focused on the huge quantities of mostly Chinese objects. The *Jewel of Muscat* project broadened the focus beyond these objects by drawing attention to where the vessel itself had originated. This was, of course, not a new question. But additional analysis of the ship's timbers, published as an addendum by Flecker a decade after the *Belitung* had been salvaged, appeared to provide a more definitive answer to this question.[32] The new analysis suggested that the timber species were quite mixed, coming from Africa, Arabia, and South Asia.[33] This effectively ruled out India, Sri Lanka, Africa, or Southeast Asia as the site of construction, all of which have "very good" local shipbuilding material and therefore no need to import timber.[34] Instead, the analysis pointed to the ship having been built in "Arabia or Persia, which lacked nearly all of these boatbuilding timbers and were therefore importing [those that were] the most useful."[35]

Flecker's interpretation of the results, in which he suggested that the vessel may have been constructed "in the region of Oman or Yemen," effectively created an opportunity for one of these countries to claim a piece of the *Belitung*'s story.[36] Yet it was not Oman or Yemen that initiated the *Jewel of Muscat* project, but Singapore. Shortly after Flecker's article was published in 2008, Singapore approached the Sultanate of Oman, proposing a joint initiative that would reimagine the *Belitung* shipwreck using experimental archaeological reconstruction, and strengthen bilateral relations in the process.[37] Oman agreed to fund the construction of the new vessel, to be known as the *Jewel of Muscat*, and sail it to Singapore.[38] In return, Singapore would cover the expenses of the voyage and build a museum to display the vessel.[39] This was the impetus that had been missing in the debates about Singapore's new maritime museum.

Oman's interest in the project was linked to pride in its "illustrious maritime history."[40] Sewn-plank vessels had been a feature of the Arabian Peninsula since at least the first century CE, with Omani seafarers later using such vessels to sail "the longest network of commercial routes of the Medieval period, commonly referred to collectively as the Maritime Silk Route."[41] The *Jewel of Muscat* was the second of three medieval sewn-plank reconstructions undertaken by Oman. The first of these was the *Sohar*, which sailed from Oman to China in the early 1980s under British explorer Tim Severin—a journey known as the "Sindbad Voyage."[42] More recently, the *al-Hariri Boat*, built at three-quarter scale in 2013 for museum display, was based on illustrations accompanying the thirteenth-century *Maqamat al-Hariri* (Arabic literary tales).[43] Whereas the construction of the *Sohar* can best be described as a modified ethnographic reconstruction that used limited iconographic evidence, and the *al-Hariri Boat* as an experimental iconographic reconstruction based on a manuscript, the *Jewel of Muscat* reconstruction was unique in its primary reliance on archaeological—rather than textual, iconographic, or ethnographic—evidence.[44]

The construction was overseen by Tom Vosmer, considered to be one of the world's leading authorities on the history of Arabic shipbuilding.[45] He was joined by Flecker as consultant archaeologist, as well as Nick Burningham, who brought with him experience in ancient ship reconstruction. They were supported by a team of twenty experienced shipwrights and rope-workers from Kerala, India, plus fourteen Omani trainees from a local technical college.[46] The project team reviewed the archaeological evidence and settled on an approach that incorporated "information, direct and indirect, with elements of naval architecture and common sense."[47] "Mindful that the reconstruction was based on a shipwreck—possibly not the optimum model for a reconstruction—we paid close attention to every detail," Vosmer wryly observed.[48] The process was extensive, involving everything from research, experimentation, construction, and sea trials to sailing and navigation.[49] It was underpinned by a firm instruction from the sponsoring ministry in Oman: "There is no room for failure—this ship must get to Singapore."[50]

The *Belitung* had not been a particularly long vessel, probably around sixty-five to seventy-two feet, but it had to have been sufficiently capacious to house the seventy thousand-odd objects in its cargo.[51] Burningham's design, a vessel sixty feet in length and twenty-one feet wide, sought to capture what he described as its "fullness."[52] Each step in the construction brought its own challenges. The hull was most difficult, not only from an engineering perspective but also in terms of the effort required to accurately interpret the archaeological evidence without straying beyond it.[53] Because sewn boats are built shell-first (as opposed to frame-first), each plank of timber had to be preformed to the correct shape. The team experimented with the best way of softening the planks to make them supple enough to bend, including soaking them in seawater for days before clamping them with oversized wooden forks; fire bending, in which heat was applied to one side of the plank while the reverse was kept wet with water or oil; and steam bending, which was most effective but quickly exhausted supplies of firewood.[54] The process of sewing was not only extremely time intensive, but also involved complex engineering, requiring numerous decisions to be made about the hole size, hole spacing, and thickness of the planks.[55] Fiber remains from the *Belitung* wreck indicated wadding had been tightly packed along both the inside and outside of the plank seams to make the ship watertight. This double-wadding technique added yet more complexity to the process.[56] Each hole, once stitched, was plugged with fresh coconut fiber, primed with fish oil, and covered in a mixture of calcium carbonate and rendered goat fat to create a thick seal against any seawater that might seep through the stitched planks.[57] Similarly pungent materials were used elsewhere on the ship, leading Vosmer to describe the hull's odor as "enough to gag a maggot."[58]

Although there was a great degree of certainty behind many of the design and construction decisions, there were some elements that required the project team to look beyond the archaeological evidence to iconographic or ethnographic

Figure 9. The *Jewel of Muscat* during sea trials off the coast of Oman in early 2010 prior to its voyage to Singapore. This magnificent reconstruction yielded significant new insights into sewn-plank ship construction and its performance at sea, and primed researchers for new data revealed by the 2013 discovery of the *Phanom Surin* shipwreck in Thailand. The project was also a diplomatic triumph, heralding strengthened bilateral cooperation between Singapore and Oman. Photo by John Tsantes and Robert Harrell, Arthur M. Sackler Gallery, 2010.

sources or experimental techniques. There was no archaeological evidence of the number or position of the masts, for example, or the shape of the sails. The steering system was another unknown. Meanwhile, a number of compromises were made to ensure the safety and comfort of the crew, such as the installation of a deck and modern communication systems.[59] No engine was installed, however; just as the *Belitung* had in the ninth century, the *Jewel of Muscat* had to rely entirely on the wind and the currents to take it to its destination. The entire process—from the construction of a 1:9 model of the hull and the felling of trees in Ghana, to the smearing of animal blood on the stem post and the selection of the captain—was extensively documented.[60] Scholars even created a detailed stitching history, an ambitious objective given the final vessel had some 37,371 holes—plugged by the husks of 1,300 coconuts—and over 132,600 stitches in the planking alone.[61] The construction took over a year, plus sea trials and final adjustments.

The *Jewel of Muscat* finally sailed from Oman in February 2010, making four stops—in Cochin (India), Galle (Sri Lanka), and Penang and Port Klang (both in Malaysia)—en route to Singapore.[62] The journey totaled over 3,800 nautical miles and took 139 days, 68 of which were spent at sea.[63] The remaining days were spent in port, including an extensive layover in Galle to replace both masts following storm damage. Aboard were a crew of sixteen to twenty, depending on the leg, as well as a brood of chickens, which Vosmer said were "more trouble than they were worth," and two goats (who "had a habit of eating the rigging") for food.[64] The vessel arrived in Singapore in early July 2010 where it was met with a "spectacular and joyous welcome" before being formally presented as a gift from the Sultanate of Oman to the Singapore government.[65] Testament to the skill of those involved in its construction was that the *Jewel of Muscat* was hauled from the water "without a single sound of complaint emanating from the hull—an amazing occurrence for a wooden vessel."[66]

This was much more than an experimental archaeological reconstruction, however. The project coincided with the twenty-fifth anniversary of diplomatic relations between Oman and Singapore. As recorded on a commemorative plaque for the *Jewel of Muscat* at the Maritime Experiential Museum, the project was "a cultural, historical and diplomatic initiative with educational and scientific objectives" that "celebrates the peaceful relations enjoyed by Oman and Singapore."[67] At a gala dinner at the Asian Civilisations Museum to celebrate the ship's arrival, George Yeo reflected:

> We are so fortunate that because of a decision taken years ago to acquire some pieces of pottery, we have re-established an ancient link between Singapore and Oman, between Southeast Asia and the Middle East.[68]

In Yeo's telling, the importance of the objects (mere "pieces of pottery," a phrase that belied their true value) was downplayed, while ancient global connections were foregrounded. The *Jewel of Muscat* project represented nothing less than "a new Asia, a new age of globalisation, a new silk road much larger than the one before, which will connect us altogether again."[69]

But there was nowhere to house the *Jewel of Muscat* when it arrived in Singapore in mid-2010. It was not until October 2011, when the Maritime Experiential Museum opened on Sentosa Island, that the *Jewel of Muscat* was placed on permanent display.[70] The museum was part of Resorts World Sentosa, which had opened the year before and included not only a casino but also hotels, restaurants, and theme parks.[71] Although it was a private venture, entrance fees were more in line with those of Singapore's public museums: SGD$5 for adults, and SGD$2 for children.[72] The museum sought to distinguish itself from "traditional" galleries with their "artifacts encased in pristine glass panels and behind retractable queue barriers."[73] Instead, this was the museum as entertainment.

The *Jewel of Muscat* was positioned at the heart of this interactive, multisensory, and experiential space, supported in a huge steel cradle that hung from two large columns in apparent defiance of gravity.[74] Entering the museum was intended to feel like "embarking on an adventure" to discover the historical maritime silk route. Visitors were invited to "discover Southeast Asia's maritime history" by participating in a journey of adventure that included "bustling bazaars, Typhoon Theatre, interactive exhibits, shipwreck artefacts [and] life-sized ship replicas."[75] Berthed in the water outside the museum were five replica vessels from around Asia, intended to bring to life "ancient seafaring ways by allowing visitors onboard, further enhancing the 'maritime' experience."[76]

The ship's hull was visible, at a distance, from most places in the main hall. But a closer look at the *Jewel of Muscat* was only possible by purchasing a ticket to the museum's Typhoon Theatre. Visitors then had to pass through a turnstile and enter a waiting area level with the *Jewel of Muscat*'s deck. Close inspection of the ship was possible from here, and here only. The space included bilingual (English and Mandarin Chinese) interpretive panels—rendered in blue to make the maritime connection more obvious—on topics such as Tang dynasty maritime trade, traditional dhows, materials, sewing techniques, and the Southeast Asian trade winds. There was also a tabletop computer game featuring a ship navigating through an unidentified archipelago under threat from pirates, sea monsters, and the monsoon.[77] The presence of the computer game, positioned low and pitched at children rather than the average-size adult, conveyed the sense that this was a space for waiting and playing. Any efforts to connect the *Jewel of Muscat* with its broader historical context were dismantled by the fact that the vessel, and its crew, were depicted as Chinese.

The Typhoon Theatre itself constituted the *Belitung*'s imagined homeward journey, an experiential shipwrecking rendered entertaining and safe.[78] The overall experience was more theme park than museum, encapsulating what Balloffet and others have described as the "hybridisation of museum offerings characterised by growing porosity . . . between museums and amusement parks."[79] In this "amazing historical journey," up to 150 visitors entered a circular theater and took their places on the bench seating, intended to resemble an Arabia-bound sailing ship. Vents and jets then emitted "wind and rain to conjure a storm out at sea."[80] As the ship hit a wave, the seating platform, mounted on a hydraulic lift platform, dropped eighteen feet to mimic the sinking of a vessel. Surrounded by corals and jellyfish, the "survivors" endured no more than a fine mist of water.[81] Once the "ride" was over, visitors were channeled away from the Typhoon Theatre through a separate exit that led to an enormous aquarium containing a reproduction wrecked vessel, real fish, and an overflowing treasure chest surrounded by replica ceramic artifacts. Visitors did not have an opportunity to return to the *Jewel of Muscat* display. Instead, their ability to make the connection between the *Jewel of Muscat* and the Typhoon Theatre was contingent on the time they spent in the waiting area before being ushered into the theater for their immersive adventure.

The *Jewel of Muscat* has become a victim of Singapore's changing vision for the Tang Shipwreck Collection, permanently separated from the *Belitung* objects to which it is necessarily connected. Inspired by an ancient shipwreck, yet a modern marvel in its own right, the *Jewel of Muscat* was reduced to a decorative backdrop at the Maritime Experiential Museum. The *Belitung* objects were never displayed, even temporarily, alongside their ship's replica. Their absence was heightened by the display of other shipwreck artifacts elsewhere in the museum— including, at one time, objects from the *Bakau* wreck, which had been purchased by Resorts World.[82] The Maritime Experiential Museum closed in 2020, with plans for the *Jewel of Muscat* to be incorporated within the adjacent aquarium; however, it remains inside the shuttered museum's main hall. It may never leave, as the entire roof of the building would have to be lifted to remove it.

A Major Exhibition

As the *Jewel of Muscat* reconstruction was coming together, another project was in the pipeline: a major international exhibition of the *Belitung* objects. *Shipwrecked: Tang Treasures and Monsoon Winds* opened on February 19, 2011, at the ArtScience Museum, one of Singapore's newest exhibition venues.[83] Developed in partnership with the Smithsonian Institution, *Shipwrecked* had been in the works since as early as 2007 following a conversation between Pamelia Lee and Julian

Raby, director of the Freer Gallery of Art and the Arthur M. Sackler Gallery, which together form the American National Museum of Asian Art under·the Smithsonian umbrella.[84]

The development of this traveling exhibition was affected by the 2008 global financial crisis, which meant that many international museums did not have the funds to afford the loan fee. The Smithsonian Institution was not dissuaded, however, and work on the project began in December 2009. As it gained momentum, the range of partners expanded to include not only the Singapore Tourism Board but also the National Heritage Board and the Asian Civilisations Museum, represented by curator Heidi Tan.[85] After its debut in Singapore, *Shipwrecked* was scheduled to travel to Washington D.C., where it was to open at the Sackler Gallery in March 2012 in time for the gallery's twenty-fifth anniversary.[86] From there, it was to have continued on an extended world tour of five to six years in "major museums in Asia, the United States, Europe, the Near East and Australia."[87]

The evocative words in the exhibition title left no room for speculation about the rarity, significance, and sheer drama of the production. *Shipwrecked* featured approximately four hundred objects, including dozens of the Changsha bowls, the dragon head ewer, and the bronze mirrors, plus a miniature *Jewel of Muscat*. In her review of the exhibition, Leow (2011) describes how the exhibition design built up to a dramatic finale:

> The first gallery is cast in shadowy, warm wooden hues, redolent of the hull of a ship. We then move gradually into colder underwater colours—deep blues, turquoises, aquamarine. The exhibition saves the true treasures for the last few rooms—the solid gold, silver and green-splashed porcelain wares, submerged in near pitch blackness and illuminated as though by search spotlights. They have become beautiful, mysterious icons of the *Belitung* wreck.[88]

In this final gallery, visitors were greeted with a huge wall emblazoned with questions in English and Mandarin Chinese, layered in different-sized white font on a black background.[89] The questions ranged from the prosaic to the profound: Why were there so few blue-and-white ceramics? How typical was the cargo? How did the captain pay for goods in China? Who financed the voyage? How many languages might have been spoken by those on board? How long did the entire round trip take? What devices were used to navigate the ship?

This wall placed value on public engagement and introspection by providing an opportunity for the audience to pause and reflect on what questions they may have had after taking in the exhibition. However, as Leow observed, "one question nagged at me throughout the exhibition, and was no less interesting for its omission from the wall. The question is this: What does Singapore *really* have to do with the *Belitung* wreck at all?"[90] This was the US$32 million question that Singapore's curators and creative minds had been wrestling with since the purchase of the objects some six years earlier, the answer to which appeared to be in a conceptualization of Singapore as the modern equivalent of the ancient dynasties and trade relationships that had dominated the ninth-century world.

The marketing campaign for *Shipwrecked* reinforced Singapore's claims to the shipwreck, centering the city-state within the maritime silk route narrative and as modern inheritor of its material legacy. Waterproof posters, featuring images of the salvaged cargo arranged to resemble Singapore, were plastered to the bottom of community pools.[91] Exhibition banners featuring weathered masts and life-sized replicas of the ship's sails were erected; rope rigging and tattered sails, each one individually handcrafted, added to the sense of authenticity. These sails, printed with the catchphrase "Discover Asia's Sunken Past" and details about the exhibition, adorned prime tourist locations, including outside the Singapore Visitor Centre on Orchard Road.[92] The campaign was complemented by print advertising in both English and Mandarin Chinese daily newspapers.

The opening of *Shipwrecked* coincided with the opening of the ArtScience Museum in which it was displayed, adding to the sense of occasion and anticipation. The museum was designed by modernist architect Moshe Safdie to resemble a human hand, and has been likened to a white lotus. Its distinctive form and prime location on the Marina Bay foreshore meant that it quickly became part of Singapore's rapidly changing skyline. Described in a press release as "the premier venue for major international touring exhibitions from the most renowned collections in the world," the ArtScience Museum was part of Singapore's other integrated resort, the Las Vegas Sands Corporation.[93]

As the cultural offering at a casino-based development, the ArtScience Museum was to Las Vegas Sands Corporation what the Maritime Experiential Museum was to Resorts World Sentosa.[94] This casino-backed funding model attracted criticism that the museum lacked cultural legitimacy. Asked one academic, "Is the museum even a proper one? Or are we talking about something that we'd see in a sort of Las Vegas sideshow?"[95] The profit-focused nature of the venture was evident in the museum's entrance fees, which were significantly higher than those of the Maritime Experiential Museum or Singapore's national museums.[96] Compounding these concerns was the fact that there was no permanent collection, a key component of a museum as defined by ICOM.[97] Instead, *Shipwrecked* was one of three temporary "blockbusters" on show (and the only one that was locally produced) sitting alongside a longer-term, but not permanent, exhibition.[98]

Director Thomas Zaller was undeterred. He envisioned a museum that departed from the traditional model with its "relics and dusty old objects. I want to shake things up a little bit. I want parents to go in there and have fun with their children."[99] Zaller's perspective was informed by his role as founder, president, and CEO of Imagine Exhibitions, the US-based traveling blockbuster exhibition development company responsible for the original *Titanic* exhibition. *Titanic: The Artifact Exhibition* opened at the ArtScience Museum in October 2011, immediately after *Shipwrecked*, doing further damage to the cultural credentials of the museum in the eyes of the international maritime archaeology community.[100] The *Titanic* exhibition coincided with the one hundredth anniversary of the sinking of the eponymous vessel on April 15, 1912, and attracted over 286,000 visitors in its six-month run. Another 96,000 people had visited the ArtScience Museum in the five months *Shipwrecked* was on display.[101] Despite the high entrance fees, there was clearly an appetite for shipwreck exhibitions in Singapore.

A Swell of Disapproval

The *Shipwrecked* exhibition was the culmination of Singapore's efforts to position itself as the global fulcrum around which pivoted the maritime histories not only of Southeast Asia, but of the Indian Ocean and South China Sea as well. But international criticism had begun to bubble to the surface even before the exhibition opened. As early as March 2011, museums such as the Australian National Maritime Museum in Sydney had declined *Shipwrecked* due to ethical concerns relating to the commercial nature of the salvage.[102] And, before long, rumors began circulating in Washington that some of the Smithsonian Institution's own research organizations—including members of the anthropology department and the Senate of Scientists at the National Museum of Natural History—were critical of the exhibition.[103]

Soon there was "a swell of disapproval in international scientific circles."[104] Internal memos from the Smithsonian Institution were leaked to the media, and on March 10, 2011, an article appeared in the influential journal *Science* quoting a letter from Melissa Songer (chair of the Smithsonian Congress of Scholars) to Wayne Clough (secretary of the Smithsonian Institution), in which Songer had expressed concern about the potential reputational damage to the Smithsonian Institution:

> We agree that there was unprofessional and unethical conduct associated with the recovery of this wreck, regardless of the "letter of the law," and that at the least, the perception of impropriety and the potential for the

Smithsonian's engagement with this project could set a negative precedent and reflect ill on this institution.[105]

Another *Science* article was published on March 18 of the same year, stating that, despite growing concerns—including from a number of major American archaeological associations and three of the Smithsonian's own research organizations—Director Raby was standing firm on the grounds that the salvage operation had been legal.[106] But this scandal was not going away. Other organizations joined the chorus.[107] Coverage gained traction in outlets including CNN, the *New York Times*, Voice of America, the *Washington Post*, and National Public Radio.[108] The Smithsonian Institution struggled to stay on top of the volume of correspondence it was receiving from institutions and individuals.[109]

One of the clearest expressions of these concerns was articulated by the Archaeological Institute of America in a public statement:

> The *Belitung* was salvaged unscientifically by commercially-motivated treasure hunters. Although the excavation and disposition of these materials may be technically "legal," it is the AIA's position that involvement by the Smithsonian Institution in the exhibition of these artifacts will serve to blur the distinction between bona fide nautical archaeology and treasure hunting. Following this path puts the Smithsonian in the indefensible position of aiding those who believe that antiquities are a commodity to be mined for personal or corporate financial gain. They are not—they are part of the world's cultural patrimony.[110]

Criticisms of the *Belitung* salvage had centered on three main points: failure to preserve the wreck *in situ*; the involvement of a commercial salvage company in the recovery of the wreck; and the failure of this company to adhere to professional archaeological standards. The *Shipwrecked* exhibition introduced an additional consideration: that to display these objects in a museum—let alone a taxpayer-funded institution with "iconic" national status—would be akin to supporting and legitimizing treasure hunting and the commercial exploitation of heritage sites.[111]

Because the salvage had been legal under Indonesian law and the assemblage remained intact, Raby had not anticipated backlash.[112] He had viewed *Shipwrecked* as an exhibition that would raise awareness about the issues facing underwater cultural heritage in Southeast Asia, allowing audiences to make up their own minds.[113] It was also, in his words, an opportunity for "both the public and politicians in the ASEAN (Association of Southeast Asian Nations) region to value their maritime heritage" and a "catalyst for investment across the region in the structures and institutions that can best study and preserve the underwater archaeological record."[114]

There were also criticisms of the lavishly illustrated catalog, which drew from the two monographs produced earlier by Seabed Explorations. The catalogue, which was copublished and co-branded with the Smithsonian Institution, was a significant addition to the literature. One reviewer described it as the "standard reference for this extremely important archaeological site," and "an excellent summary of the data in our current state of knowledge."[115] But, in the storm of controversy surrounding *Shipwrecked*, many dismissed it as lacking in substance. For example, another reviewer opined, "It should have been written, or edited, by a maritime archaeologist, but that is just a dream."[116] Instead, he continued, "it showcases treasure-hunting, or, in different terminology, commercial salvage. It does absolutely nothing for archaeology, and that is really worrying."[117] The difference in these reviews epitomized the variety of perspectives on the ethics of exhibiting to the public objects from the ocean that had been commercially salvaged.

In the face of mounting pressure, a review was conducted by the Smithsonian Institution's Office of General Counsel, which confirmed that legal title to the *Belitung* cargo was indeed valid and that there was no evidence that the objects had been illegally salvaged or exported by Seabed Explorations.[118] The question, therefore, was one of ethics, not legality. According to the Office of the General Counsel's report, almost all of the ethical standards and policies governing professional organizations and institutions "condemn and prohibit the commercial exploitation and unscientific excavation of archaeological sites, including underwater sites."[119] To manage underwater cultural heritage ethically, it cannot be sold, traded, or bartered as commercial goods. Furthermore, any excavation has to involve qualified archaeologists, and has to be conducted in accordance with established scientific archaeological standards.

To address these issues, the Smithsonian Institution convened a "604 review" meeting on April 25, 2011, with prominent archaeologists and museum directors from within and beyond the institution to discuss the ethics of exhibiting *Shipwrecked*.[120] The review was called such because it was guided by Smithsonian Directive 604, an internal policy that sought to uphold "the integrity of its research activities in a conscientious and responsible manner and to encourage scholarly inquiry while ensuring compliance with applicable laws and regulations."[121] The tensions were palpable. Those who were in favor of displaying the objects pointed to the potential for *Shipwrecked* to spark a discussion about the threats to underwater cultural heritage. Ford Bell, president of the American Association of Museums (2007–2015), described it as a "teachable moment," while a professor from the University of Pennsylvania observed that "those who have called for the cancellation of the exhibition are, in effect and in fact, denying access to the wealth of information embodied in the *Belitung* shipwreck."[122] This was, they argued, an opportunity to "educate the public about the consequences of the commercialization of underwater heritage."[123] There was also a sense that to cancel *Shipwrecked* altogether would set an almost impossible standard for museums when it came to displaying underwater cultural heritage.[124] Said one attendee, "I came away strongly convinced that the Smithsonian should stand up and be counted. As a world museum, it can illustrate how this area of study can be better understood. They must be bold."[125]

But others saw it differently, arguing that widespread condemnation of commercial salvage would not only be "greatly weakened if institutions with the standing of the Smithsonian mount exhibitions of such material," but that hosting the exhibition was akin to aiding and abetting such practices.[126] They contended that displaying the objects, let alone in one of the Smithsonian Institution's museums, was a tacit endorsement of looting and treasure hunting and would only hasten the loss of the world's underwater cultural heritage. There were also concerns about the standing of the ArtScience Museum. One vocal and well-placed individual directed his attentions at the museum's owner, the Las Vegas Sands Corporation, asking, "Is this a savory group that the Smithsonian wants to be doing business with, that a federal government museum wants to be in partnership with?"[127]

Equally difficult discussions were taking place in Singapore. In June, the Asian Civilisations Museum convened a symposium "to explore some of the challenges and contradictions of undersea archaeology in Southeast Asia."[128] Contributors consisted of a broad cross-section of experienced stakeholders from Asia and beyond, including Kwa Chong Guan (adjunct associate professor of history at the National University of Singapore, member of the National Heritage Board, and chairman of its National Archives Board); John Miksic (associate professor in Southeast Asian studies at the National University of Singapore); Bobby Orillaneda (director of the Philippine Maritime Archaeology Foundation); Erbprem Vatcharangkul (director of Thailand's Underwater Archaeology Division); Gatot Gautama (deputy director for Underwater Archaeology in Indonesia); Phann Nady (deputy director-general in Cambodia's department of cultural heritage); Bill Jeffery (coordinator for the maritime and underwater cultural heritage program at CIE-Centre for International Heritage Activities); Robert Parthesius (director of the CIE-Centre and associate professor at the University of Leiden); and a representative from the Bangkok-based SEAMEO-SPAFA archaeology initiative. Michael Flecker also contributed, as did Ellen Gerth and Sean Kingsley from Odyssey Marine Exploration. This was a potent mix of maritime archaeologists, scholars, government officials, heritage professionals, and commercial salvagers.

Significantly, two representatives from the Sackler Gallery also attended, as speakers: Nancy Micklewright, head of research, and Cheryl Sobas, head of exhibitions.[129] Taking the dragon head ewer as a case study, Micklewright reflected on how *Shipwrecked* had revealed a gap in how maritime archaeologists and art historians "think about the material and the kinds of questions they ask about it."[130] Hinting at the internal tensions within the Smithsonian Institution, she said that the objects "have stories to tell us," but there were also multiple ways of seeing and interpreting them.[131] Sobas, meanwhile, proposed that the *Belitung* case had legal and ethical implications for the management of threatened underwater cultural heritage not only in Southeast Asia but worldwide. Underwater cultural heritage was "shared heritage," she reminded the audience, and *Shipwrecked* offered lessons about what the sharing of heritage actually looked like in a practical sense.[132] The *Belitung* had problematized accepted discourses around what constituted protection and preservation of underwater cultural heritage, Sobas argued, demanding other models of engagement beyond those articulated by the 2001 UNESCO Convention.

Speaking as representatives of the Smithsonian Institution at a time when their organization was under extreme scrutiny and pressure, Micklewright's and Sobas's presentations were quite extraordinary. It is notable that theirs were among the only papers not to be published in the symposium's formal proceedings.[133] Their presentations, which remain available online, offer an insight into the consideration that Smithsonian Institution curatorial staff gave to both this specific exhibition and to broader questions about the right of the public to access the maritime past.[134] But critics saw the symposium as a last-ditch effort to legitimize the collection and the exhibition. The same individual who had earlier questioned the credentials of the ArtScience Museum dismissed the symposium as a "shell maritime archaeology conference" designed to "validate" their scientific credentials. "I know Bobby Orillaneda," stated this individual, but—despite the caliber of many of the contributors—"all the rest were pretty much not so legitimate. Lots of tea, lots of discussion, lots of meals, not a whole lot of substance."[135] UNESCO, although invited, chose not to send any delegates for fear that to do so would be seen to be endorsing the exhibition. It meant a lost opportunity for this Paris-based organization to engage in a frank discussion—in Southeast Asia, with local experts—and gain valuable context about the region's circumstances and challenges. In the process of upholding their ethical principles, *Shipwrecked*'s critics had revealed their profoundly dismissive attitudes to Southeast Asian knowledge and expertise.

Ten days after the symposium in Singapore, the Smithsonian Institution made an announcement: *Shipwrecked* was to be postponed.[136] Rather than proceeding with the exhibition in its current iteration, a formal advisory council would instead continue discussions with "professional archaeologists and cultural heritage experts regarding the ethical and professional issues raised by the *Belitung* shipwreck."[137] The announcement was followed by celebratory emails "flying from archaeologists and maritime museum professionals across the United States and beyond, exulting in victory after a prolonged and passionate battle for a good cause."[138] According to a Smithsonian Institution insider, this had been "an amazingly powerful and professional movement . . . unprecedented in the Smithsonian's long history."[139]

Shipwrecked had become a flashpoint exhibition, drawing attention not only to the role and responsibilities of the Smithsonian Institution, but to the broader question of how any public museum should proceed when its ethical principles brought it into conflict with its educative mission. Should a principled stance be prioritized, and what might be the cost of doing so? Was exhibiting *Shipwrecked* akin to supporting treasure hunting, or could it instead be an opportunity for museums to define "protection and preservation" differently? Was it possible, or even desirable, for museums to manage and adjudicate such profound disagreements within the communities they worked with and sought to engage? And what might the answers to these questions mean for the ownership, display, and interpretation of the past in the present?

The postponement had a ripple effect in Singapore. Given that public money had been spent on acquiring the assemblage, journalists asked, why was the first major exhibition of the *Belitung* objects taking place in a private rather than a public museum? And why were there still no definitive plans to put the collection on permanent display?[140] The Singapore Tourism Board's response was defensive: the decision to display the objects at the ArtScience Museum, rather than a public institution, had allowed the museum to have "a blockbuster opening," they countered.[141] Nevertheless, steps were taken to mitigate the criticisms that the objects should have been shown in a public museum, including a new preferential ticketing structure "to encourage more Singaporean visitors."[142] It is reasonable to suggest that there was a connection between the timing of this announcement and the pressure Singapore was under by that time in relation to *Shipwrecked*, including criticisms in a national newspaper that the exhibition should have been shown in a public rather than a private museum.[143]

In late July, the Singapore Tourism Board and Marina Bay Sands announced that *Shipwrecked* would be extended from July 31 to October 2, 2011, ostensibly due to public demand.[144] The same press release also announced that entry to *Shipwrecked*—not to the museum, but to the *exhibition*—would be free to all visitors and residents during the week of Singapore's National Day (August 8–14).[145] It is hard to interpret this announcement as anything other than an attempt to deflect criticisms that *Shipwrecked* was not accessible to the general public. Meanwhile, representatives from the National Heritage Board and the Singapore Tourism Board continued to state that the collection would eventually be housed in a national museum.[146] They were unable to specify when or where.

An Act of Hubris

The postponement of *Shipwrecked* had bought the Smithsonian Institution some time, but a decision still needed to be made about whether the exhibition would proceed in an altered state or indeed at all. In December 2011, the Smithsonian Institution convened a Shipwreck Advisory Committee, attended by influential American maritime archaeologists and researchers.[147] After two days of discussions, it announced that not only was it canceling *Shipwrecked* altogether, but that it intended to re-excavate the wreck site in Indonesia to "reveal context that was lost or ignored in the original salvage operation" and "eventually build an exhibition from those findings."[148] This was, as one participant described it, "the solution of our dreams."[149] Some members of the Shipwreck Advisory Committee even developed a list of mini-exhibits, "which the Smithsonian could mount by engaging archaeologists, scientists and curators from several of the [Smithsonian's Institutions] museums."[150]

But the decision to re-excavate betrayed a fundamental lack of understanding about the Indonesian context. Apparently unbeknownst to the Shipwreck Advisory Committee, the site had *already* been surveyed, by Indonesian archaeologists from the Jambi Office for Cultural Heritage Protection, in 2010. The survey results had been presented at the Asia/Pacific Conference on Underwater Cultural Heritage in Manila in November 2011—just one month prior to the Smithsonian's cancellation.[151] The Shipwreck Advisory Committee's announcement was also hubristic, predicated as it was on the assumption that Indonesia—which had not been consulted in the making of this decision—would allow an excavation. The Indonesian archaeologists had made three recommendations in their report: legal protection, site rehabilitation, and the establishment of a maritime museum in Belitung regency. Nowhere was re-excavation recommended. The Shipwreck Advisory Committee also seemed to be unaware of sensitivities regarding foreign involvement in Indonesian archaeology: five years earlier, in March 2006, two foreign divers had been arrested by Indonesian authorities for allegedly salvaging another shipwreck, the *Cirebon*, without the required permits.[152] The absence of Indonesian researchers in the *Belitung* salvage had been noted in the report prepared by the Jambi Office for Cultural Heritage Protection, indicating this remained a live issue.[153]

Many Singaporean academics spoke out against the Smithsonian Institution's decision. One scholar emphasized the importance of public access to the objects, and the need to make a "sharp distinction" between "the controversies over professional ethics and the right of the public to have direct access to these artefacts and expert interpretation of them."[154] The Singaporean media condemned the proposal, pointing to its failure to engage with the real world:

> All told, it does seem that the proposal to re-excavate the *Belitung* site comes from armchair academics paying laughable lip service to an ideal, while ignoring the very real problems marine archaeologists face in the field.[155]

A senior staff writer at *The Straits Times* was more forceful: "The Smithsonian should not cave in to people with doctrinal blinders who think nothing of hijacking the whole show for their own parochial interests."[156] "The knee-jerk reaction," wrote another local journalist, "is to assume that Singapore has on its hands a white elephant."[157] Having committed so much financial and cultural capital to the project, Singapore could not afford for it to fail. But if even its curatorial partner was not willing to display *Shipwrecked*, what future did this international traveling exhibition have?

Should, asked Derek Fincham, professor at South Texas College of Law, the sixty thousand objects "be returned to the ocean floor" as a disincentive for treasure hunters and commercial salvagers?[158] Or was it possible to develop an exhibition of these objects that both disavowed looting while also ensuring the public's right to learn from, and about, the world's underwater cultural heritage? The cancellation of *Shipwrecked* at the Sackler Gallery, with the scheduled opening just three months away, was a gesture toward the creation of an "exclusive club of academic archaeologists" that spoke to the power of "a museum culture where certain artifacts are hidden away from the general public," wrote one researcher. Rather than setting a legal, ethical, and professional precedent, it was instead "an act of distrust in the general public's ability to reach its own conclusions."[159] This was the authorized heritage discourse at work, exercising control through institutional means about what stories could be told and by whom.

Conclusion

Having purchased and taken delivery of the objects in 2005, the Sentosa Development Corporation grappled for years with the question of how to integrate them into the Singapore Story. Eventually, it identified a historical narrative that aligned these ancient objects with the city-state's vision for the future. *Shipwrecked* was a major statement about Singapore's place in the modern world. The exhibition connected Singapore both temporally and spatially with the maritime trade networks of the past, and helped to "tell the story of how Singapore grew from a fishing village into the modern metropolis it is today."[160] The *Jewel of Muscat* project confirmed and extended this vision of Singapore as the modern inheritor of this cultural legacy, taking the story beyond Asia by asserting an "ancient link" between Southeast Asia and the Middle East.[161] But the question of how to accommodate the objects within the Singapore Story resulted in international controversy and wasted resources. The more important issue was, and had always been, how to manage objects that had been commercially recovered from the ocean. Singapore's search for a grand narrative had distracted it, and by the time the magnitude of the controversy became evident, it was too late.

As complicated as this issue of "orphaned" objects from the sea was, Singapore was also up against a much more difficult challenge—the lack of knowledge of, and engagement with, Southeast Asia in the global cultural heritage sector. It is disappointing that the coordination and energy mustered by the anti-*Shipwrecked* campaigners did not yield efforts to share knowledge, build institutional links, or develop capacity-building programs with Southeast Asian colleagues. There is no doubt that the criticism leveled at *Shipwrecked*, specifically its curators' failure to address ethical concerns regarding the management of commercially salvaged underwater cultural heritage, was justified. But in their vehement opposition to the exhibition, critics silenced the voices of those who had valid questions about the practical realities of protecting and preserving underwater cultural heritage in an under-resourced region. As safe spaces for dangerous ideas, the museums involved in displaying *Shipwrecked* were ideally positioned, yet ultimately failed, to advance these conversations.

There was, however one positive—albeit unexpected—outcome arising from the cancellation of *Shipwrecked*: whereas its initial connection to the *Belitung* cargo was tenuous, Singapore was now, for better or for worse, indelibly associated with these objects. Canceled plans to develop *Shipwrecked* into a long-term traveling exhibition forced Singapore to reevaluate its international strategy and the projection of its own place in history. While the controversy that swirled around the objects in 2011 had the potential to threaten the afterlives of the objects, Singapore's post-*Shipwrecked* response, as I argue in the following chapter, instead ensured their longevity.

CHAPTER FIVE

Reimagined

Singapore's response to the cancellation of *Shipwrecked* required a profound reimagining of not only the exhibition strategy, but of the objects themselves. Was it still (if indeed it ever had been) appropriate to use these objects for tourism, leisure, and development, as their management by the Sentosa Development Corporation implied? And what would it take for these objects to be recognized for their heritage value, and managed accordingly?

Singapore responded with agility. Its first step, less than a month after the Smithsonian's announcement, was to open a new exhibition. Of significance was that the exhibition was held at a public museum, thereby minimizing the possibility Singapore could be seen as profiting from the objects through high entrance fees. It also gave Singapore time to develop strategies to avoid a repeat of the Smithsonian Institution controversy.

Transferring responsibility for the objects from the tourism to the heritage portfolio was another important step in Singapore's reimagining of them. This transfer symbolized a reconceptualization of the objects based on their heritage rather than their economic value, and precipitated the installation of a permanent exhibition at Singapore's own Asian Civilisations Museum. Singapore also sought to ensure the objects would be shown internationally, including in Canada, France, the United States, Korea, and the Netherlands—even, after years of negotiation, in China.[1] Although each of these exhibitions has been different, they have all served a common purpose: the legitimization of the objects through museum exhibits. This has occurred with each new display of the objects, but the effect has been cumulative, embedding the objects within a museological context. Each exhibition has provided museums in Singapore and internationally with the opportunity to reassess the display of these objects, and to introduce an increasingly broad range of national, ethical, and art historical narratives into their interpretations. While some of these exhibitions have been met with criticism, most have not. The controversy, although by no means dissipated, has been subsumed within these other stories. This has created a space for the objects to come into their own.

Singapore's Response

In the wake of the cancellation of *Shipwrecked*, Singapore did not attempt to por-tray the salvage as ethical or seek to defend the methods that had been used to recover the objects. These were arguments that could not be won. Instead, Singa-pore's early responses were directed at mitigating perceptions that the manage-ment of the Tang Shipwreck Collection was a for-profit venture that deprioritized public access. Thus, although the Tang Treasures Suite had already been open at the Goodwood Park Hotel for five years, Singapore's daily newspaper published an article reminding readers that these objects were accessible to the public and "displayed with the aim of sharing a part of history with hotel guests and visi-tors."[2] This free display provided a counterbalance to criticisms made at the height of the controversy that *Shipwrecked* had been shown at a private museum "that charges visitors [SGD]$30 for entry, instead of a national museum, where fees are cheaper."[3]

A renewed emphasis on public accessibility was also evident in the new exhibition, *The Tang Shipwreck: Gold and Ceramics from Ninth-Century China* (January 12–June 24, 2012), at the Asian Civilisations Museum.[4] This was no casino-backed cultural add-on: it was an established public museum that consti-tuted part of Singapore's "organizational ecology of museums," each doing its part "to create citizens."[5] Organizers had no way of knowing that the very same venue would, in a few years' time, become the objects' permanent home; in the immediate aftermath of the controversy, and within the context of Singapore's rapidly evolving museum sector, the Asian Civilisations Museum was simply an available public institution with space for a small temporary exhibition.

While this exhibition was much smaller than *Shipwrecked*—130 objects in-stead of *Shipwrecked*'s 400—it did include never-before-exhibited pieces, such as a number of the blue-and-white ceramic dishes and the gilt silver flask.[6] The new exhibition signaled a shift from the usual modus operandi of museums, in which people have only limited opportunity to "directly, physically, engage with the things on display."[7] It also departed from the artificial interactivity of the Maritime Experiential Museum and the ArtScience Museum. This shift was achieved through a simple curatorial intervention: the incorporation of a section where visitors could "get a feel" of some of the ceramic sherds.[8] In the words of the exhibition's curator, Kan Shuyi,

> Most of the time when people go to a museum, the things are behind glass cabinets and we thought it would be good if people can actually handle some of these objects and develop maybe another kind of appreciation for

these ceramics as well because you can feel the form of the object, the pot-
ter inscribing words and the glaze.[9]

By removing physical barriers between the public and the objects, meta-
phorical barriers were also dismantled. These objects, and the larger assemblage
they were drawn from, constituted a visceral connection to the past; a past that
visitors were now able to hold in their hands. Singapore had, quite literally, handed
the objects to the public.

Multisensory engagement with objects in a museum setting is both educational and affective.[10] It allows a certain type of learning to take place. Holding a
ceramic sherd in our hands gives us a greater sense of the weight, texture, and
other qualities of the object, and how it interacted with its surroundings. Museums scholar Sandra Dudley considers this sort of multisensory experience to be
a form of analysis more meaningful than a purely visual approach because, as she
explains, touching, tapping, or even smelling an object "can confirm or contra-
dict the evidence of one's eyes."[11] Further, she suggests, touching an object is a two-
way exchange: a person touches an object, and is also touched by it, allowing "an
intimacy with the material thing . . . an intimacy I cannot feel if I only gaze at the
thing on a plinth behind a sheet of glass."[12] Other scholars suggest that holding
objects develops empathy because it encourages people to connect with the hands
of the maker and to imagine "the feelings of those who originally held the objects, cherished them, collected them, possessed them."[13] This effect is heightened
with shipwrecked objects, which, having never reached their intended destination, were lost to those who had made them as well as those who anticipated them.
To hold a shipwrecked sherd is to wonder about its interrupted voyage, and to
question how, despite being wrecked, it came to be in one's hands. Encouraging
people to hold such objects is rich with opportunities to interrogate how the objects finished their voyage, as it were.

Shipwrecked may have been canceled at the Smithsonian, but the Singaporean public could see these objects for free in a hotel and for a nominal fee at the
Asian Civilisations Museum. This took the pressure off Singapore to a certain extent, and provided some much-needed space in which to make decisions about
the longer-term plans for the objects. It is not clear whether Singapore considered
selling them, although that was surely an attractive option: in June 2012 the Tang
Shipwreck Collection was independently valued at over US$60 million, almost
double what Singapore had paid for it just seven years earlier.[14] But who would
buy it at that price? And what would the loss of it mean for Singapore's efforts to
position itself as central to Southeast Asian and global maritime histories? Instead,
with the weight of responsibility for this contentious and valuable collection grow-

ing each year, Singapore doubled down on its efforts to turn the collection into a traveling exhibition.

A Shipwreck by Any Other Name

Singapore finally found an international partner willing to host an exhibition of the objects in late 2014. *The Lost Dhow: A Discovery from the Maritime Silk Route* opened at the Aga Khan Museum in Toronto, Canada, on December 13, 2014, and continued until April 26, 2015. Like the ArtScience Museum, the Aga Khan was a new museum in a "sublimely detailed" building designed by Pritzker Prize–winning architect Fumihiko Maki and opened just two months earlier, on September 18, 2014.[15] Funded by the Aga Khan Development Network, through the Aga Khan Trust for Culture, the new museum's mission was to "foster a greater understanding and appreciation of the contribution that Muslim civilizations have made to world heritage."[16] Despite the museum's distance from the center of Toronto and its high entrance fees, it had reasonable attendance figures (85,000) in the first six months of visits by the public, which included the period in which *The Lost Dhow* was shown.[17]

Previous displays of the objects had highlighted the Chinese connection, because that is where the objects had been made. But *The Lost Dhow* was the first exhibition to amplify an element that had largely been missing: the Islamic connection, and the question of where the objects were (presumed to be) traveling to. Even the exhibition title, with its use of the term "dhow"—a blanket term for wooden sailing vessels from the Indian Ocean, particularly from the western Indian Ocean—was an indication of the distinctly Islamic elements that the Aga Khan Museum was seeking to develop.[18] This re-centered the exhibition away from Tang dynasty China and toward a different identity altogether. As the director of the Aga Khan Museum, Henry Kim, explained, "the cross-cultural exchange exemplified by the dhow's cargo is exactly what our collection and programming both celebrate and explore."[19] Speaking at the opening of the exhibition, Asian Civilisations Museum director Alan Chong—who had flown in from Singapore—emphasized the ancient connections between China, Southeast Asia, and the Islamic world.[20] The focus on the objects' Islamic connections, which contrasted with the approach taken in *Shipwrecked*, was an indication of the ways in which different aspects of this vessel and cargo could be highlighted depending on context and purpose.

The Lost Dhow was curated by guest curator John Vollmer, an independent North America–based curator with expertise in Asian art, textiles, and dress, and was accompanied by a sixty-four page catalogue.[21] The exhibition featured a ship's silhouette on the gallery's wooden floorboards, a useful technique by which the museum could convey the size of the vessel.[22] A ship's model was also on show, one of four copies made by the Omanis of the *Jewel of Muscat*.[23] Printed fabric banners hanging from the ceiling divided the gallery into sections and provided context on the origins of the vessel and cargo, how the wreck was dated, and speculation about its destination. One banner posed the question "What is treasure?" followed by an acknowledgment that the exhibition "evokes a familiar cliché of sunken treasure."[24] But, as it also noted, "treasure can be more than the value assessed in monetary terms. Rarity, age, use, importance and curiosity are also ways of measuring value and gauging our own perceptions against those of other times."[25] Treasure was not something that related to monetary value, but to knowledge. Whereas *Shipwrecked: Tang Treasures and Monsoon Winds* had been an exhibition with treasure at its heart, *The Lost Dhow* was about knowledge, discovery, and information.

This exhibition highlighted the wreck's connections with the Islamic world, but did not do so in a narrow or exclusionary way. Of the three hundred–odd objects on display, Vollmer's curation prioritized the dragon head ewer which, with its incised lozenge motif and leafy fronds, clearly suggested a connection with the Persian Gulf.[26] But Vollmer also prioritized a double-fish ovoid jar from the kilns of Yue, its intertwined fish considered to be a Buddhist symbol of harmony and abundance.[27] The gold cup was displayed not alone, as "star" objects often are, but in a cabinet alongside two of the silver ingots. Other objects on display in the exhibition included two blue-and-white dishes, a tumble of Changsha bowls (which constituted more than half the objects on display), and the oversized ceramic storage containers.[28] There was also a selection of mirrors, coins, and a number of non-Changsha bowls and jars. By placing the spotlight on the ewer and ovoid jar rather than the gold, the display supported the message conveyed in the graphic banner: that treasure, as it is often conceived, is not necessarily that which is most financially valuable. It can instead be an object that provides new information or insight into the exchange of ideas or the production of material culture—in this case, the foregrounding of Buddhist symbols in a museum dedicated to Islamic civilization.

The Lost Dhow was the first exhibition to position museums, as institutions, as part of the solution rather than as part of the problem. Although there was no way of rectifying the complications arising from commercial salvage and sale of the objects, there was a growing appreciation of the possibility of mitigating these issues through the future ethical management of the collection. The Aga Khan achieved this both through its display, which did not go down the treasure route, and through the preparation and programming associated with the exhibition.

Anticipating a "potential storm of controversy," the Aga Khan developed a position paper that provided background on the legal and ethical aspects of *Shipwrecked* and the nature of the opposition to the exhibition, and discussed potential Canadian responses to a version of the exhibition being shown at the Aga Khan Museum.[29] Reflecting on the "maelstrom of media attention" directed at the Smithsonian Institution in 2011, it warned that the Aga Khan Museum could "expect a similar response to news of the exhibition coming to Toronto"[30] but proposed that the public should have an opportunity to see the objects and decide for themselves. It argued:

> The Aga Khan Museum cannot ignore or downplay the issues surrounding the excavation and sale of the Belitung shipwreck . . . Moreover, not to address the issues and the preservation of underwater cultural heritage would be a disservice to the public—as would not exhibiting the shipwreck's cargo.[31]

Telling the shipwreck's story fitted neatly with the museum's mandate of promoting cross-cultural interactions through heritage. The Aga Khan Museum also recognized that *The Lost Dhow* was an opportunity to stimulate discussion about the protection and preservation of underwater cultural heritage and encourage reflection on the responsibilities of managing this and other shared heritage. The Aga Khan Museum's approach was informed and considered. It was positioned to manage any backlash to *The Lost Dhow* in a way that the organizers of *Shipwrecked* had not been.

But when Chong addressed the media at the exhibition opening in Toronto, there were no questions about the archaeological methods that had been used to salvage the collection.[32] It is considered likely that the lack of critical scrutiny in Toronto was because the connection between *The Lost Dhow* and *Shipwrecked* was unclear, and not because the controversy had died down. This is not to suggest that the Aga Khan Museum had kept this information hidden: a press release issued by the museum prior to the opening of *The Lost Dhow* clearly stated that the objects had been recovered and conserved by Tilman Walterfang, were traveling for the first time since their acquisition by Singapore, and that their acquisition had been made possible by a donation from the Khoo Teck Estate.[33] At the same time, however, it was not specifically stated that this was the Tang Shipwreck Collection, or that these objects had formed the basis of the aborted *Shipwrecked* exhibition.

To "encourage conversation about the importance of preserving and sharing maritime heritage," the exhibition was accompanied by programming initiatives including an international symposium, film screening, and musical performances inspired by the Silk Road.[34] The one-day symposium, "The *Belitung* Shipwreck and the Maritime Silk Route," was held at the exhibition's halfway point on February 28, 2015.[35] The morning session featured speakers discussing the discovery and salvage of the wreck, the objects themselves, and the insights the shipwreck offered into the ninth-century commercial maritime silk route.[36] A roundtable discussion in the afternoon sought to broach the "recent" controversy through "a discussion of the historical and ethical implications of shipwrecks and the role of museums as venues for exploring and showcasing archaeological materials."[37] The symposium aligned with the objective articulated in the Aga Khan's position paper, namely that the museum wished to "encourage dialogue between the public, representatives of archaeological organizations, and commercial salvors."[38]

Whereas much of the academic and institutional criticism of *Shipwrecked* had focused on whether the objects should have been salvaged at all, the roundtable was dominated by the question of whether the public should have a right to view the objects. James Delgado, who participated in the roundtable, had long condemned the sale of the objects but remained of the view he had first put forward in 2011 that exhibiting the objects was an opportunity to "educate the public about the consequences of the commercialization of underwater heritage."[39] He also indicated his satisfaction with the Aga Khan Museum's display, which went beyond simply presenting the objects as art historical treasures.[40] Another roundtable participant, Chen Shen, emphasized the need to prioritize the right of the public to decide for themselves, rather than being dictated to by archaeologists and museums.[41] Shen, who was senior curator of Chinese Art and Culture at the Royal Ontario Museum, feared that patronizing the public by deciding what was best for them would drive people away from museums. There was also a growing awareness of the complexity of the salvage. During the question-and-answer session that followed the roundtable, for example, the discussion focused on why "developing countries such as Indonesia" were expected to adhere to international standards articulated in the 2001 UNESCO Convention when "even Canada" was not investing in its maritime archaeology research.[42]

Discussions at the symposium confirmed that a subtle shift had taken place. In 2011, museums that had entertained the possibility of exhibiting *Shipwrecked* had been characterized as complicit in the destruction of underwater cultural heritage. Opponents to *Shipwrecked* contended that the cargo should never have been commercially salvaged and sold; questions of display and access were moot because the objects themselves were effectively invalidated due to the means by which they had been salvaged. By 2015, however, the question was less about how the objects had been recovered and more about whether the North American public should continue to be refused access to them. There was no denying the problems arising from the commercial salvage and sale. But there was also a growing recognition that the objects, having been salvaged, needed to be managed ethically, and that to achieve this, those responsible for the objects needed to actively promote public access—including, for example, by removing high entrance fees—and provide additional interpretive information about the context in which they had been recovered and acquired. Alongside this was a growing acknowledgement of the role that museums, as places to display the objects and make them available for public access, could play.

A Permanent Home

Two days after *The Lost Dhow* closed in Toronto, Singapore's Minister for Culture, Community and Youth, Lawrence Wong, made a major announcement about the future of the Tang Shipwreck Collection. In a speech delivered on April 28, 2015, at Singapore's Patron of Heritage Awards, Wong announced that the collection would go on permanent display at the Asian Civilisations Museum.[43] What Wong did not mention was that this was only possible because of the consolidation, in 2013, of Singapore's national collections into a single collection managed by the National Heritage Board. As a Statutory Board under the Ministry of Culture, Community and Youth, the National Heritage Board owns and operates Singapore's national museums, interpretive centers, and heritage institutions. Following the consolidation, it was responsible for a vast repository of more than two hundred thousand artworks and artifacts.[44] As part of the process, the 53,227 objects in the Tang Shipwreck Collection were transferred from the Singapore Tourism Board (under the Ministry of Trade and Industry) to the National Heritage Board, a move that effectively reframed the objects as a heritage rather than a tourist attraction.[45] It was just one of many collections to be transferred to the National Heritage Board, so the transfer should not necessarily be interpreted as directly related to the 2011 controversy. However, it did follow considerable lobbying by key players in Singapore's museum sector, who had long viewed the tourism portfolio as the wrong home for the objects. The consolidation was a critical step in reconceptualizing these as heritage, rather than tourist, objects.

At the time of Wong's announcement, the Asian Civilisations Museum was undergoing a SGD$25 million renovation. Whereas it had previously been organized geographically, the renovation placed a stronger emphasis on trade and interconnectivity—a narrative that the Tang Shipwreck Collection was well positioned to support. The museum reopened on November 14, 2015, with the Tang Shipwreck Collection on permanent display in the new Khoo Teck Puat Gallery, strategically located adjacent to the Singapore River.[46] This location reinforces the message that,

> until airplanes and the Suez Canal changed things, almost every ship travelling from India to China passed through the Singapore Straits. As far back as Vasco de Gama, sailors rode the monsoon winds, which change direction every six months, in and out of Singapore's harbor.[47]

At the entrance to the gallery, visitors are greeted with an oversized black-and-white photograph of the *Jewel of Muscat* during sea trials off the coast of Oman. This photograph is effectively a replica of the "original" replica, which remains in the former Maritime Experiential Museum. Inside the gallery itself, reflections of light and water bounce off masses of objects encased in glass. Overhead, circular skylights "bathe the precious artefacts with daylight and allow their exquisite craftsmanship to shine."[48] These elements—glass, sunshine, and the reflections from the nearby Singapore River—posed significant challenges for curator Stephen Murphy, who needed to manage the exposure of objects to light for conservation purposes. But the Khoo Teck Puat Foundation had made clear its expectations that the collection would be displayed in a prominent position at the center of the ground-floor galleries.[49]

The donors also requested that as many objects be displayed as possible, thus highlighting one of the dilemmas for a museum in managing a large collection of similar objects—how to display (and store) them, and how, with so many to choose from, to decide which ones to display.[50] One curatorial solution was to create a sculptural "wave" of Changsha bowls and to integrate one of the ship's models within this ceramic wave. Featuring hundreds of bowls, this display creates an impression of a powerful ocean wave tossing about a small boat.[51] Numerous other Changsha bowls are coiled inside one of the large storage jars in which many of them would have originally traveled. This display, near the entrance of the gallery, gives visitors an idea of the volume of the cargo, the size of the ship, how the bowls traveled, and the organization of trade in the ninth century. Because the bowls are coiled, their unique designs are not clearly visible to viewers. However, there is another large display case in the gallery in which hundreds of bowls are on show, with interpretive text accompanying the more significant designs. The multiple uses of the bowls—as visual cue for a replica ship's last voyage, as demonstration of packing technique, as *objet d'art* in a traditional glass case—is made possible by the size of the assemblage the museum has at its disposal. The quantity of bowls reminds us of the sheer volume of ceramic production in Changsha. But it also makes a powerful statement about the collection itself, namely that this

Figure 10. A wave of Changsha bowls greets visitors at the entrance to the Khoo Teck Puat Gallery inside Singapore's Asian Civilisations Museum. The use of bowls to create a sculptural wave upon which a ship's model appears to float is one of a number of curatorial solutions to the question of how to do justice, in a limited space, to such an enormous assemblage. Photo by Natali Pearson, 2017.

was an *assemblage* of objects—that they traveled together, and that even though the cargo featured rare and exquisite objects, it was dominated by one type of object in particular.[52]

Although many of the objects on display appear to be in new condition, there are also a significant number that clearly show signs of having been underwater for centuries. The contrast of coral-encrusted objects alongside those in pristine condition allows the former to retain "vestiges of its life in, and passage through, the outside world."[53] For museums, leaving objects in a state of semi-conservation can be a practical decision—removing the encrustations might irreversibly damage the objects, or be prohibitively expensive—as well as aesthetic one. The effect is a display that speaks to experiences of time spent underwater, making the recovery of these objects, and their display in a museum, appear all the more remarkable. The effect is heightened by the juxtaposition of seemingly "perfect" and semi-conserved objects alongside the replica boats (in photographic and miniature

Figure 11. On display at the Asian Civilisations Museum are dozens of Changsha bowls coiled helically inside a storage container as they would have been packed. Image courtesy of the Asian Civilisations Museum, 2015.

form) that feature throughout the exhibition.[54] This "trifecta of objects"—those that have been restored, those that have been left in their original state or semi-conserved, and replicas—represents the stages of preservation, decay, and re-creation. Scholars Elizabeth Greene and Justin Leidwanger describe its effect—used by contemporary artist Damien Hirst in his 2017 *Treasures from the Wreck of the Unbelievable* exhibition in Venice—as the foregrounding of "the role of the archaeological process in viewers' enchantment with the deep."[55] By presenting this process of decay, restoration, and re-creation as synchronous rather than sequential, the museum creates an impression of time collapsing, of history being made before the visitor's own eyes.

The permanent exhibition is accompanied by a new catalog, replacing the one produced with the Smithsonian Institution. *The Tang Shipwreck: Art and Exchange in the 9th Century* is a lavish production with detailed scholarly essays and plentiful color photographs. The Asian Civilisations Museum also released a free virtual reality app "that allows the user to step into the shoes of a member of the ship's crew or those of a marine archaeologist recovering the cargo."[56] This app allows a visitor to hold a curated interpretation of the objects in their hands, an echo of the 2012 *The Tang Shipwreck* exhibition in which the audience could hold the objects themselves. In its use of technology, the app is also reminiscent of the multisensory Typhoon Theatre at the Maritime Experiential Museum, although the information it provides is far richer and more nuanced. The app includes a special functionality that allows visitors to (virtually) "collect" artifacts in order to unlock the "next stage" of the app. Although this is reminiscent of a treasure hunt, it also encourages visitors to explore the gallery, engage closely with the objects, and extend their time in the museum.

This is an arresting exhibition that does justice to the objects in the Tang Shipwreck Collection. The Asian Civilisations is a small museum, and the Khoo Teck Puat Gallery, in which the Tang Shipwreck Collection is housed, is hard to miss. The display has been refined in the years since it opened—the ceramic wave has been bulked out with the addition of more bowls, for example, and the creation of a small alcove provides some much-needed darkness and intimacy by which to display the shining gold. At the entrance to the gallery, wall panels draw attention to issues of maritime trade and archaeology in Singapore; inside the gallery, there is information on the objects themselves, including the commercial context in which they were recovered. Much as the Aga Khan did, they encourage visitors to reflect on the challenges of managing underwater cultural heritage in the region. Looking through the glass display cabinets and beyond to the Singapore River, it is hard not to imagine the *Jewel of Muscat*, just a few miles away on Sentosa Island, and how it might look on display by the waterfront.

Escaping the Spotlight

Because of the quantity of objects in the Tang Shipwreck Collection, Singapore was able to pursue a permanent display and a traveling exhibition simultaneously. Nineteen objects went on display in France in late 2016 as part of the *Ocean Explorers: From Sindbad to Marco Polo* (*Aventuriers des Mers: De Sindbad à Marco Polo*) exhibition, which focused on the maritime worlds of the Mediterranean and Indian Ocean from the seventh to the seventeenth centuries. Except for *Southeast Asian Ceramics* at the NUS Museum in 2009–2010, previous exhibitions of the Tang Shipwreck Collection had been solely dedicated to objects recovered from the *Belitung* shipwreck. *Aventuriers des Mers* was different, as the nineteen objects from the Tang Shipwreck Collection made up just a fraction of the more than two hundred objects on display. Subsumed as they were within the exhibition—shown first at the Institute of the Arab World (Institut du Monde Arabe, or IMA) in Paris and then at the Museum of European and Mediterranean Civilisations (Musée des Civilisations de l'Europe et de la Méditerranée, or MuCEM) in Marseille—they again managed to escape controversy.[57]

The exhibition was divided into themed galleries. The first theme related to the notion of the ocean as dangerous and wild. Representations of sea monsters and imperiled vessels reinforced the text of the wall panels, which told of the vastness and endlessness of the ocean, and of the mythological creatures that lived beneath its waves—and the barbarians who inhabited its farthest shores. The second gallery focused on the role of navigation in these early maritime voyages. With its marine-blue walls and its extraordinary objects—early maps of the world, astrolabes, ship's models, and old photographs of monsoonal voyages—this gallery communicated the creativity and ingenuity required to chart global sea routes without modern navigational equipment. This gallery contained evidence of the often-invisible connections between objects, places, and people across time and space: one of the ship's models on display in this gallery, a replica of a boat from India's Malabar Coast, was made by Nick Burningham, who had also made the first model of the *Jewel of Muscat*. Furthermore, Burningham's model in *Aventuriers des Mers* was owned by the Aga Khan Trust for Culture, which had funded the Aga Khan Museum in Toronto. The replica had been made in 2010, thus predating the Aga Khan Museum's *The Lost Dhow* exhibition yet serendipitously anticipating the future connections that would unfold.

The nineteen objects from the Tang Shipwreck Collection were displayed in the third gallery. This gallery was themed around merchandise and mercantilism and was differentiated from the previous gallery by its rich red walls. Wall panels described an ancient world in which traders created commercial networks "to obtain supplies from ever more distant lands and in ever greater quantities."[58] The emphasis in this gallery was the fascination of traders and adventurers with spices, ivory, ceramics, silk, cotton, pearls, and precious woods. Merchants from the Arabian Peninsula were ideally located to take advantage of the maritime trade between the Mediterranean and the Indian Ocean, and it flourished in the eighth to thirteenth centuries. Objects traveled across the ocean from China to the Persian Gulf, from where they were transported by caravans to the southern Mediterranean for distribution to wealthy ports such as Venice and Constantinople. The *Belitung*'s place in this ancient and connected world was evident. The objects were assembled together in a long, low display case, and included a number of Changsha wares including bowls and ewers, coins, bronze mirrors, a silver dish, and a selection of other ceramics including a blue-and-white dish.

This was not a display of the collection's highlights, but instead one that was more representative of the *Belitung* assemblage as a whole. Visitors could look down at the objects through the display case, and at a nearby video explaining the ship's discovery and significance. The exhibition then turned to the theme of new markets and new merchandise, and the adaptations made by traders and craftsmen to these new demands. The final gallery set the stage for colonial expansionism by situating the historical focus of the exhibition within an increasingly interconnected world made possible by the voyages of Christopher Columbus, Vasco de Gama, and Ferdinand Magellan. Consisting of one medium-sized display case in a large exhibition spread across five thematic galleries, the *Belitung* objects were not lost, but contextualized. When they were first made, these objects were part of complicated networks of commercial exchange; their display in the *Aventuriers des Mers* exhibition reinforced these broader connections.

Aventuriers des Mers opened first at the IMA in Paris (November 15, 2016–February 26, 2017), where it was co-curated by IMA staff Agnès Carayon and Nala Aloubat. The concept of the IMA dates to the 1980s, when a group of Arab countries developed a plan to promote and share information about Arab culture, art, and civilization in France. Designed by architect Jean Nouvel and constructed as part of an urban redevelopment project, the IMA includes a museum, library, auditorium, restaurant, and offices. It is co-funded by France and member states of the Arab League and seeks to inhabit a space between the European and the Arab world. The opening of *Aventuriers des Mers*, which coincided with the thirtieth anniversary of the IMA's establishment in 1987, was attended by the French Minister of Foreign Affairs and International Development, Jean-Marc Ayrault, and the Ambassador of the Sultanate of Oman to France, Humaid Al Maani. A traditional Omani fishing vessel, the *Nizwa*, was positioned outside the IMA, boldly announcing the exhibition's themes of maritime adventure and exploration within a European, as well as an Indian Ocean, context.[59]

From Paris, the exhibition traveled to the MuCEM in Marseille (June 7–October 9, 2017). There, *Aventuriers des Mers* was displayed in partnership with the IMA under the oversight of MuCEM conservator and curator Vincent Giovannoni. A much newer venue than the IMA, having opened in June 2013, MuCEM was the first national museum exclusively located outside the French capital.[60] Although a relatively new museum, much of its extensive collection of over one million objects dates to the nineteenth century and the collections of three Paris-based ethnographic museums, which it has supplemented with Mediterranean-focused acquisitions.[61] There was no vessel positioned outside Mu-CEM to herald the presence of *Aventuriers des Mers*, although the location of MuCEM at the old port suggested a maritime connection. Visitors were greeted at the entrance of the exhibition by an enormous shark jaw, spotlit in a darkened room. Positioned adjacent to a video depicting a roiling sea, this object immediately established the exhibition's focus as one of exploration and adventure. An introductory wall panel emphasized the Mediterranean's place within an unpredictable and dangerous world, in which seafaring adventurers pursued "the exotic riches" that lay beyond their familiar coasts and, in the process, developed new maritime trade routes that led to exchanges across the Indian Ocean.[62] From there, it followed a similar exhibition structure to that used at the IMA.

There is no evidence to indicate that the inclusion of objects from the Tang Shipwreck Collection in the *Aventuriers des Mers* exhibition attracted negative publicity or controversy in France, or indeed elsewhere. This was a significant change from the media coverage of 2011. The avoidance of negative publicity is even more surprising given the fact that this exhibition was shown in France, where UNESCO headquarters are located. This was not a function of the controversy going away; instead, it seemed that the critics had simply not noticed.

American Debut

In 2017, objects in the Tang Shipwreck Collection went on display at the Asia Society Museum in New York. *Secrets of the Sea: A Tang Shipwreck and Early Trade in Asia* (March 7–June 4, 2017) was an important exhibition. The objects were finally making their much-anticipated US debut, despite the campaign mounted in 2011 to ensure otherwise. Furthermore, they were doing so in an institution of the caliber of the Asia Society Museum. Unlike *The Lost Dhow* at the Aga Khan Museum or *Aventuriers des Mers* at IMA and MuCEM, the Asia Society was an established institution with a strong international reputation. Its museum, on Park Avenue, is adjacent to Manhattan's "museum mile," home to a concentration of the world's most celebrated cultural institutions. It was impossible to mount the argument, as had been made about Singapore's ArtScience Museum, that this was some kind of "sideshow."[63]

The Asia Society is not funded publicly but by donations from foundations, corporations, and philanthropic individuals.[64] This model distinguishes it from the taxpayer-funded Smithsonian Institution, and is a legacy of its philanthropic origins: it was established by John D. Rockefeller III in 1956, at the height of the Cold War. Rockefeller's intention was to promote mutual understanding and engagement between America and Asia, and he saw art as fundamental to this mission. Throughout the 1960s and 1970s, he and his wife, Blanchette, worked together with their advisor, Sherman E. Lee—who was also then the director of the Cleveland Museum of Art—to assemble the now-renowned *Mr. and Mrs. John D. Rockefeller III Collection* with the intention of ultimately giving it to an institution for public view. Following Rockefeller's death in 1978, part of the collection was bequeathed to the Asia Society, forming the beginnings of the society's small but spectacular collection of Asian antiquities.[65]

Rather than bringing in a guest curator as the Aga Khan Museum had done, the Asia Society drew upon the expertise of its in-house curator, Adriana Proser. *Secrets of the Sea* featured around seventy-five objects, and, as is evident from its title, reintroduced the Tang moniker to reflect the involvement of the Tang Center for Early China at Columbia University in the exhibition and one of the associated symposia. This was the first premodern exhibition to open at the Asia Society Museum under director Tan Boon Hui. Described as a "trailblazer," Tan had come to Asia Society from the National Heritage Board, most recently as director of the Singapore Art Museum,[66] and was therefore deeply familiar with the history of the collection. He brought with him knowledge of the Singaporean, and Southeast Asian, context—qualities that had been notable for their absence in earlier efforts to bring the objects to America.

Whether it was because the use of the word "Tang" made the exhibition's provenance clearer than it had been in Canada and France, or because the exhibition was appearing in America for the first time since the aborted *Shipwrecked* exhibition, *Secrets of the Sea* attracted attention in a way the Canadian and French iterations had not. The opening-night reception for *Secrets of the Sea* was attended by over six hundred people, including many high-profile donors. But the opening also attracted a small number of protesters outside the Asia Society Museum's Park Avenue building, signaling not only a public awareness of the controversy but a physical manifestation of the contested terrains museums now occupy.[67] It also raised attention in the media.[68] In an interview with the *New York Times*, Tan acknowledged the exhibition's potential to attract controversy:

> We're not shying from it—we do acknowledge that it is a problem. We intend to collate together material, including newspaper reports and other commentaries, in the exhibition because we think people do need to be aware of these kinds of issues.[69]

Curator Proser was also aware of the issues at stake, and expressed her desire to use the exhibition to explore a middle ground:

> The matters surrounding preservation and provenance and looting are complex, and yet there is a tendency to see these issues in terms of black and white. At times, taking a purist approach can mean one ends up with destruction rather than what one is hoping to achieve.[70]

The exhibition was not only about educational outcomes, however.[71] Within the context of an increasingly isolationist America, it was seen by many, including Tan, as a valuable reminder of the early—and enduring—nature of international trade and cultural exchange in foreign waters.[72] Such messages were particularly salient in light of the changing and increasingly contested political situation in the United States.

The exhibition design emphasized Tan's messages of international connection. Outside the main gallery space, visitors to *Secrets of the Sea* were greeted with information and photos of the *Jewel of Muscat*, explaining how and where the ship had been constructed and the nature of its relationship to the objects on display. The exhibition itself conjured the ocean, with sea-green walls and lighting effects mimicking water rippling across the floorboards. The fragile dragon head ewer, which had also appeared at the Aga Khan Museum's *The Lost Dhow* exhibition, was highlighted. It was separate from other objects, standing under a spotlight in a glass case around which visitors could circle. There were also four of the bronze mirrors, one of the blue-and-white-dishes, and a representative selection of the ceramics.

One of the first wall panels in the exhibition related to the controversy surrounding the objects' recovery. This wall panel contextualized the wreck's discovery with reference to the economic troubles and racial riots following Suharto's resignation, and emphasized the legality of the salvage. It stated:

This exhibition and its related programming provide an opportunity to discuss underwater cultural heritage and the complex questions surrounding archaeology, preservation, commercial salvaging, looting, and international law. The recovery and sale of the cargo by Seabed Explorations were commercial transactions, which is problematic. The wreck, however, is one of the most important discoveries from the last fifty years and it is important that we share this historic story of global interaction.[73]

This was one of the clearest statements to be made about the controversy in, and by, a museum thus far. Visitors were given more opportunities to explore these issues in the final alcove, which took the form of a breakout space with a number of folders displayed on wooden desks. One of these contained the Aga Khan Museum position paper.[74] Another held eleven journal and newspaper articles pertaining to underwater cultural heritage, archaeological ethics, the *Belitung* shipwreck, and the controversy.[75] A significant omission from this folder were any articles by Michael Flecker, who had overseen the second salvage season in 1999 and subsequently published extensively on both the wreck and the ethical issues associated with managing underwater cultural heritage in Southeast Asia.[76] The alcove also featured a large wall panel titled "Marine Salvage and Recovery: A Conversation." This wall panel noted the "ground breaking reappraisal" of the maritime silk route made possible as a result of the *Belitung*'s discovery, before acknowledging that "a number of international and professional organizations dedicated to underwater archaeology oppose the display of this extraordinary material at museums because it was commercially salvaged." The wall panel also recognized concerns about the loss of information caused by "fast-paced, less scrupulously scientific commercial operations," while noting that looting had occurred at the site and that the majority of the cargo had been sold not to a private organization but to a subsidiary of the Singapore government. Reminding visitors of the objects' "global historical importance," the wall panel acknowledged "both the importance of sharing these works of major historical significance with the public and educating them about how critical full-fledged scientifically conducted archaeology is to understanding our past." From the first wall panels to the final alcove, then, the entire exhibition was effectively bracketed within the context of the controversy. As Tan had promised in his interview with the *New York Times*, the Asia Society was not shying away from the issues first raised in 2011.[77]

The final alcove also included a large photo of the *Jewel of Muscat*, forming a connection with the images of the vessel's construction shown at the beginning of the exhibition. This photo was identical to the one displayed at the entrance to the Khoo Teck Puat gallery at the Asian Civilisations Museum, although rendered in color rather than black and white. The foregrounding of the *Jewel of Muscat*, both in *Secrets of the Sea* and also in the permanent display at the Asian Civilisations Museum, is a reminder of the significance of the replica vessel to the objects themselves. The *Jewel of Muscat* is often referred to as evidence of how much archaeological information was recovered during the salvage, including construction materials and techniques, but its purpose here was also prosaic, reminding visitors of the maritime interlude experienced by these objects.

On the same floor of the museum as *Secrets of the Sea*, the Asia Society displayed a selection of Tang dynasty objects from its own collection. The objects in *Art of the Tang Dynasty (618–906): Selections from the Asia Society Museum Collection* (March 7–June 4, 2017) echoed those on display in *Secrets of the Sea*. Although from the same dynastic period, the objects in *Art of the Tang Dynasty* were sourced from terrestrial rather than maritime sites. The effect of this separate gallery was to anchor the *Secrets of the Sea* exhibition within the Asia Society's own museological narrative, by demonstrating that *Secrets of the Sea* was closely aligned with the permanent collection. This effectively embedded the *Belitung* objects within a wider historical, as well as museological, context. This was not just a one-off exhibition about a single shipwreck; it spoke to objects already in the Asia Society's own collection. The objects on display from the permanent collection were similar enough to be recognizable as from the same period as the *Belitung* objects, yet different enough in form and color to be distinguishable from the shipwrecked objects. This created a conversation across galleries, between the temporary exhibition and the permanent collection, and a point of difference from previous displays of the *Belitung* objects.

In addition to this novel curatorial intervention, *Secrets of the Sea* was accompanied by two public symposia. These created opportunities for scholars and the public to engage more closely with the issues raised by the exhibition. The first of these was "The *Belitung* Shipwreck Symposium: Intersections of History, Archaeology, and Capitalism," held on March 4, 2017.[78] This symposium was organized at New York University by the New York Centre for Global Asia and the Institute of Fine Arts, and supported by the Centre for the Humanities. Prior to the symposium, Marco Meniketti, chair of the Advisory Council on Underwater Archaeology (ACUA), an independent and international advisory body, had written to organizer David Ludden, professor of History at New York University, to express deep concern about the symposium:

> While we have no objections to a frank discussion of the relevant ethical issues surrounding the shipwreck's recovery, we object to exhibiting arti-

facts from commercially salvaged shipwreck sites and using the artifacts in scholarly presentations.[79]

Meniketti's letter noted that a number of ethical principles had been violated.[80] Meniketti's letter also referred to the sale of *Belitung* objects online as evidence that the salvage company's "intent was to provide a monetary reward for the excavation as opposed to protecting the site in the public trust."[81] ACUA vice chair Kimberly Faulk had made a similar argument in 2011 in her letter to the Smithsonian Institution about *Shipwrecked*, whereby "artifacts in excellent condition from the Belitung wreck can be found for sale on internet sites including eBay and WorthPoint."[82] Both Meniketti and Faulk were correct. There were, and occasionally still are, objects from the *Belitung* available for sale online. But the conclusions they have drawn are misguided.[83] There is no evidence to indicate that Seabed Explorations attempted to sell salvaged objects online. Instead, the objects for sale on online auction sites are likely among those to have been opportunistically looted from the site prior to, or in between, salvage seasons.

Discussions at the symposium centered on the historical implications of the wreck—its discovery, the broader Southeast Asian maritime context, and the connections between China, South Asia, and the Persian Gulf.[84] A prevailing theme was the need to reassert Southeast Asian agency within conversations about ninth-century maritime trade networks, and the opportunities provided by the *Belitung* wreck to do this. In the afternoon, a two-hour roundtable was dedicated to "The *Belitung* Controversy: Archaeology and Capitalism." Audience participation and questions were encouraged. The Asian Civilisations Museum's curator, Stephen Murphy—already in New York to oversee the exhibition installation—participated, as did John Guy, Asian curator at the Metropolitan Museum; Philippe de Montebello, former director of the Metropolitan Museum and now affiliated with New York University; and Roxani Margariti from Emory University. Asia Society staff did not participate in the symposium, though some were in the audience. Flecker, the archaeologist who had overseen the second salvage season, was not invited to participate. A UNESCO representative was invited, but declined. The absence of such participants—representing the two extremes in terms of how to manage and protect underwater cultural heritage in Southeast Asia—was a missed opportunity to advance discussion and knowledge about the implications of the *Belitung* salvage and display. Nevertheless, there was extensive discussion about the ethics of underwater cultural heritage, and a reiteration of a message that had been articulated by Cheryl Sobas at the "Marine Archaeology in Southeast Asia" symposium in Singapore some years earlier: that this was shared heritage.

The second symposium was organized by the Asia Society and the Tang Center for Early China at Columbia University.[85] It was preceded by a keynote lecture on April 21 by Regina Krahl (a renowned expert of Tang ceramics, and editor of the *Shipwrecked* catalog) at the Asia Society Museum, which focused on the stylistic connections between the ceramics and the precious metals of the *Belitung* cargo.[86] The symposium itself, held on April 22, 2017, at Columbia University, sought to place the *Belitung* shipwreck and cargo in its historical context.[87] The entire symposium was recorded and can be accessed online through the Tang Center for Early China's website.[88] Unlike the first symposium, which devoted time to discuss the circumstances by which the objects had been recovered, this second symposium did not address the salvage at all.

Ancient Objects, New Narratives

Most post-*Shipwrecked* exhibitions of the objects have failed to attract the same level of criticism they endured during the controversy, or indeed any at all. In some instances, as with *The Lost Dhow*, the exhibition appears to have simply slipped under the radar, despite being in Canada and therefore easier for the English-speaking critics to identify. In other cases, as with *Aventuriers des Mers*, the inclusion of a handful of *Belitung* objects in a broader exhibition appears to have allowed them to escape critical attention. The controversy and criticism have not disappeared, as *Secrets of the Sea* in New York demonstrated. But a space has been created whereby the objects have become more malleable. They are now part of other narratives, and used to advance different stories.

Although these stories may differ, they have in common a shared purpose: to advance national claims that use the past to legitimize the present. Just as Singapore made space for the *Belitung* objects within its Singapore Story, so too has China sought to frame them within a national narrative: the Belt and Road Initiative. This international project is both economic and strategic in ambition, connecting China with Europe, West Asia, Africa, and the Indian Ocean through land- and sea-based infrastructure investments.[89] As Chinese president Xi Jinping has indicated, the *Belitung* shipwreck is evidence that these modern initiatives have ancient roots.[90] As such, its display in China remains highly desirable, despite or perhaps because of that country's failed efforts to purchase the objects. In 2020, a selection of the objects went on display at the Shanghai Museum (*The Baoli Era: Treasures from the Tang Shipwreck Collection*, September 15, 2020–January 10, 2021), a deeply symbolic exhibition given that museum's active, and ultimately unsuccessful, negotiations with Seabed Explorations in 2004. The exhibition was planned to coincide with the thirtieth anniversary of diplomatic relations between

China and Singapore, again showing how the *Belitung* has been used to support and solidify national and bilateral narratives.

However, this was not the first display of *Belitung* objects in China. In September 2017, local media reported that the administration office of the Tongguan Imperial Kilns complex, located in Changsha, had purchased 162 objects from Tilman Walterfang's own collection for US$1.485 million. The objects, of which more than ninety were from Changsha, went on permanent display as part of the *Tongguan Kiln Porcelain Culture* exhibition on May 15, 2018.[91] Yet more *Belitung* objects, purchased from an unknown source, were displayed in the *China and the World: Shipwrecks and Exported Porcelain on the Maritime Silk Road* exhibition (May 8–August 7, 2018) at the China Maritime Museum in Pudong, Shanghai. The exhibition included objects from eleven shipwrecks, including the *Belitung*, and had previously been shown elsewhere in China.[92] These "other" objects, originating from Walterfang's collection and from an unknown source, have received little media or scholarly attention in English-language publications. But their appearance on the market is a sharp reminder that the assemblage sold to Singapore was never fully intact, and that there remain other objects, and other stories, from the *Belitung* still in circulation. China's embrace of the objects, through both museum loans and potentially less official channels, stems from the view that these objects, being made in China, are Chinese. In doing so, it overlooks the other, global elements of this story.

In particular, China's confidence stands in contrast to that of Indonesia. Of all the modern nations with a stake in telling the *Belitung*'s story, it was Indonesia that had the strongest claim. It was in Indonesian territorial waters that the wreck was found, and Indonesia had legal ownership of the wreck. There was no need to search for a grand narrative into which these objects could fit; such a narrative already existed in this shipwreck near Sumatra that dated to the Sriwijaya period. But with the sale of the objects, Indonesia lost the opportunity to tell its story as Southeast Asia's true maritime center. Despite this loss, Indonesia still has in its possession the seven thousand objects withheld from Tilman Walterfang when the *Intan/Belitung* deal collapsed in 2004. In March 2017, the Ministry of Marine Affairs and Fisheries opened a Marine Heritage Gallery at its offices in Jakarta.[93] The gallery is designed to raise awareness, among both the public as well as government officials, of the cultural and historical value of underwater objects. It features hundreds of shipwreck artifacts, including objects from the *Belitung* as well as other wrecks including the *Cirebon* and the *Buaya*.[94] Notwithstanding the mismanagement of underwater cultural heritage under previous administrations, Indonesia is increasingly engaged in telling the stories embodied in this heritage. Indonesia's interest in its maritime histories is part of a growing maritime nationalism under President Joko Widodo, who has articulated his vision of Indonesia as a global maritime axis (*poros maritim dunia*). More recently, Director-General of Culture Dr. Hilmar Farid has embarked on a journey to reconstruct and revitalize the Spice Routes concept, including through proposed a UNESCO World Heritage listing. The concept is a vital counterbalance to the discursive supremacy of China's Silk Road narrative, and a strong indicator of Indonesia's growing assertiveness in claiming and telling the region's maritime histories. Like Singapore and China, Indonesia has shown its ability to adapt the story of the *Belitung* and the objects it carried for its own nationalistic purposes.

The Middle East has been less involved in this conversation than expected. Oman has thus far been unable to capitalize on the success of the *Jewel of Muscat* project by hosting a traveling exhibition, despite its interest in doing so. Notwithstanding the vessel's possible connections to the Middle East and the fact that many of the objects appeared destined for the Persian and Arabian market, this is one element of the story that remains underdeveloped.

Conclusion

Forced to reconceptualize its vision for the objects in its care, Singapore's strategy has been notable for both its patience and its agility. This has allowed the objects to slowly settle into an international traveling routine, albeit of a different sort than that initially anticipated. This strategy has effectively ensured the longevity of the objects' afterlives by providing distance from the controversy, thereby enabling them to become part of a museological context.

In the process, it has become clear that the *Belitung* objects have multiple entry points for engagement. They speak to Chinese manufacturing, to Arabian-style shipbuilding, to Southeast Asian maritime histories, and to global connections facilitated by the ocean. These transnational elements mean that the objects can be used to support diverse narratives, in different ways and simultaneously. But the ship's journey has also been reimagined in modern, and political, terms, to support narratives about infrastructure, security, and the nation. Their profile is such that they have been used to support national narratives even when no direct connection is evident. In Korea, for example, the objects have been used to demonstrate the "shared cultural connections between Singapore and Korea."[95] *Secret of the Sea: The Tang Shipwreck* (December 11, 2018–March 17, 2019) was initiated by the Republic of Korea's National Research Institute of Maritime Cultural Heritage. It brought together "two of the most important shipwrecks to have been discovered in Asian waters," namely the *Belitung* shipwreck and the *Sinan* shipwreck.[96] With the National Research Institute of Maritime Cultural Heritage gaining a reputation for its significant financial investment in developing maritime archaeology programs and capacity, the exhibition of this increasingly high-profile collection in Korea was as much about credentialing as it was about shipwrecks in Asian waters.

As with so many shipwrecks, the *Belitung* traversed multiple seascapes when it sailed, in the process implicating diverse communities of makers, traders, and consumers. It continues to do so through the afterlives of its objects, bringing in communities and nations who all seek to claim a part of this story for themselves. The implications for these objects, and for other commercially salvaged underwater cultural heritage, are profound. In the next and final chapter, I consider these implications and offer some suggestions about how they can be used as the basis for a reappraisal of the roles and responsibilities of museums in displaying underwater cultural heritage.[97]

Conclusion

This book tells the story of an ancient shipwreck. It begins with raw materials and human ingenuity, which came together in a vessel capable of sailing beyond the horizon. It considers the skills required to navigate by the stars in harmony with the rhythm of the winds and currents, and the support systems, on board and on shore, that made such a journey possible. The thousands of objects it transported are an essential part of this story, as are the networks of craftspeople, laborers, and merchants who brought these objects into being. Dwelling on the *Belitung*'s first life reminds us that this shipwreck was once part of a living, connected world. The vessel then became part of another world altogether, both protected and destroyed by the warm waters in which its wreckage lay. New connections were established with marine animals and, in time, with local communities. Time spent underwater transformed it from a seafaring vessel to a reef where jars grew, confounding fishers whose search for sea cucumbers instead yielded ancient ceramics.

Just as the wrecking was a turning point, so too was its discovery and recovery. At this point, its fate was determined by the invisible lines that had come to crisscross the ocean floor, delineating maritime zones and vesting ownership in Indonesia, in whose territorial waters this shipwreck lay. The process by which the objects were salvaged delegitimized them in the eyes of the international standard setters. But accusations that this was looting were quite simply wrong. As much as the international community may have disagreed with Indonesian legislation—and as flawed as that legislation was—it could not deny that, as a sovereign nation, Indonesia was within its rights to determine the management of heritage in its territorial waters. Singapore, too, acted legally when it purchased the objects, which it did not through a private entity, as some critics claimed, but through a statutory body of the Singaporean government.

In short, the *Belitung*'s salvage was not a heritage crime, and these objects were not looted. These orphaned objects were proof, rather, of the inadequacies of national ownership models for the management of trans- and pre-national heritage, and of an international failure to develop mechanisms that accounted for the complexities of heritage located in a context as mobile and fluid as the ocean. These subtleties were lost in the controversy that followed, which was characterized by willfully dismissive and even ignorant attitudes toward both Indonesia and Singapore. This was authorized heritage rendered visible, as powerful institutional actors used the considerable tools at their disposal to dictate how a formerly colonized nation should manage the heritage in its waters.

Heritage Contested

It is difficult to conjure a shipwreck that better exemplifies the concept of contested heritage than the *Belitung*. The circumstances of its recovery were undoubtedly the driving factor behind the controversies that have accompanied the wreck. But there is also the fact that so many actors, from states and institutions to communities and individuals, had a stake in the narrative. These actors straddled local, national, and international arenas, colliding as they sought to exercise control over the story and justify why their perspective should prevail. In mapping these contested claims, it is worth considering which voices are being amplified, and which are being silenced.

Many of these claims were compelling. The ship's identity could be traced to western Indian Ocean boatbuilding traditions, explaining Qatar's early interest in purchasing the salvaged objects to fill its museums. The presence of turquoise-glazed earthenware and blue glass evoked a connection with Persia and the Arab world. But whether it was Middle Eastern (or, more specifically, Arabian) or built somewhere else entirely by shipwrights skilled in sewn-plank techniques, Oman's intervention through the *Jewel of Muscat* project created a situation in which it became easy to simply conflate the two vessels and attribute Omani origin to the *Belitung*. As this suggests, determining the origin of the vessel was a product of contemporary influences, rather than ancient, and testament to the extent to which this wreck has been constructed in the present. Other claims can also legitimately be made. The *Belitung*'s cargo told a distinctly Chinese story—though, even then, Middle Eastern influences were evident. The ceramics it carried were made in China, but they were produced for a non-Chinese market. Regardless, the cargo was extremely desirable from the perspective of China's cultural institutions. The fact that the Shanghai Museum almost succeeded in purchasing these objects makes bittersweet the willingness of Singapore, after years of negotiations, to loan objects from the collection as part of a temporary exhibition.

The most cogent claim of all belonged to Indonesia, due to the location of the shipwreck in its territorial waters and its discovery by Indonesian fishing communities. It is tempting to dismiss Indonesia's role in this story as nothing more than a consequence of fate; the ship just happened to be wrecked in these waters as it transited between the Indian Ocean and China. But this framing, which renders Indonesia the passive host of foreign voyages, is too simple. Unexplained anomalies relating to the origin of its timbers, cordage, wadding, and anchor suggest a closer Southeast Asian connection than previously countenanced. Certain elements—the use of local navigators, the wreck's location at the center of the Sriwijayan sphere of influence, and the likelihood that some of its cargo was en route to Java—confirm the involvement of local actors. The ship and its cargo may not have been Indonesian, but Indonesia was and is nevertheless an important part of this story. By selling the rights to the shipwreck, Indonesia relinquished the opportunity to tell the Belitung's tale within the context of Southeast Asia's central role in global maritime histories. Since then, however, its government has demonstrated a growing awareness of the geopolitical value of heritage within an international context. The story of the Belitung could have been, and perhaps may still be, mobilized to support national narratives—in this case, the reemergence of Indonesia as a global maritime nexus.

Although Singapore does not feature as part of the Belitung's origin story, the city-state is central to the wreck's afterlives, for it is here that the majority of the objects have found their forever home. It took some time for Singapore to identify a narrative that these objects could speak to, eventually settling on an idea of a historic maritime silk route that was not so much weighted toward China as centered on Singapore. This decision reflected a subtle shift in how Singapore has sought to conceptualize itself in the decades following independence in 1965. The Singapore Story—the nation's government-backed foundation narrative—has typically traced its origin to the idea of Singapore as a "sleepy fishing village" that has undergone rapid transformation to become one of the region's leading economies.[1] Recently, however, Singapore has thrown its efforts into extending the claims it makes to the past, teasing out a pre-independence, indeed precolonial history.[2] This broader conceptualization of its historic roots has made it possible for Singapore to claim a stronger position within China's Belt and Road Initiative, its Silk Road of the Sea narrative providing a way for Singapore to claim "centre stage" through telling stories such as the Belitung's.[3] The Belitung must be understood within the context of these ambitions.

In each of these examples, certain "slices" of the past have been fashioned into what scholar Tim Winter describes as a "geocultural resource," in which culture and history, through heritage, are used to not only articulate but also accumulate power.[4] This modus operandi is exemplified by China's nationalization of ancient "narratives of connectivity" through the Belt and Road Initiative.[5] Heritage is less a luxury than an essential tool within a broader geocultural strategy that seeks to redefine the global political, social, and economic landscape by reimagining the past.

To the extent that the *Belitung* shipwreck has been constructed and appropriated by modern nation-states, it has also been implicated within an institutional context. This vessel is both one of the most significant shipwreck discoveries and one of the most controversial underwater exhibitions of recent times. For UNESCO and the Smithsonian Institution, this shipwreck exemplified approaches to the management and display of underwater cultural heritage that, if not illegal, are certainly unethical. The willingness of Singaporean institutions to work with these objects represents an entirely different form of institutional engagement, one that has gained traction around the world through a program of temporary traveling exhibitions. The dissonance between these two very different institutional approaches was at first distinctly neocolonial in tone, not only in the Smithsonian Institution's last-minute decision to cancel the exhibition but also in its announcement, made without consulting Indonesia, that the wreck site would be re-excavated. However, Singapore's willingness for the objects to travel and be told in different ways has subverted dominant institutional models by demonstrating what is possible in a museological context with orphaned objects.

It is through these archaeological and museological contexts that the *Belitung* continues to cause ripples more than a thousand years since it was wrecked. Since being pulled from the ocean, its objects have accumulated meanings and significance beyond their original purpose. In the process, they have been infused with their own power, shaping the very institutions and debates that have shaped them.[6] They have been used performatively to celebrate museum openings and diplomatic anniversaries, and to advance national and institutional narratives. In their permanent installation at a public museum, coral-encrusted objects are juxtaposed with those that appear as-new, reminding audiences of the journey these objects have taken from maker to merchant to museum. Increasingly, they have been displayed in a way that addresses issues relating to the ownership, appropriation, and commodification of underwater cultural heritage. They have also found resonance with other sites and stories, including Thailand's *Phanom Surin* shipwreck and Oman's *Jewel of Muscat*, sparking new knowledge about the Indian Ocean world as well as further questions about Southeast Asia's role in this maritime space. As such, the *Belitung* has become more, not less, entangled in the world.

Fragile Frameworks

In retelling the *Belitung*'s story, I have given equal billing not only to the original vessel and the shipwreck it became, but also to its post-discovery afterlives. Doing so has allowed me to identify the extent of the errors that were made, particularly during its first salvage season. This account contextualizes the actions of the salvage crew within Indonesia's regulatory framework, which, although deeply problematic, was also sufficiently flexible that neither the *Belitung* nor the *Intan* cargoes were split up. It also provides clarity around some of the most persistent rumors surrounding the thousands of objects that came to be buried in sand, the presence of ceramic sherds around the wreck site itself, the reasons why the hull and anchor were not recovered, and the whereabouts of some seven thousand missing objects.

More urgently, telling the full story of the *Belitung*, with all its contradictions and complexities, reveals the fragility of current approaches to managing the premodern past in an underwater context. Around the world, underwater cultural heritage is being damaged and destroyed at an unprecedented rate. Although the story of this commercially salvaged shipwreck poses a threat to established approaches, it also presents new ways of thinking about what protection and preservation mean in an underwater context. In doing so, it lays bare the paradox with which this book began—that, despite being managed contrary to the international standards on underwater cultural heritage embodied by the 2001 UNESCO Convention, the *Belitung* assemblage is largely intact, publicly accessible, and being used as both an educational and scholarly resource.

What allowance, if any, do existing frameworks make for such an outcome? Can orphaned objects be accommodated in circumstances where the benefits of recovering the objects outweigh the costs? And, if not, what is the cost of such a rigid adherence to ethical principles? The mere act of asking these questions runs the risk of one being labeled an apologist. But it is overly simplistic to conflate orphaned objects with those recovered by treasure hunters. Doing so overlooks the broad range of management approaches that lie on the spectrum between UNESCO compliance and treasure hunting. These considerations are particularly relevant in Indonesia, where historic shipwrecks were long valued as commodities rather than as heritage, and actively managed as such. Although the 2010 moratorium on commercial salvage brought Indonesia closer to international standards, there are many who believe that this ban has come at the expense of the very heritage it seeks to preserve and protect.

Although the commercial salvage had its limitations, it gave the *Belitung* objects another life. Were the *Belitung* discovered today, a commercial salvage permit would not be issued.[7] Nor would the wreck be preserved *in situ*, as the fate of its hull and anchor demonstrates. Instead, the objects that are now on permanent display in Singapore's Asian Civilisations Museum would have been looted and dispersed, to the detriment of the viewing public and international scholarship.

This reality has grave implications for other wrecks in Indonesia, particularly at a time when knowledge of the archipelago's maritime histories is overshadowed by the powerful political narratives evoked by the Belt and Road Initiative. Ironically, this may well be one of the *Belitung*'s lasting legacies: the fostering of an understanding of the significance of shipwrecks beyond their economic value, and the subsequent elevation of underwater cultural heritage to a level of critical scholarly attention usually reserved for its terrestrial counterparts.

Despite efforts by UNESCO to stimulate regional interest in its underwater cultural heritage convention, formal compliance with the international standards is, in the short term at least, neither desirable nor achievable for many states. This includes Indonesia, which continues to refuse to sign the Convention, citing concerns about how sovereignty is exercised, the difficulties of monitoring and enforcing protection across its vast expanse of sea territory, and the lack of input on the Convention from formerly colonized countries. The looming presence of China in Southeast Asia, and the tension between the heritage diplomacy of that nation's Belt and Road Initiative and the aggression of its expansionist policies in the South China Sea, also gives cause for pause. In the absence of widespread ratification of the Convention, it is even more important to broaden the notion of what constitutes an ethical approach to underwater cultural heritage beyond (and even alongside) international compliance. This is where museums can make a critical contribution. But are they willing, or even able, to take on this role?

Museums are uniquely placed to increase awareness of, and access to, threatened underwater cultural heritage. Yet, although they have undergone significant transformation in recent decades, the sector is not yet ready to take on the role of advocating for a new approach to protection and preservation in an underwater context. In 2019, a renewed commitment was made by maritime museums to an ethical code through the Åland Accord, named after the archipelago in the Baltic Sea where the agreement was signed. The accord governs standards expected of maritime museums "in caring for and bringing to life" the maritime past.[8] Signatories commit to acting as repositories for objects recovered "in a legal, professional and ethical manner," and expressly rule out the acquisition or display of maritime cultural material recovered illegally, unprofessionally, or unethically.[9] One clause warrants further scrutiny:

> We will only act to preserve material, including associated archival documentation, after recovery has occurred in an illegal, unprofessional or unethical manner, if the material is culturally significant and at serious risk of destruction, damage or irretrievable dispersal.[10]

This clause echoes the ICOM Code of Ethics for Museums, which makes allowances for the collection of unprovenanced objects if they make an "inherently outstanding contribution to knowledge."[11] Here, then, is acknowledgement that ethical codes must incorporate a degree of flexibility. Some argue this is not enough; that, even with this flexibility, ethical codes can constrain rather than enable.[12] If we accept this criticism, then it becomes clear that a new framework is needed to transform museum ethics from a professional practice that limits dialogue to a social practice that facilitates critical reflection and discussion. This approach incorporates what Marstine and others describe as three distinct, overlapping spheres, consisting of not only ethical codes but also case studies and values and principles.[13]

This model extends the postcolonial critique of museums that has been gathering momentum in recent decades.[14] Such critiques have resulted in an increasingly inclusive and diverse approach to representation in museums, both in the sense of what is displayed (and how) as well as whose stories are being told. Support for restitution, reparation, and decolonization continues to mount, as evidenced by institutional efforts to return cultural items stolen in the name of empire and the groundswell of support for the toppling of racist statues. These developments testify to the complexity of the world museums inhabit, and the pressures they face to serve an ever-widening range of stakeholders, often without a commensurate increase in financial or human resources. Within this context, it is all too easy to view underwater cultural heritage as irrelevant to the postcolonial project, serving merely to distract with "the lure of the deep, the thrill of discovery, and the commodification of objects."[15] What can old ceramics and waterlogged timbers possibly tell us about justice, or power, or inclusion?

The answer lies in how museums use this heritage, and whether the afterlives of the objects displayed—how they were recovered, how they came to be in the museum—are understood to be part of the story told. As this book has shown, there are multiple turning points and influences on the lives of these objects to consider. Doing so moves the *Belitung*'s story beyond one of global connection and exchange, as important as that story is, into a much bigger debate about who owns the past. It is here that underwater cultural heritage confronts justice, power, and inclusion—in the way certain frameworks determine what is ethical and what is not, and in how these frameworks are deployed. As Janet Marstine observes, "the technical, legalistic approach to museum ethics has functioned to oversimplify issues and scope and deaden the vitality of the discourse."[16] This is not to say that this approach does not have merit. But in its rigid understanding of what constitutes protection and preservation of underwater cultural heritage, it runs the risk of overlooking or even suppressing the stories that arise through alternate heritage management models, such as that in place in Indonesia when the *Belitung* was salvaged.

Reappraising the role of museums in protecting and preserving underwater cultural heritage is not an add-on to the postcolonial project; it is part of this work. Museums are increasingly being called on to embrace the dark heritage and difficult stories in their collections, and to acknowledge the role privilege, power, and colonialism have played in allowing them to acquire these objects in the first place. In museums, the echoes of these legacies reverberate not only in objects and collections but also in structures and systems. Orphaned underwater objects are the ideal starting point for examining these legacies, because they force museums to question their very reason for being. Embracing these objects does not condone looting and treasure hunting; in fact, it creates an opportunity for museums and their communities to conceptualize underwater cultural heritage beyond treasure and tragedy, and to explore not only its historic value but also the insights it offers into the sociocultural and geopolitical uses of heritage.

This is a new form of museum ethics, in which social responsibility, radical transparency, and shared guardianship of heritage emerge as factors that warrant consideration and perhaps even priority.[17] Museums allow people to place the object, and their own response to it, "within a framework of cognitive understanding."[18] In doing so, they play a vital role in establishing the biography of an object: how it was made, what the turning points in its life were, and how its legacy will be told.[19] This involves consideration not only of where the object came from, but how it came to be in the museum and how it changes, and is changed, within the museum context. Precisely because of their fundamental responsibilities to the objects in their care, museums are capable of disrupting the authorized heritage discourse. Critically, however, objects are the means by which these new and complex ethical issues can be explored, not the end in themselves.

A New Approach

This book has rendered visible the institutions, structures, and individuals that have constructed meaning, value, and knowledge about the *Belitung*. In doing so, its intention has been to demonstrate the benefits of extending a critical approach to underwater cultural heritage. This approach is questioning, contextual, interdisciplinary, and reflective. It understands heritage as something constantly created and recreated, "a set of attitudes to, and relationships with, the past."[20] In seeking to go beyond the authorized heritage discourse that privileges "old, grand, prestigious, expert approved sites . . . that sustain Western narratives of nation, class and science," it embraces a more democratic, diverse, and nuanced way of understanding how we use the past, and its material remains, in the present to shape the future.[21] In doing so, it draws attention to the power relations that heritage is invoked to sustain, recognizing that, while notions of shared heritage can be inclusive, they can also be deployed to exclude local stakeholders from decision-making processes.

In an increasingly divided and polarized world, it is more important than ever to interrogate why heritage matters. Heritage is not about dusty objects hidden in museums, or corroded relics at the bottom of the sea. It is about how the echoes of the past continue to resonate today, and how the tension between national and international interests plays out at the local level. As such, it serves as a flashpoint for the biggest issues of our times, bearing upon and extending outward from heritage across multiple scales and geographies.[22] It is where these debates—about identity, inequality, privilege, opportunity, sustainability, climate change, modernity, colonialism, the nation-state—come together, and where the ideas and legacies of the past intersect with the present to create both friction and opportunities. The ocean is the biggest museum in the world, and it offers new ways of thinking about the past and for the future. In this regard, the *Belitung* is only the beginning.

Appendix
Exhibition list

Date	Exhibition title	Exhibition type	Venue	City/Country
15 June–31 July 2005	Tang Treasures from the Sea	Temporary	Asian Civilisations Museum	Singapore
2007–present	Tang Treasures Suite	Permanent	Goodwood Hotel	Singapore
14 November 2009–25 July 2010	Southeast Asian Ceramics: New Light on Old Pottery	Temporary; mixed	National University of Singapore Museum	Singapore
19 February–2 October 2011 (original end date 31 July)	Shipwrecked: Tang Treasures and Monsoon Winds	Temporary	ArtScience Museum	Singapore
12 January–24 June 2012	The Tang Shipwreck: Gold and Ceramics from Ninth-Century China	Temporary	Asian Civilisations Museum	Singapore
14 November 2015–present	The Tang Shipwreck Collection	Permanent	Asian Civilisations Museum	Singapore
13 December 2014–26 April 2015	The Lost Dhow: A Discovery from the Maritime Silk Route	Temporary	Aga Khan Museum	Toronto, Canada
15 November 2016–26 February 2017	Aventuriers des Mers: De Sindbad à Marco Polo	Temporary; mixed	l'Institut du Monde Arabe	Paris, France
7 March–4 June 2017	Secrets of the Sea: A Tang Shipwreck and Early Trade in Asia	Temporary	Asia Society Museum	New York, USA

Date	Exhibition	Type	Institution	Location
13 March 2017–present	*Marine Heritage Gallery Collection*	Permanent; mixed	Marine Heritage Gallery	Jakarta, Indonesia
7 June–9 October 2017	*Aventuriers des Mers: De Sindbad à Marco Polo*	Temporary; mixed	Musée des Civilisations de l'Europe et de la Méditerranée	Marseille, France
8 May–7 August 2018	*China and the World: Shipwrecks and Exported Porcelain on the Maritime Silk Road*	Temporary	China Maritime Museum	Shanghai, China
15 May 2018–present	*Tongguan Kiln Porcelain Culture*	Permanent	Tongguan Imperial Kilns Museum	Changsha, China
11 December 2018–17 March 2019	*Secret of the Sea: The Tang Shipwreck*	Temporary	National Research Institute of Maritime Cultural Heritage	Republic of Korea
7 September 2019–28 June 2020	*Sunken Treasures: Secrets of the Maritime Silk Road*	Temporary; mixed	Princessehof National Museum of Ceramics	Leeuwarden, The Netherlands
15 September 2020–10 January 2021	*The Baoli Era: Treasures from the Tang Shipwreck Collection*	Temporary	Shanghai Museum	Shanghai, China

Notes

Introduction

1. Article 2.5 of the 2001 UNESCO Convention states "The preservation in situ of underwater cultural heritage shall be considered as the first option before allowing or engaging in any activities directed at this heritage." This suggests material can be recovered, especially if it is under threat. The Annex of the 2001 UNESCO Convention contains rules for assisting with this work, such as project design.

2. "Underwater cultural heritage" is not just shipwrecks, and in fact the word *shipwreck* does not appear once in the text of the 2001 UNESCO Convention. Article 1(a) defines underwater cultural heritage as "all traces of human existence having a cultural, historical or archaeological character which have been partially or totally under water, periodically or continuously, for at least 100 years, such as: (i) sites, structures, buildings, artefacts and human remains, together with their archaeological and natural context; (ii) vessels, aircraft, other vehicles or any part thereof, their cargo or other contents, together with their archaeological and natural context; and (iii) objects of prehistoric character."

3. Laurajane Smith, *Uses of Heritage* (London: Routledge, 2006).

4. Laurajane Smith, "A Pilgrimage of Masculinity: The Stockman's Hall of Fame and Outback Heritage Centre," *Australian Historical Studies* 43, no. 3 (2012): 474.

5. Smith, *Uses of Heritage.*

6. Cornelius Holtorf, "Averting Loss Aversion in Cultural Heritage," *International Journal of Heritage Studies* 21, no. 4 (2015): 406.

7. Rodney Harrison, *Heritage: Critical Approaches* (London and New York: Routledge, 2013), 128.

8. Marieke Bloembergen and Martijn Eickhoff, *The Politics of Heritage in Indonesia: A Cultural History*, ed. Sunil Amrith, Tim Harper, and Engseng Ho (Cambridge: Cambridge University Press, 2020).

9. Marieke Bloembergen and Martijn Eickhoff, "Decolonizing Borobudur: Moral Engagements and the Fear of Loss. The Netherlands, Japan and (Post)Colonial Heritage Politics in Indonesia," in *Sites, Bodies and Stories: Imagining Indonesian History*, ed. Susan Legêne, Bambang Purwanto, and Henk Schulte Nordholt (Singapore: NUS Press, 2015).

10. Susan Legêne, Bambang Purwanto, and Henk Schulte Nordholt, eds., *Sites, Bodies and Stories: Imagining Indonesian History* (Singapore: NUS Press, 2015), 8.

11. Marieke Bloembergen and Martijn Eickhoff, "Critical Heritage Studies and the Importance of Studying Histories of Heritage Formation," *International Institute for Asian Studies* 70 (Spring 2015).

12. Tim Winter, "Clarifying the Critical in Critical Heritage Studies," *International Journal of Heritage Studies* 19, no. 6 (2013).

13. Tim Winter, "Geocultural Power: China's Belt and Road Initiative," *Geopolitics* (2020), doi: 10.1080/14650045.2020.1718656.

14. Edward Rodley, "The Ethics of Exhibiting Salvaged Shipwrecks," *Curator* 55, no. 4 (2012): 383.

15. *Mary Rose Museum.* Last updated 2021. Accessed July 8, 2021. https://maryrose.org/.

16. Bruce D. Doar, "China Maritime Silk Road Museum." *China Heritage Quarterly.* Last updated 2005. Accessed July 8, 2021. http://www.chinaheritagequarterly.org/articles.php ?searchterm=001_maritimesilk.inc&issue=001.

17. James Clifford, *Routes: Travel and Translation in the Late Twentieth Century* (Cambridge, MA: Harvard University Press, 1997); Kylie Message, "Contentious Politics and Museums as Contact Zones," in *Museum Theory*, ed. Andrea Witcomb and Kylie Message (Hoboken, NJ: John Wiley & Sons, 2020).

18. China is the obvious exception.

19. Michael Flecker, *Legislation on Underwater Cultural Heritage in Southeast Asia: Evolution and Outcomes*, Trends in Southeast Asia (Singapore: ISEAS-Yusof Ishak Institute, 2017).

20. The International Council of Museums defines education as core to the definition of museums. However, its Code of Ethics precludes the display of "material of questionable origin." Museums will therefore be increasingly constrained in their ability to tell the stories of the deep (*educating*) using objects with established provenance (*being ethical*).

21. Rodley, "Exhibiting Salvaged Shipwrecks," 384.

22. C. M. Counts, "Spectacular Design in Museum Exhibitions," *Curator* 52, no. 3 (2009): 282.

23. Richard Sandell, *Museums, Prejudice and the Reframing of Difference* (London and New York: Routledge, 2007).

24. Pierre Balloffet, François H. Courvoisier, and Joëlle Lagier, "From Museum to Amusement Park: The Opportunities and Risks of Edutainment," *International Journal of Arts Management* 16, no. 2 (2014): 4.

25. Tim Winter, "Heritage and the Politics of Cooperation," in *The Oxford Handbook of Public Heritage Theory and Practice*, ed. Angela Labrador and Neil Silberman (Oxford: Oxford University Press, 2018).

26. Rodley, "Exhibiting Salvaged Shipwrecks," 383.

27. Elaine Heumann Gurian, *Civilizing the Museum: The Collected Writings of Elaine Heumann Gurian* (London and New York: Routledge, 2006); Andrea Witcomb, "Book Review: Civilizing the Museum: the Collected Writings of Elaine Heumann Gurian," *reCollections* 1, no. 2 (2006).

28. Charles Saumarez-Smith, "Museums, Artefacts, and Meanings," in *The New Museology*, ed. Peter Vergo (London: Reaktion Books, 1989).

29. Felwine Sarr and Bénédicte Savoy, *The Restitution of African Cultural Heritage: Toward a New Relational Ethics* (Paris, 2018).

30. Paul Forsythe Johnston, "Treasure Salvage, Archaeological Ethics and Maritime Museums," *International Journal of Nautical Archaeology* 22, no. 1 (1993); Kieran Hosty, "A Matter of Ethics: Shipwrecks, Salvage, Archaeology and Museums," *Bulletin of the Australasian Institute for Maritime Archaeology* 19, no. 1 (1995).

31. As Witcomb explains, *Titanic: The Artifact Exhibition* was an "emotional rollercoaster" for audiences and, with its replica blankets and flatware, a great shopping experience. But there

was "no open discussion on the desirability of salvaging these objects in the first place. We are encouraged to wonder at the capability and achievement of the technology, but not to question the propriety of using it." Andrea Witcomb, "Exhibition Review: *Titanic: The Artefact Exhibition*," *reCollections* 5, no. 2 (2010).

32. Jeremy Green, "Book Review: Shipwreck [*sic*]: Tang Treasures and Monsoon Winds," *International Journal of Nautical Archaeology* 40, no. 2 (2011): 452.

33. These include the International Council of Museums (ICOM), the International Congress of Maritime Museums (ICMM), the International Council on Monuments and Sites (ICOMOS), the Advisory Council on Underwater Archaeology (ACUA), the Society for Historical Archaeology (SHA), and the Council of American Maritime Museums (CAMM).

34. UNESCO, *Convention on the Protection of the Underwater Cultural Heritage* (Paris: United Nations Educational, Scientific and Cultural Organization, 2001).

35. ICOM, *Code of Ethics for Museums*, Article 3.4. (Paris: International Council of Museums, 2004). Museums have undergone radical transformations in recent decades. In 2019 ICOM proposed a new definition of museums that focuses on inclusiveness, diversity, and a willingness to acknowledge and address the conflicts and challenges of the present.

36. Harrison, *Critical Approaches*.

37. Deborah Cherry, "The Afterlives of Monuments," *South Asian Studies* 29, no. 1 (2013): 1.

38. Igor Kopytoff, "The Cultural Biography of Things: Commoditization as Process," in *The Social Life of Things: Commodities in Cultural Perspective*, ed. A. Appadurai (Cambridge: Cambridge University Press, 1986); Neil G. W. Curtis, "Universal Museums, Museum Objects and Repatriation: The Tangled Stories of Things," *Museum Management and Curatorship* 21, no. 2 (2006).

39. Christopher Gosden and Yvonne Marshall, "The Cultural Biography of Objects," *World Archaeology* 31, no. 2 (1999).

40. Ibid., 169.

41. Bloembergen and Eickhoff have described these experiences as boundary-crossing. The objects are entangled with the heritage politics of the state, yet they also enable us to think "beyond the boundaries of empire and national states, without ignoring these boundaries, and to study the dynamics of heritage formation from multiple perspectives." Marieke Bloembergen and Martijn Eickhoff, "Exchange and the Protection of Java's Antiquities: A Transnational Approach to the Problem of Heritage in Colonial Java," *The Journal of Asian Studies* 72, no. 4 (2013): 894. See also Bloembergen and Eickhoff, *The Politics of Heritage in Indonesia: A Cultural History*.

42. Patrick Coleman, "UNESCO and the Belitung Shipwreck: The Need for a Permissive Definition of 'Commercial Exploitation'," *The George Washington International Law Review* 45, no. 4 (2013): 854.

43. Noel Hidalgo Tan, "Whose Treasure Is it Anyway?" *The Southeast Asian Archaeology Newsblog*. Last updated September 11, 2007. Accessed July 8, 2021. http://www.southeastasianarchaeology.com/2007/09/11/whose-treasure-is-it-anyway/.

44. Glenn Lowry, "Keynote," in *Making a Museum in the 21st Century*, ed. Melissa Chiu (New York: Asia Society, 2014).

45. Sandell, *Museums, Prejudice and the Reframing of Difference*; Kylie Message, *The Disobedient Museum: Writing at the Edge* (Oxford; New York: Routledge, 2018).

46. Akshita Nanda, "Salvaging a Wrecked Opportunity," *The Straits Times*, December 28, 2011, 2.

47. Rachel Leow, "Curating the Oceans: The Future of Singapore's Past." *A Historian's Craft.* Last updated July 14, 2009. Accessed July 8, 2021. https://idlethink.wordpress.com/2009/07/14 /curating-the-oceans-the-future-of-singapores-past/.

Chapter 1. Created

1. Tim Winter, *Geocultural Power: China's Quest to Revive the Silk Roads for the Twenty-First Century* (Chicago: University of Chicago Press, 2019).

2. George Bass and Peter Throckmorton, *Cape Gelidonya: A Bronze Age Shipwreck*, Transactions of the American Philosophical Society (Philadelphia: American Philosophical Society, 1967), 165.

3. Matthew Harpster, "Shipwreck Identity, Methodology, and Nautical Archaeology," *Journal of Archaeological Method and Theory* 20, no. 4 (2013).

4. Michael Flecker, "The Origin of the Tang Shipwreck: A Look at Its Archaeology and History," in *The Tang Shipwreck: Art and Exchange in the 9th Century*, ed. Alan Chong and Stephen Murphy (Singapore: Asian Civilisations Museum, 2017), 23.

5. Tom Vosmer et al., "The 'Jewel of Muscat' Project: Reconstructing an Early Ninth-Century CE Shipwreck," *Proceedings of the Seminar for Arabian Studies* 41 (2011); Michael Flecker, "A 9th-Century Arab or Indian Shipwreck in Indonesian Waters," *International Journal of Nautical Archaeology* 29, no. 2 (2000).

6. Vosmer et al., "Reconstructing an Early Ninth-Century Shipwreck."

7. Michael Flecker, "A Ninth-Century AD Arab or Indian Shipwreck in Indonesia: First Evidence for Direct Trade with China," *World Archaeology* 32, no. 3 (2001): 345.

8. Ian Kenneth McCann, "The Binh Chau Anchors: A 7th–8th CE Composite Conundrum" (Master's thesis, University of New England, 2019); Stephen Haw, "The Genus Afzelia and the Belitung Ship," *Journal of the Royal Asiatic Society* 29, no. 3 (2019).

9. Flecker, "A 9th-Century Arab or Indian Shipwreck."

10. Teak is a "magnificent" timber for shipbuilding, due to its durability, strength, weight, workability, and resistance to the voracious timber-eating teredo worm. Flecker, "Origin of the Tang Shipwreck," 36.

11. Michael Flecker, "A 9th-Century Arab or Indian Shipwreck in Indonesian Waters: Addendum," *International Journal of Nautical Archaeology* 37, no. 2 (2008).

12. For other limitations of timber analysis, see ibid., 385.

13. Ibid.

14. See Flecker, "A 9th-Century Arab or Indian Shipwreck"; Flecker, "Addendum."

15. According to this analysis, *Afzelia africana* had been used for the stempost, frames, hull planks, anchor shank, and dunnage, and the *Afzelia bipindensis* for the keelson, a key structural element. Another, probably *Juniper procera* (African juniper), had been used for the ceiling planks. The only timber sample of Indian origin was *Tectona grandis* (teak), used for the through beams. Flecker, "Addendum."

16. The prevalence of African timbers has led some scholars to speculate that the *Belitung* was in fact an African ship, though this theory has not been widely accepted. See Marco Viganò, "The Lost Wood: African Seamasters across the Indian Ocean" (paper presented at *Anno Domini 1000, Finale Ligure, Italy, August 31–September 1, 2013*).

17. Flecker, "Origin of the Tang Shipwreck," 36.

18. Haw, "The Genus Afzelia and the Belitung Ship."

19. Structural timbers included *Tectona grandis* but also *Afzelia bipindensis*, which, while native to Africa, is found farther from the Middle East than is *Afzelia Africana*. Nonstructural elements used lesser-quality timbers such as *Afzelia africana* and *Juniperus* spp. Flecker, "Addendum"; Vosmer et al., "Reconstructing an Early Ninth-Century Shipwreck."

20. Charlotte Minh Hà Pham, "Asian Shipbuilding Technology," in *Training Manual for the UNESCO Foundation Course on the Protection and Management of Underwater Cultural Heritage in Asia and the Pacific* (Bangkok: UNESCO Bangkok, 2012).

21. Flecker, "Addendum," 386.

22. Flecker, "A 9th-Century Arab or Indian Shipwreck," 215.

23. Haw, "The Genus Afzelia and the Belitung Ship," 514, 518.

24. Vosmer et al., "Reconstructing an Early Ninth-Century Shipwreck," 411.

25. Ibid.

26. These observations of the wadding and cordage were based on an inspection of small salvaged pieces of remains of the hull, and were never identified scientifically. Further analysis is needed to identify these materials. Tom Vosmer, personal communication, *Belitung Afterlives*, June 10, 2021.

27. Vosmer et al., "Reconstructing an Early Ninth-Century Shipwreck"; Pauline Burger et al., "The 9th-Century-AD Belitung Wreck, Indonesia: Analysis of a Resin Lump," *International Journal of Nautical Archaeology* 39, no. 2 (2010).

28. Preeyanuch Jumprom, "The Phanom Surin Shipwreck: New Discovery of an Arab-style Shipwreck in Central Thailand," *Southeast Asian Ceramics Museum Newsletter* VIII, no. 1 (2014).

29. Vosmer et al., "Reconstructing an Early Ninth-Century Shipwreck."

30. David Gibbins and Jonathan Adams, "Shipwrecks and Maritime Archaeology," *World Archaeology* 32, no. 3 (2001): 280.

31. Given the cost of putting to sea, it is likely that the *Belitung* carried cargo on its outward journey. This cargo might have included glass, ceramics, metal, precious stones, myrrh and frankincense, olive oil, cotton, and cobalt. Stephen Murphy, "Asia in the Ninth Century: The Context of the Tang Shipwreck," in *The Tang Shipwreck: Art and Exchange in the 9th Century*, ed. Alan Chong and Stephen Murphy (Singapore: Asian Civilisations Museum, 2017), 12.

32. Roxanna M. Brown and Sten Sjostrand, *Turiang: A Fourteenth-Century Shipwreck in Southeast Asian Waters*, ed. David Kamansky (Pasadena, CA: Pacific Asia Museum, 2000); Alan Chong and Stephen Murphy, eds., *The Tang Shipwreck: Art and Exchange in the 9th Century* (Singapore: Asian Civilisations Museum, 2017), 41.

33. Unlikely. When the *Jewel of Muscat* arrived in Georgetown, Malaysia, in June 2010, people told the crew they had been able to smell the vessel before it docked. Vosmer, personal communication.

34. Flecker, "Origin of the Tang Shipwreck," 30.

35. Burger et al., "Analysis of a Resin Lump."

36. Flecker, "Origin of the Tang Shipwreck."

37. Kan Shuyi, "Ceramics from Changsha: A World Commodity," in *The Tang Shipwreck: Art and Exchange in the 9th Century*, ed. Alan Chong and Stephen Murphy (Singapore: Asian Civilisations Museum, 2017).

38. John Guy, "Hollow and Useless Luxuries: The Tang Shipwreck and the Emerging Role of Arab Traders in the Late First Millennium Indian Ocean," in *The Tang Shipwreck: Art and Exchange in the 9th Century*, ed. Alan Chong and Stephen Murphy (Singapore: Asian Civilisations Museum, 2017), 160.

39. *Secrets of the Tang Treasure Ship*. Documentary. Distributed by National Geographic, 2010.

40. Shuyi, "Ceramics from Changsha," 54.

41. The Yue region is around modern-day Shaoxing.

42. Shuyi, "Ceramics from Changsha," 51.

43. "The lonely goose has flown to the far southern skies and the cold wind startles one with mournful whispers. The maiden pines for that guest from beyond the river who sooner or later will come back to cross the frontier." Chong and Murphy, *Art and Exchange*, 69.

44. Victor Mair and Erling Hoh, *The True History of Tea* (London: Thames & Hudson, 2009); Shuyi, "Ceramics from Changsha," 54; Chong and Murphy, *Art and Exchange*, 137.

45. Amanda Respess, "Islamic Inscriptions on the Belitung Bowls: Ninth-century Changsha Designs for the Abbasid Market" (paper presented at *China and the Maritime Silk Road: Shipwrecks, Ports and Products, Asian Civilisations Museum, Singapore, August 21–23, 2020*); Amanda Respess, "The Abode of Water: Shipwreck Evidence and the Maritime Circulation of Medicine between Iran and China in the 9th through 14th Centuries" (PhD dissertation, University of Michigan, 2020).

46. Daniel James Waller, "Curious Characters, Invented Scripts, and . . . Charlatans? 'Pseudo-Scripts' in the Mesopotamian Magic Bowls," *Journal of Near Eastern Studies* 78, no. 1 (2019): 119. See also Respess, "Islamic Inscriptions on the Belitung Bowls"; Respess, "The Abode of Water."

47. Rachel Leow, "Curating the Oceans: The Future of Singapore's Past." *A Historian's Craft*. Last updated July 14, 2009. Accessed July 8, 2021. https://idlethink.wordpress.com/2009/07/14/curating-the-oceans-the-future-of-singapores-past/.

48. Shuyi, "Ceramics from Changsha," 52–54.

49. Andrew Chittick, "Maritime Trade and the Transformation of the Chinese Ceramics Industry" (paper presented at *China and the Maritime Silk Road: Shipwrecks, Ports and Products, Asian Civilisations Museum, Singapore, August 21–23. 2020*).

50. Ibid.; Shuyi, "Ceramics from Changsha," 52–59.

51. Shuyi, "Ceramics from Changsha," 54.

52. Stephen Murphy, "Asia in the Ninth Century," 18.

53. Qi Dongfang, "Gold and Silver on the Tang Shipwreck," in *The Tang Shipwreck: Art and Exchange in the 9th Century*, ed. Alan Chong and Stephen Murphy (Singapore: Asian Civilisations Museum, 2017), 184.

54. Derek Heng, "The Tang Shipwreck and the Nature of China's Maritime Trade during the late Tang Period," in *The Tang Shipwreck: Art and Exchange in the 9th Century*, ed. Alan Chong and Stephen Murphy (Singapore: Asian Civilisations Museum, 2017), 152.

55. Flecker, "Origin of the Tang Shipwreck," 28. Regina Krahl, "Green, White, and Blue-and-White Stonewares," in *The Tang Shipwreck: Art and Exchange in the 9th century*, ed. Alan Chong and Stephen Murphy (Singapore: Asian Civilisations Museum, 2017), 103.

56. Flecker, "Origin of the Tang Shipwreck."

57. Simon Worrall, "Made in China: A 1,200-year-old Shipwreck Opens a Window on Ancient Global Trade," *National Geographic Magazine*, June 2009.

58. Guy, "Hollow and Useless Luxuries," 161.

59. Alan Chong and Stephen Murphy, "Green-Splashed Ceramics for the Middle East," in *The Tang Shipwreck: Art and Exchange in the 9th Century*, ed. Alan Chong and Stephen Murphy (Singapore: Asian Civilisations Museum, 2017), 125.

60. My thanks to Dr. Cheng Nien Yuan for this translation.

61. Guy, "Hollow and Useless Luxuries," 161.

62. Ibid.

63. Baoping Li, "The Origin of Blue and White: Research Progress, Latest Finds and Their Significance," *The Oriental Ceramic Society Newsletter* 16 (2008); Krahl, "Green, White, and Blue-and-White Stonewares." Renowned architect I. M. Pei attended the opening of *Secrets of the Sea* in New York, March 2017, specifically to see one of these dishes. Asia Society, "Photos: Asia Society Members Celebrate and Discover 'Secrets of the Sea'." *Asia Society*. Last updated March 8, 2017. Accessed July 8, 2021. http://asiasociety.org/new-york/photos-asia-society -members-celebrate-and-discover-secrets-sea.

64. Geraldine Heng, "An Ordinary Ship and Its Stories of Early Globalism: World Travel, Mass Production, and Art in the Global Middle Ages," *Journal of Medieval Worlds* 1, no. 1 (2019): 37.

65. Guy, "Hollow and Useless Luxuries," 161.

66. Ibid., 160.

67. Krahl, "Keynote: Precious Metals, Precious Earths: Luxury Goods in Ninth-Century China" (paper presented at *Exhibition Symposium "Secrets of the Sea: A Tang Shipwreck and Early Trade in Asia," Tang Center for Early China, New York, April 21, 2017*).

68. John Guy, "Rare and Strange Goods: International Trade in Ninth-Century Asia," in *Shipwrecked: Tang Treasures and Monsoon Winds*, ed. Regina Krahl et al. (Singapore: Arthur M. Sackler Gallery, Smithsonian Institution, Washington D.C.; National Heritage Board, Singapore; Singapore Tourism Board, 2010), 20.

69. Krahl, "Keynote."

70. The Xing kilns were considered to be the leading producers of porcellaneous white ware in China in the Tang period. Although the Ding kilns produced very similar wares, they were consistently described in Tang literature as inferior to their Xing counterparts. Krahl, "Green, White, and Blue-and-White Stonewares," 81.

71. Ibid.

72. Alan Chong and Stephen Murphy, "As Green as Jade: Celadon," ibid.

73. Krahl, "Green, White, and Blue-and-White Stonewares," ibid., 80.

74. Ibid.

75. Ibid., 81.

76. Qi Dongfang, "Gold and Silver on the Tang Shipwreck," ibid., 184.

77. Ibid., 186.

78. Ibid.

79. Ibid., 188.

80. Flecker, "Origin of the Tang Shipwreck," 31.

81. Ibid.

82. Qi Dongfang, "Gold and Silver on the Tang Shipwreck," 186.

83. Regina Krahl et al., *Shipwrecked: Tang Treasures and Monsoon Winds (Special Souvenir Edition)*, Special Souvenir Edition (Singapore: Arthur M. Sackler Gallery, Smithsonian Institution, Washington D.C.; National Heritage Board, Singapore; Singapore Tourism Board, 2011), 59.

84. François Louis, "Metal Objects on the Tang Shipwreck," in *The Tang Shipwreck: Art and Exchange in the 9th Century*, ed. Alan Chong and Stephen Murphy (Singapore: Asian Civilisations Museum, 2017), 208.

85. Ibid.

86. These include the wine flask, a fan-shaped and a lobed triangular silver box, and two lobed oval gold bowls. See Heng, "An Ordinary Ship," 42.

87. Regina Krahl et al., *Shipwrecked: Tang Treasures and Monsoon Winds* (Singapore: Arthur M. Sackler Gallery, Smithsonian Institution, Washington D.C.; National Heritage Board, Singapore; Singapore Tourism Board, 2010), 59.

88. Only a small number of comparable cups have ever been found. The closest examples are three cups unearthed in Hejia village near Xi'an in 1970, all of which have an octagonal shape, Central Asian entertainers in relief, a ring handle with a thumb plate featuring bearded men, and a high, flared foot. Only one of these is gold (the other two are gilt bronze and gilt silver). The Hejia cups are earlier (late seventh or early eighth century) and smaller than the *Belitung* cup. François Louis, "Gold and Silver," in *The Belitung Shipwreck: Sunken Treasures from Tang China,* ed. Jayne Ward, Zoi Kotitsa, and Alessandra D'Angelo (New Zealand: Seabed Explorations, 2004), 154.

89. François Louis, "Bronze Mirrors," in *Shipwrecked: Tang Treasures and Monsoon Winds*, ed. Regina Krahl et al. (Singapore: Arthur M. Sackler Gallery, Smithsonian Institution, Washington D.C.; National Heritage Board, Singapore; Singapore Tourism Board, 2010), 213.

90. Louis, "Metal Objects," 204.

91. Ibid.

92. Ibid., 206.

93. Flecker, "Origin of the Tang Shipwreck."

94. Louis, "Metal Objects," 204.

95. J. Keith Wilson and Michael Flecker, "Dating the Belitung Shipwreck," in *Shipwrecked: Tang Treasures and Monsoon Winds*, ed. Regina Krahl et al. (Singapore: Arthur M. Sackler Gallery, Smithsonian Institution, Washington D.C.; National Heritage Board, Singapore; Singapore Tourism Board, 2010); Louis, "Mirrors."

96. Guy, "Hollow and Useless Luxuries," 163.

97. If silk were stowed on board it is highly unlikely that it survived the wrecking process. Silk would have been stowed above the ceramics, and therefore would not have been buried in an anaerobic environment. Michael Flecker, personal communication, *Draft Book*, September 19, 2020.

98. Guy, "Hollow and Useless Luxuries," 176.

99. Harpster, "Shipwreck Identity, Methodology, and Nautical Archaeology," 606.

100. Chong and Murphy, "Chinese on Board," in *The Tang Shipwreck: Art and Exchange in the 9th Century,* ed. Alan Chong and Stephen Murphy (Singapore: Asian Civilisations Museum, 2017), 256.

101. Shuyi, "Ceramics from Changsha," 55.

102. Himanshu Prabha Ray, *Coastal Shrines and Transnational Maritime Networks across India and Southeast Asia* (London: Routledge India, 2021).

103. For information on tonnage see Chong and Murphy, *Art and Exchange,* 266. Regarding the size of the vessel, Flecker gives an overall length of around twenty to twenty-two meters (65.6–72.2 feet) and a maximum beam of about eight meters (26.2 feet). See Flecker, "First evidence for Direct Trade with China," 339. By comparison, the *Jewel of Muscat* was constructed with a length of approximately 18.5 meters (60.7) feet and a beam of 6.5 meters (21.3 feet), and even then it was considered "extraordinarily beamy" (wide). Vosmer, personal communication.

104. Flecker, "A 9th-Century Arab or Indian Shipwreck," 205.

105. The voyage of the *Jewel of Muscat* in 2010 included goats and chickens.

106. Chong and Murphy, *Art and Exchange*, 252.

107. Ibid., 57, 250, 264.

108. Ibid., 250.

109. Eric Staples, "An Experiment in Arab Navigation: The Jewel of Muscat Passage," in *The Principles of Arab Navigation*, ed. Anthony R. Constable and William Facey (London: Arabian Publishing, 2013).

110. Ibid., 48.

111. Ibid. The *Jewel of Muscat* was equipped with GPS and other modern navigational equipment for safety reasons, and experiments with Arab navigation techniques were therefore just that—experiments.

112. Murphy, "Asia in the Ninth Century," 18.

113. Flecker, "Origin of the Tang Shipwreck," 38.

114. Heng, "An Ordinary Ship."

115. Pierre-Yves Manguin, "Austronesian Shipping in the Indian Ocean: From Outrigger Boats to Trading Ships," in *Early Exchange between Africa and the Wider Indian Ocean World*, ed. Gwyn Campbell, Palgrave Series in Indian Ocean World Studies (Montreal: Palgrave Macmillan, 2016).

Chapter 2. Wrecked

1. This means that the original ceramic cargo would have numbered around seventy thousand pieces. There would have been breakage at the time of the initial wrecking event as the vessel impacted the reef/rock and then the seabed. However, most breakage takes place slowly, over many years, with cargo continuing to spill out as the hull planks rot and the packaging disintegrates. Only after decades does the wreck achieve near-equilibrium. Michael Flecker, "The Origin of the Tang Shipwreck: A Look at Its Archaeology and History," in *The Tang Shipwreck: Art and Exchange in the 9th Century*, ed. Alan Chong and Stephen Murphy (Singapore: Asian Civilisations Museum, 2017), 28. Michael Flecker, personal communication, *Draft Book*, September 19, 2020.

2. "Tektites." *Australian Museum*. Last updated November 12, 2018. Accessed April 2, 2020. https://australianmuseum.net.au/learn/minerals/shaping-earth/tektites/.

3. One publication even refers to the *Belitung* as the *Batu Intan* (the *Intan* being a different shipwreck altogether, albeit salvaged by the same company). See Darrel J. Kitchener and Heny Kustiarsih, eds., *Ceramics from the Musi River, Palembang, Indonesia: Based on a Private Collection*, vol. 22 (Australian National Centre of Excellence for Maritime Archaeology, 2019), 26.

4. Noel Hidalgo Tan, "The Belitung Shipwreck." *The Southeast Asian Archaeology Newsblog*. Last updated June 28, 2007. Accessed July 8, 2021. http://www.southeastasianarchaeology.com/2007/06/28/the-belitung-shipwreck/.

5. Stephen Haw, "The Maritime Routes between China and the Indian Ocean during the Second to Ninth Centuries C.E.," *Royal Asiatic Society* 27, no. 1 (2017).

6. Dashu Qin and Kunpeng Xiang, "Sri Vijaya as the Entrepôt for Circum-Indian Ocean Trade," *Études Océan Indien* 46–47 (2011); John Miksic, "Sinbad, Shipwrecks and Singapore," in *The Tang Shipwreck: Art and Exchange in the 9th Century*, ed. Alan Chong and Stephen Murphy (Singapore: Asian Civilisations Museum, 2017).

7. Dashu Qin, "Sri Vijaya—The Entrepôt for Circum-Indian Ocean Trade—The Evidence from Chinese Documentary Records and Materials from Shipwrecks of the 9th–10th Centuries" (paper presented at *ST Lee Annual Lecture in Asian Art and Archaeology, The University of Sydney, September 2, 2014*).

8. Flecker, "Origin of the Tang Shipwreck," 37.

9. Hsieh Ming-liang, "The Navigational Route of the Belitung Wreck and Late Tang Ceramic Trade," in *The Belitung Wreck: Sunken Treasures from Tang China*, ed. Jayne Ward, Zoi Kotitsa, and Alessandra D'Angelo (New Zealand: Seabed Explorations, 2004).

10. Andrew Chittick, "Maritime Trade and the Transformation of the Chinese Ceramics Industry" (paper presented at *China and the Maritime Silk Road: Shipwrecks, Ports and Products, Asian Civilisations Museum, Singapore, August 21–23, 2020*); Derek Heng, "The Tang Shipwreck and the Nature of China's Maritime Trade during the Late Tang Period," in *The Tang Shipwreck: Art and Exchange in the 9th Century*, ed. Alan Chong and Stephen Murphy (Singapore: Asian Civilisations Museum, 2017).

11. Austronesians, Indians, Arabs, and Persians all acted as intermediaries during the Tang period. Philippe Beaujard, "Tang China and the Rise of the Silk Roads," in *The Worlds of the Indian Ocean: A Global History* (Cambridge: Cambridge University Press, 2019).

12. Stephen Murphy, "Asia in the Ninth Century: The Context of the Tang Shipwreck," in *The Tang Shipwreck: Art and Exchange in the 9th Century*, ed. Alan Chong and Stephen Murphy (Singapore: Asian Civilisations Museum, 2017), 19.

13. Ibid.; Michael Flecker, "Origin of the Tang Shipwreck"; Mahirta Sasongko et al., *Dieng Temple Complex Excavation Report* (Singapore: NUS Press, 2010).

14. Andaya explains that resins were valued in China, western Asia, and Europe for their "much-vaunted" medical properties and their scarcity. Leonard Y. Andaya, *Leaves of the Same Tree: Trade and Ethnicity in the Straits of Melaka* (Honolulu: University of Hawai'i Press, 2008).

15. Flecker, "Origin of the Tang Shipwreck," 37.

16. Janice Stargardt, "Indian Ocean Trade in the Ninth and Tenth Centuries: Demand, Distance, and Profit," *South Asian Studies* 30, no. 1 (2014): 36.

17. Pierre-Yves Manguin, "Southeast Asian and Other Shipwrecks, Cosmopolitan Cargoes: A Distorted View of the Maritime Scene in the Java Sea" (paper presented at *Belitung Shipwreck Symposium: Intersections of History, Archaeology, and Capitalism, New York University, March 4, 2017*).

18. Justin Leidwanger, "From Time Capsules to Networks: New Light on Roman Shipwrecks in the Maritime Economy," *American Journal of Archaeology* 121, no. 4 (2017).

19. John G. Butcher and R. E. Elson, *Sovereignty and the Sea: How Indonesia Became an Archipelagic State* (Singapore: NUS Press, 2017).

20. Adrian B. Lapian, *Orang Laut, Bajak Laut, Raja Laut: Sejarah Kawasan Laut Sulawesi Abad XIX* (Jakarta: Komunitas Baru, 2009).

21. Hilmar Farid, "The Backward Current of Culture—History as Critique" (paper presented at *Cultural Lecture, Arts Council of Jakarta, November 10, 2014*).

22. Michael Leadbetter, "Beyond the Temple Trail: The Sacred Landscapes of Southeast Asia," *TAASA Review* 25, no. 4 (2016).

23. Nia Naelul Hasanah Ridwan, "Maritime Archaeology in Indonesia: Resources, Threats, and Current Integrated Research," *Journal of Indo-Pacific Archaeology* 36 (2015); Mai Lin Tjoa-Bonatz, "Struggles over Historic Shipwrecks in Indonesia: Economic Versus Preservation Interests," in *Cultural Property and Contested Ownership: The Trafficking of Artefacts and the Quest*

for Restitution, ed. Brigitta Hauser-Schäublin and Lyndel V. Prott (Abingdon and New York: Routledge, 2016); Judi Wahjudin, "Human Resources Development in Indonesia's Underwater Archaeology" (paper presented at *Asia/Pacific Regional Conference on Underwater Cultural Heritage, Manila, The Philippines, November 8–12, 2011*).

24. KKP, "FAQ Barang Muatan Kapal Tenggelam (BMKT)." *Kementerian Kelautan dan Perikanan Republik Indonesia*. Last updated September 1, 2017. Accessed January 1, 2018. http://kkp.go.id/2017/09/01/faq-barang-muatan-kapal-tenggelam-bmkt/.

25. Cahyo Junaedy, "Arkeologi Bawah Air Nusantara." *Arkaeologi Bawah Air*. Last updated 2011. Accessed March 3, 2018. http://arkeologibawahair.blogspot.com.au/2011/03/arkeologi-bawah-laut-nusantara.html; Jhohannes Marbun, "An Advocacy Approach on Underwater Heritage in Indonesia, Case Study: An Auction on Underwater Heritage from Cirebon Waters in 2010" (Yogyakarta: Masyarakat Advokasi Warisan Budaya [MADYA], 2011); Tamalia Alisjahbana, "Indonesia Is Not Signing UNESCO's Convention for the Protection of Underwater Cultural Heritage." *Independent Observer*. Last updated November 28, 2019. Accessed April 6, 2020. https://observerid.com/indonesia-declines-to-sign-unesco-convention-for-protection-of-underwater-cultural-heritage/.

26. KKP, "FAQ BMKT."

27. Tjoa-Bonatz, "Struggles over Historic Shipwrecks," 92.

28. Junaedy, *Arkaeologi Bawah Air*; Robin McDowell, "Indonesia's Shipwrecks Means Riches and Headaches," *San Diego Union Tribune*, March 31, 2012; Yurnaldi, "Melacak Kapal Karam." *Arkeologi Bawah Air*. Last updated April 28, 2010. Accessed April 7, 2022. https://arkeologibawahair.wordpress.com/2010/12/16/arkeologi-bawah-air-melacak-kapal-karam/.

29. Jean Gelman Taylor, *Indonesia: Peoples and Histories* (New Haven, CT and London: Yale University Press, 2003).

30. See, for example, Marieke Bloembergen, *Colonial Spectacles: The Netherlands and the Dutch East Indies at the World Exhibitions, 1880–1931*, trans. Beverly Jackson (Singapore: Singapore University Press, 2006); Marieke Bloembergen and Martijn Eickhoff, "Exchange and the Protection of Java's Antiquities: A Transnational Approach to the Problem of Heritage in Colonial Java," *The Journal of Asian Studies* 72, no. 4 (2013); Marieke Bloembergen and Martijn Eickhoff, "Conserving the Past, Mobilizing the Indonesian Future: Archaeological Sites, Regime Change and Heritage Politics in Indonesia in the 1950s," *Bijdragen tot de Taal-, Land- en Volkenkunde* 167, no. 4 (2011); Marieke Bloembergen and Martijn Eickhoff, "Save Borobudur! The Moral Dynamics of Heritage Formation in Indonesia across Orders and Borders, 1930s–1980s," in *Cultural Heritage as Civilizing Mission: From Decay to Recovery*, ed. Michael Falser (Switzerland: Springer International Publishing, 2015); Marieke Bloembergen and Martijn Eickhoff, "Decolonizing Borobudur: Moral Engagements and the Fear of Loss. The Netherlands, Japan and (Post)Colonial Heritage Politics in Indonesia," in *Sites, Bodies and Stories: Imagining Indonesian History*, ed. Susan Legêne, Bambang Purwanto, and Henk Schulte Nordholt (Singapore: NUS Press, 2015); Ana Dragojlovic, Marieke Bloembergen, and Henk Schulte Nordholt, "Colonial Re-Collections: Memories, Objects, and Performances," *Bijdragen tot de Taal-, Land- en Volkenkunde* 170, no. 4 (2014); Susan Legêne, Bambang Purwanto, and Henk Schulte Nordholt, eds., *Sites, Bodies and Stories: Imagining Indonesian History* (Singapore: NUS Press, 2015).

31. Zainab Tahir, "Cultural Attitude and Values towards Underwater Cultural Heritage and Its Influences on the Management Actions in Indonesia" (paper presented at *Asia/Pacific Regional Conference on Underwater Cultural Heritage, Honolulu, Hawaii, May 14, 2014*);

Gatot Gautama, "Underwater Archaeology in Indonesia: Experiences and Prospects," in *Marine Archaeology in Southeast Asia: Innovation and Adaptation*, ed. Heidi Tan (Singapore: Asian Civilisations Museum, 2012).

32. Nayati argues it was in Indonesian waters, citing Indonesian news sources, but notes that Marx and Marx hold that "the *Geldermalsen* lay at the bottom of the South China Sea, far from the Riau Islands." See Pudak Nayati, "Ownership Rights over Archaeological/Historical Objects Found in Indonesian Waters: Republic of Indonesia Act No. 5 of 1992 on Cultural Heritage Objects and its Related Regulations," *Singapore Journal of International and Comparative Law* 2 (1998): 143. See also Robert F. Marx and Jenifer Marx, *The Search for Sunken Treasure: Exploring the World's Great Shipwrecks* (Toronto: Key-Porter Books, 1993), 20–21, 148.

33. John Dyson, "Captain Hatcher's Richest Find," *Reader's Digest* (1986). George L. Miller, "The Second Destruction of the Geldermalsen," *Historical Archaeology* 26, no. 4 (1992).

34. Nick Habermehl, "Shipwrecks and Lost Treasures of the Seven Seas—Famous Wrecks— VOC Geldermalsen: Porcelain and Gold Bullion from Asia." *Shipwrecks and Lost Treasures of the Seven Seas*. Last updated. Accessed July 8, 2021. http://www.oceantreasures.org/pages /content/famous-wrecks/old-treasures-and-shipwreck-news-voc-geldermalsen.html. See also Natali Pearson, "Heritage Adrift." *Inside Indonesia*. Last updated July 5, 2016. Accessed July 8, 2021. http://www.insideindonesia.org/heritage-adrift.

35. Miller, "The Geldermalsen," 126.

36. Ibid.; John Austin, "Our New Dinner Service is 235 Years Old and Has Never Been Used," *Colonial Williamsburg News* 39, no. 8 (1986).

37. Miller, "The Geldermalsen," 127.

38. Jeremy Green, "Book Review: The Nanking Cargo by Michael Hatcher with Max de Rham and Other Books on the Geldermalsen," *International Journal of Nautical Archaeology* 17, no. 4 (1988): 359.

39. Nayati, "Ownership Rights."

40. Green, "Book Review: The Nanking Cargo." See also Jennifer Rodrigues et al., "The UNESCO Convention on the Protection of the Underwater Cultural Heritage: A One-Day Workshop Held on 23 May 2004." *Department of Maritime Archaeology, WA Maritime Museum*. Last updated 2005. Accessed May 2, 2015. http://museum.wa.gov.au/maritime-archaeology-db /sites/default/files/no._189_uneco_report.pdf.

41. At the time of the *Geldermalsen*'s salvage in the mid-1980s, legislation in Indonesia relating to cultural heritage was limited to the Monuments Ordinance No. 19 of 1931, a relic from the Dutch colonial era. This ordinance focused on tangible objects and sites older than fifty years of age. As would be expected from legislation dating to this period, the ordinance made no specific provisions for underwater sites or objects.

42. As a party to the 1982 United Nations *Convention on the Law of the Sea* (UNCLOS) (which it ratified in 1985), Indonesia had special rights to the exploration and use of marine resources in its territorial waters and its Exclusive Economic Zone. However, Indonesia's early legislative reforms in relation to maritime issues were focused on establishing sovereignty and exclusive economic zones under UNCLOS, and gave minimal attention to underwater cultural heritage.

43. Tahir, "Cultural Attitude and Values towards Underwater Cultural Heritage and Its Influences on the Management Actions in Indonesia."

44. For a more detailed discussion of Indonesian heritage-related legislation in this period, see Natali Pearson, "Salvaging a Wreck: The Afterlife of the *Belitung* Shipwreck" (PhD dissertation, University of Sydney, 2018).

45. National Committee for the Salvage and Utilisation of Valuable Objects from Sunken Ships (*Panitia Nasional Pengangkatan dan Pemanfaatan Benda Berharga Asal Muatan Kapal yang Tenggelam*, or PanNas BMKT). The chair of PanNas BMKT was the Coordinating Minister for Political and Security Affairs (*Menteri Koordinator Bidang Politik dan Keamanan*), and the vice chair was the Minister of Education and Culture (Article 5).

46. Michael Flecker, "The Ethics, Politics, and Realities of Maritime Archaeology in Southeast Asia," *International Journal of Nautical Archaeology* 31, no. 1 (2002): 20. These were the Ministry of Defence and Security (*Departemen Pertahanan Keamanan*), Ministry of Education and Culture (*Departemen Pendidikan dan Kebudayaan*), Ministry of Home Affairs (*Departemen Dalam Negeri*), Ministry of Foreign Affairs (*Departemen Luar Negeri*), Ministry of Justice (*Departemen Kehakiman*), Ministry of Finance (*Departemen Keuangan*), Ministry of Transportation (*Departemen Perhubungan*), Ministry of Trade (*Departemen Perdagangan*), and the Headquarters of the Armed Forces of Republic of Indonesia (*Markas Besar Angkatan Bersenjata Republik Indonesia*).

47. Gautama, "Underwater Archaeology in Indonesia," 116.

48. Shipwreck assemblages often consist of multiple duplicates (for example, the tens of thousands of similar Changsha bowls found on the *Belitung*). A representative set is a selection of objects from these multiple duplicates. Representative objects are in addition to "unique" objects, of which there may be one or only a few examples. Distinguishing objects within an assemblage based on their "representative" or "unique" character is anathema in maritime archaeology, in which the value of the assemblage lies in the whole, not in the individual. Nevertheless, some countries, including in Southeast Asia, have used this distinction to manage objects recovered from shipwrecks—see, for example, the seventeenth-century Chinese *Binh Thuan* shipwreck in Vietnam. In this case, the provincial authority retained all unique objects and four representative sets, and the remaining multi-duplicate ceramics were sold at auction with the intention that profits from the sale of the objects would be used to fund a dedicated museum. Natali Pearson, "Maritime Archaeology in Vietnam: Australian Involvement," *TAASA Review* 25, no. 4 (2016). See also Michael Flecker, "Wrecked Twice: Shipwrecks as a Cultural Resource in Southeast Asia," in *Rethinking Cultural Resource Management in Southeast Asia: Preservation, Development and Neglect*, ed. John Miksic, Geok Yian Goh, and Sue O'Connor (London and New York: Anthem Press, 2011).

49. Tahir, "Cultural Attitude and Values towards Underwater Cultural Heritage and Its Influences on the Management Actions in Indonesia."

50. Emphasis added. The other two characteristics necessary to assert state ownership were that the object in question had a distinct and unique style; and that the number and type of object was limited and rare.

51. Nayati, "Ownership Rights."

52. While it is accurate to conceive of the *Geldermalsen* as a critical moment in legislative terms, the valuation of shipwrecks in Indonesian waters as economic, rather than historical or archaeological, resources predates the *Geldermalsen* case by decades, as evidenced by the profit-motivated, state-sanctioned salvage of key objects from allied warships such as HMAS *Perth* (I) and USS *Houston*. Natali Pearson, "Naval Shipwrecks in Indonesia" (paper presented at *Asia/Pacific Regional Conference on Underwater Cultural Heritage, Hong Kong SAR, November 27–December 2, 2017*).

53. Michael Flecker, *Legislation on Underwater Cultural Heritage in Southeast Asia: Evolution and Outcomes*, Trends in Southeast Asia (Singapore: ISEAS-Yusof Ishak Institute, 2017), 7.

54. Ibid., 8.

55. Alisjahbana, "Indonesia is not Signing UNESCO's Convention."

56. Laurajane Smith, *Uses of Heritage* (London: Routledge, 2006), 11.

57. Rodney Harrison, *Heritage: Critical Approaches* (London and New York: Routledge, 2013), 42.

58. Ibid.

59. Craig Forrest, *International Law and the Protection of Cultural Heritage* (Abingdon: Routledge, 2010), 286.

60. Harrison, *Critical Approaches*.

61. In December 2017, the significance of South Sulawesi boatbuilding was listed by UNESCO as a form of intangible cultural heritage. The "art of boat-building" nomination recognizes a specific type of vessel, the *phinisi*, illuminating the value of cultural identity, diversity, and knowledge traditions within the maritime context in Indonesia. Jeffrey Mellefont, "UNESCO Heritage-lists Indonesian Wooden Boat Building." *Perspectives on the Past at New Mandala*. Last updated 2018. Accessed June 7, 2021. https://www.newmandala.org /unesco-heritage-lists-indonesian-wooden-boat-building/.

62. Janet Blake and Lucas Lixinski, eds., *The 2003 UNESCO Intangible Heritage Convention: A Commentary*, Oxford Commentaries on International Cultural Heritage Law (Oxford: Oxford University Press, 2020). Building on this greater attentiveness to diversity, the 2005 UNESCO Convention on the Protection and Promotion of the Diversity of Cultural Expressions has been described as a "sibling" to the 2003 UNESCO Convention. See Janet Blake, "From Traditional Culture and Folklore to Intangible Cultural Heritage: Evolution of a Treaty," *Santander Art Culture Law Review* 2, no. 3 (2017): 43.

63. Patrick Coleman, "UNESCO and the Belitung Shipwreck: The Need for a Permissive Definition of 'Commercial Exploitation'," *The George Washington International Law Review* 45, no. 4 (2013): 854. See also Elizabeth S. Greene, "What Is Underwater Cultural Heritage and Why Does It Matter?" (paper presented at *Keeping the Lid on Davy Jones' Locker: The Protection of Underwater Cultural Heritage from Titanic to Today, Washington, D.C., November 3, 2011*).

64. Indonesia is one of the states that has claimed continental shelf rights beyond two hundred nautical miles. See Arif Havas Oegroseno, "Indonesia's Maritime Boundaries," in *Indonesia Beyond the Water's Edge: Managing an Archipelagic State*, ed. Robert Cribb and Michele Ford (Singapore: ISEAS Publishing, 2009).

65. Etienne Clément, "The Elaboration of the UNESCO 2001 Convention on the Protection of the Underwater Cultural Heritage" (paper presented at *Asia/Pacific Regional Conference on Underwater Cultural Heritage, Hong Kong SAR, November 27–December 2, 2017*).

66. Patrick J. O'Keefe, "Protecting the Underwater Cultural Heritage: The International Law Association Draft Convention," *Marine Policy* 20, no. 4 (1996): 301.

67. Anastasia Strati, *Draft Convention on the Protection of Underwater Cultural Heritage: A Commentary Prepared for UNESCO by Dr. Anastasia Strati*.

68. Clément, "The Elaboration of the UNESCO 2001 Convention."

69. Ibid.

70. There were eighty-eight votes in favor, four against (Russia, Norway, Turkey, and Venezuela) and fifteen abstentions (including France, the United Kingdom, Brazil, Greece, and the Netherlands). The United States was not a member of UNESCO at that time, and did not vote.

71. Lyndel V. Prott, "The Significance of World-Wide Ratification of the 2001 UNESCO Convention on the Protection of the Underwater Cultural Heritage," in *Towards Ratification:*

Papers from the 2013 AIMA Conference Workshop, ed. Graeme Henderson and Andrew Viduka (Fremantle: Australasian Institute for Maritime Archaeology, 2014), 5. Clément, "The Elaboration of the UNESCO 2001 Convention."

72. Within the region defined by UNESCO as "Asia and the Pacific," just four countries have signed the Convention—Cambodia, Iran, Niue, and the Federated States of Micronesia.

73. The five UNESCO regions are Africa, the Arab states, Asia and the Pacific, Europe and North America, and Latin America and the Caribbean. As of April 2022, seventy-one states had ratified the 2001 UNESCO Convention. A number of other states unwilling to ratify the Convention, such as the United Kingdom, have nevertheless indicated their intention to adhere to its rules. See Mark Staniforth, "Factors Affecting the Ratification of the UNESCO Convention 2001 in the Asia and the Pacific Region" (paper presented at *ICLAFI—ICUCH Symposium, Amersfoort, The Netherlands, July 1, 2017*).

74. Indonesia's management of the *Belitung* was judged against this standard, notwithstanding that the Convention was introduced three years after the *Belitung*'s discovery and the fact that Indonesia was not then (and is not now) a signatory to the Convention. Nevertheless, it would be disingenuous to argue that Indonesia was completely unaware of the international community's efforts, which dated back to at least 1994, to develop a regulatory framework to protect and preserve underwater cultural heritage. For more information, see Nayati, "Ownership Rights."

75. Flecker, "Ethics, Politics and Realities," 13–14.

76. Debra Shefi, "The 'First Option' in Underwater Cultural Heritage Management: A Plea for the Establishment and Application of Universal Terminology and Best Practices," *The Journal of the Australasian Institute for Maritime Archaeology* 37 (2013).

77. According to UNESCO, *in situ* preservation may not be the preferred option when "the underwater cultural heritage remains are threatened by any natural or human factors (i.e. urban and port developments, pillage, environmental conditions, etc.); scientifical [*sic*] research can get results that contribute significantly to the knowledge of the history of humanity; study, research and dissemination enhance the awareness and consideration of a region towards the protection of its underwater cultural heritage." UNESCO, "In Situ Protection." *United Nations Educational, Scientific and Cultural Organization*. Last updated 2017. Accessed April 3, 2018. http://www.unesco.org/new/en/culture/themes/underwater-cultural-heritage/protection /protection/in-situ-protection/.

78. Martijn Manders, "*In Situ* Preservation: The Preferred Option," *Museum International* 60, no. 4 (2008): 32. Detailed guidance is provided in the Annex to the 2001 UNESCO Convention in the form of rules concerning activities directed at underwater cultural heritage.

79. 2001 UNESCO Convention, Rule 2. "The commercial exploitation of underwater cultural heritage for trade or speculation or its irretrievable dispersal is fundamentally incompatible with the protection and proper management of underwater cultural heritage. Underwater cultural heritage shall not be traded, sold, bought or bartered as commercial goods." I am grateful to comments provided by reviewers regarding this point.

80. Edward Aspinall, *Opposing Suharto: Compromise, Resistance, and Regime Change in Indonesia* (Stanford, CA: Stanford University Press, 2005); Edward Aspinall and Greg Fealy, eds., *Soeharto's New Order and Its Legacy: Essays in Honour of Harold Crouch* (Canberra: ANU ePress, 2010).

81. In Indonesia, the Culture portfolio had first been elevated to the ministry level in 1948 under President Sukarno, and here it had stayed for some fifty years as Education and Culture

(*Pendidikan dan Kebudayaan*). However, as President Suharto's rule reached its end, Culture was split into the extant Ministry of Education and Culture and the Department of Tourism, Arts and Culture (*Departemen Pariwisata, Seni, dan Budaya*). This split continued under Suharto's successor, President Habibie (May 1998–October 1999). Habibie's successor, President Wahid (October 1999–July 2001), consolidated Culture into the Department of Tourism and Culture (*Departemen Kebudayaan dan Pariwisata*). Under President Megawati (July 2001–October 2004), this department became a state ministry (*Kementerian Negara*). During his first five-year term, President Yudhoyono (October 2004–October 2014) renamed it the Ministry of Culture and Tourism (*Menteri Kebudayaan dan Pariwisata*). In his second five-year term, Yudhoyono moved Culture back to the Education portfolio, where it has remained under President Widodo (October 2014–present). Widodo also introduced the Coordinating Ministry for Maritime Affairs (*Kementerian Koordinator Bidang Kemaritiman*), which coordinates maritime-related policy initiatives across four ministries.

82. The Ministry of Marine Exploration (*Kementerian Eksplorasi Kelautan*). This was the predecessor to today's Ministry of Marine Affairs and Fisheries (*Kementerian Kelautan dan Perikanan*).

83. Tjoa-Bonatz, "Struggles over Historic Shipwrecks," 92.

84. Flecker, *Evolution and Outcomes*.

85. Guy Scriven, "Interview with Tilman Walterfang." *Seabed Explorations*. Last updated February 24, 2013. Accessed July 8, 2021. https://tilmanwalterfang.org/news/index.html.

86. Jürgen Kremb, "Fund Am Schwarzen Felsen," *Der Spiegel* (2004).

87. Scriven, "Interview: Scriven/Walterfang."

88. Tony Paterson, "The 1,200-year-old Sunken Treasure That Revealed an Undiscovered China," *The Independent*, April 13, 2004.

89. Flecker, "Wrecked Twice," 24–29.

90. Michael Flecker, "Treasures from the Java Sea: The 10th Century Intan Shipwreck," *Heritage Asia Magazine*, December 2004, 2.

91. William M. Mathers and Michael Flecker, *Archaeological Recovery of the Java Sea Wreck* (Annapolis, MD: Pacific Sea Resources, 1997).

92. PT: *Perseroan Terbatas*, or Limited Liability Company. *Segarajaya*: great sea.

93. Michael Flecker, *The Archaeological Excavation of the 10th Century Intan Wreck*, BAR International Series 1047 (Oxford: Archaeopress, 2002), 92.

94. Michael Flecker, "The Bakau Wreck: An Early Example of Chinese Shipping in Southeast Asia," *International Journal of Nautical Archaeology* 30, no. 2 (2001).

95. Roxanna M. Brown and Sten Sjostrand, *Turiang: A Fourteenth-Century Shipwreck in Southeast Asian Waters*, ed. David Kamansky (Pasadena, CA: Pacific Asia Museum, 2000).

96. John Miksic and Geok Yian Goh, *Ancient Southeast Asia* (Abingdon and New York: Routledge, 2017).

97. Anonymous, "Unpublished Report: Discovery of the Shipwreck "BATU HITAM" of the Tang Period in 1998" (2002).

98. Flecker, "The Bakau Wreck," 222.

99. Tilman Walterfang, personal communication, *Email correspondence with Tilman Walterfang, March–April 2018*, March 14–April 16, 2018.

100. Laura Gongaware, "To Exhibit or Not to Exhibit?: Establishing a Middle Ground for Commercially Exploited Underwater Cultural Heritage under the 2001 UNESCO Convention," *Tulane Maritime Law Journal* 37, no. 1 (2012).

101. Anonymous, "Discovery Report," page number redacted. A 2004 article in German magazine *Der Spiegel* incorrectly conflated the discovery of the *Bakau* and the *Belitung* wrecks. This has led to many sources indicating, incorrectly, that the *Belitung* came to the attention of Seabed Explorations in April 1998. My research confirms the correct date is August 1998—that is, after Suharto's resignation, not before. In ascertaining the date of the *Belitung*'s discovery, I am not suggesting that the date has been deliberately obscured but rather correcting the sometimes inaccurate information that is publicly available about these early periods in the *Belitung*'s modern history.

102. Ibid.

103. Walterfang has confirmed he was not in Indonesia when the *Belitung* wreck was brought to the attention of the Seabed Explorations team: "Our employees whose duties were among others to represent me and the company on site while I was absent, are craving for some acknowledgement for having been present in Belitung when the exact location was revealed to our license holding Indonesian partner company and to us. Over time the press was chasing me about this question and it took me some effort to get it into their heads that the fishermen discovered the site and that there was no hero and no villain available for their made up stories." Walterfang, personal communication.

104. Anonymous, "Discovery Report."

105. Meg Lambert, "Belitung Shipwreck." *Trafficking Culture.* Last updated August 8, 2012. Accessed July 8, 2021. http://traffickingculture.org/encyclopedia/case-studies/biletung-shipwreck/.

106. There are rumors about undocumented payments made by Seabed Explorations to secure the salvage license ahead of its competitors, but there is no proof to substantiate these claims.

107. There was already a small museum on the island—the *Museum Kabupaten Belitung* was established in 1963 by a Belgian geologist to showcase the island's history of tin mining. Today it features a diversity of objects, including furniture, clothing, examples of local food, and animals both taxidermied and—in a zoo out the back—alive. It does contain a number of objects from shipwrecks, including the *Belitung.*

108. Gongaware, "To Exhibit or Not to Exhibit."

109. John Guy, "Late Tang Ceramics and Asia's International Trade," in *The Belitung Wreck: Sunken Treasures from Tang China,* ed. Jayne Ward, Zoi Kotitsa, and Alessandra D'Angelo (New Zealand: Seabed Explorations, 2004).

Chapter 3. Provenanced

1. Presidential Decree No. 43/1989 on the National Committee for the Salvage and Utilisation of Valuable Objects from Sunken Ships.

2. Guy Scriven, "Interview with Tilman Walterfang." *Seabed Explorations.* Last updated February 24, 2013. Accessed July 8, 2021. https://tilmanwalterfang.org/news/index.html.

3. Ibid.

4. Email from Tilman Walterfang to Tess Davis (Director, Lawyers' Committee for Cultural Heritage Preservation), December 11, 2011. Cited in Laura Gongaware, "To Exhibit or Not to Exhibit?: Establishing a Middle Ground for Commercially Exploited Underwater Cultural Heritage Under the 2001 UNESCO Convention," *Tulane Maritime Law Journal* 37, no. 1 (2012): 216.

5. Dobberphul later worked on the salvage of the *Cirebon* shipwreck in the Java Sea, after which he and fellow diver Jean-Paul Blancan were arrested in 2006 and accused of illegally

salvaging thousands of objects. The Indonesian government alleged they had not acquired the necessary permits to salvage the wreck, but Dobberphul and Blancan protested their innocence. Dobberphul and Blancan were later released and the charges dropped.

6. The core team consisted of Walterfang, who negotiated with the government and local authorities, delegated search operations, and guaranteed financing; Dobberphul, responsible for diving equipment and repairs; the director of domestic service personnel, who acted as a translator and liaison between international and local staff; a caretaker, who acted as a contact person for informants; and a person who acted as a conservator of sorts, being responsible for "taking care of the discoveries." Anonymous, "Unpublished Report: Discovery of the Shipwreck 'BATU HITAM' of the Tang Period in 1998" (2002).

7. Ibid.

8. Simon Worrall, "Made in China: A 1,200-year-old Shipwreck Opens a Window on Ancient Global Trade," *National Geographic Magazine*, June 2009.

9. John Guy, "Arab Dhows and the Persian Gulf-China Connection in the 8th and 9th Centuries" (paper presented at *Exhibition Symposium 'Secrets of the Sea: A Tang Shipwreck and Early Trade in Asia', Tang Center for Early China, New York, April 22, 2017*).

10. Anonymous, "Discovery Report."

11. Michael Flecker, "Maritime Archaeology in Southeast Asia," in *Southeast Asian Ceramics: New Light on Old Pottery*, ed. John Miksic (Singapore: Southeast Asian Ceramic Society of Singapore, 2010).

12. Scriven, "Interview: Scriven/Walterfang."

13. Jerome Lynn Hall, "The Fig and the Spade: Countering the Deceptions of Treasure Hunters," *AIA Archaeology Watch* (2007).

14. Anonymous, "Discovery Report."

15. Ibid.

16. Ibid.

17. Ibid.

18. Scriven, "Interview: Scriven/Walterfang."

19. Michael Flecker, "A 9th-Century Arab or Indian Shipwreck in Indonesian Waters," *International Journal of Nautical Archaeology* 29, no. 2 (2000). Michael Flecker, "The Origin of the Tang Shipwreck: A Look at Its Archaeology and History," in *The Tang Shipwreck: Art and Exchange in the 9th Century*, ed. Alan Chong and Stephen Murphy (Singapore: Asian Civilisations Museum, 2017); Nancy Micklewright and Cheryl Sobas, *Shipwrecked: Tang Treasures and Monsoon Winds*, distributed by YouTube, June 18, 2011. Accessed July 13, 2021. https://www.youtube.com/watch?v=6gQbvUVWSto.

20. Smithsonian Institution, "Media Backgrounder: Discovery, Recovery, Conservation and Exhibition of the Belitung Cargo," press release, March 16, 2011, http://www.asia.si.edu/press/2011/prShipwreckedBackgrounder.asp.

21. Flecker, "Origin of the Tang Shipwreck," 22.

22. President Suharto's resignation in May 1998 had been accompanied by an outbreak of anti-Chinese sentiment and even riots in the capital, Jakarta.

23. Tilman Walterfang, personal communication, *Email correspondence with Tilman Walterfang, March–April 2018*, March 14–April 16, 2018.

24. Agus Sudaryadi, "The Belitung Wreck Site After Commercial Salvage in 1998" (paper presented at *Asia/Pacific Regional Conference on Underwater Cultural Heritage, Manila, The Philippines, November 8–11, 2011*).

25. Ibid.
26. Walterfang, personal communication.
27. Scriven, "Interview: Scriven/Walterfang."
28. Flecker, "Origin of the Tang Shipwreck," 23.
29. Flecker, "A 9th-Century Arab or Indian Shipwreck," 200–209; Flecker, "Maritime Archaeology in Southeast Asia," 85; Michael Flecker, interview by Natali Pearson, June 15, 2016, Singapore.
30. Flecker, "Origin of the Tang Shipwreck," 23.
31. Ibid. Flecker published a photo and cross-sectional drawings of the anchor. See Flecker, "A 9th-Century Arab or Indian Shipwreck," 210–211.
32. Gongaware, "To Exhibit or Not to Exhibit," 217.
33. Flecker used water dredges, which displace sediment horizontally about twelve to fifteen feet, to bury the timbers and thus protect them from shipworms. Michael Flecker, personal communication, *Draft Book*, September 19, 2020.
34. Other than scale, the *Phanom Surin* being a much bigger vessel.
35. Flecker quoted in Gongaware, "To Exhibit or Not to Exhibit," 217.
36. Walterfang, personal communication.
37. This looting is consistent with what is known about the situation in Indonesia post-*Geldermalsen*, whereby Chinese ceramics and precious metals were known targets.
38. Flecker, "Interview: Flecker/Pearson."
39. Jeremy Green, for example, wrote that "objects are only going to be recovered if they have an economic value. Hence the stern of the *Belitung* wreck still lies on the sea-bed." Jeremy Green, "Book Review: Shipwreck [*sic*]: Tang Treasures and Monsoon Winds," *International Journal of Nautical Archaeology* 40, no. 2 (2011): 452. See also Marco Viganò, "The Lost Wood: African Seamasters across the Indian Ocean" (paper presented at *Anno Domini 1000, Finale Ligure, Italy, August 31–September 1, 2013*).
40. Full recovery of a hull is extremely expensive and in fact quite rare. Exceptions include the *Mary Rose*, the *Vasa*, the *Nanhai One*, and the *Batavia*.
41. Green, "Book Review: Shipwreck," 452.
42. Michael Flecker, "Wrecked Twice: Shipwrecks as a Cultural Resource in Southeast Asia," in *Rethinking Cultural Resource Management in Southeast Asia: Preservation, Development and Neglect*, ed. John Miksic, Geok Yian Goh, and Sue O'Connor (London and New York: Anthem Press, 2011); Michael Flecker, "Rake and Pillage: The Fate of Shipwrecks in Southeast Asia," in *Marine Archaeology in Southeast Asia: Innovation and Adaptation*, ed. Heidi Tan (Singapore: Asian Civilisations Museum, 2012).
43. Flecker, "Rake and Pillage," 71, 85.
44. Natali Pearson, "Naval Shipwrecks in Indonesia" (paper presented at *Asia/Pacific Regional Conference on Underwater Cultural Heritage, Hong Kong SAR, November 27–December 2, 2017*).
45. Robyn Woodward, "The Belitung Shipwreck: To Exhibit or Not: A Question of Ethics," *INA Quarterly* 39 (2012); Heather Pringle, "Smithsonian Shipwreck Exhibit Draws Fire from Archaeologists," *Science*. Last updated March 10, 2011. Accessed April 7, 2022. https://www.science.org/content/article/smithsonian-shipwreck-exhibit-draws-fire-archaeologists; Green, "Book Review: Shipwreck"; Laura Allsop, "Shipwreck Exhibit Stirs Up Storm at Smithsonian." *CNN*. Last updated 2011. Accessed July 8, 2021. http://edition.cnn.com/2011/WORLD/asiapcf/03/19/indonesia.wreck.smithsonian.row/index.html.

46. See comments made by scientists and curators in these articles: Pringle, "Shipwreck Exhibit Draws Fire"; Allsop, "Storm at Smithsonian."

47. Gongaware, "To Exhibit or Not to Exhibit," 228. The dragon-head stopper that it is usually displayed with the ewer may not be the original stopper, as when it is fitted inside the mouth of the ewer it blocks the snake's head on the handle. Alan Chong and Stephen Murphy, "Green-Splashed Ceramics for the Middle East," in *The Tang Shipwreck: Art and Exchange in the 9th Century*, ed. Alan Chong and Stephen Murphy (Singapore: Asian Civilisations Museum, 2017), 118.

48. Meg Lambert, "Belitung Shipwreck." *Trafficking Culture*. Last updated August 8, 2012. Accessed July 8, 2021. http://traffickingculture.org/encyclopedia/case-studies/biletung-ship wreck/.

49. Pudak Nayati, "Ownership Rights over Archaeological/Historical Objects Found in Indonesian Waters: Republic of Indonesia Act No. 5 of 1992 on Cultural Heritage Objects and Its Related Regulations," *Singapore Journal of International and Comparative Law* 2 (1998); Pudak Nayati, "Ownership Rights over Archaeological / Historical Objects Found at Sea: A Study of the Republic of Indonesia's Act No. 5 of 1992" (Master's thesis, Dalhousie University, 1995).

50. Shao Da, "Sunken Chinese Treasures Rewrite History." *China Through a Lens*. Last updated May 27, 2004. Accessed July 8, 2021. http://www.china.org.cn/english/2004/May/96 658.htm.

51. Charlie Zhu, "Treasure Hunter Seeks More Shipwreck Riches in Asia." *TreasureNet*. Last updated August 20, 2006. Accessed April 7, 2022. http://www.treasurenet.com/forums /shipwrecks/25153-indonesia-far-east.html.

52. Some of the objects, including the gold, had already been sent to the University of Heidelberg in Germany for chemical analysis after the first salvage season. Nia Naelul Hasanah Ridwan, "The Belitung Shipwreck and Its Ceramic Cargo," *Southeast Asian Ceramics Museum Newsletter* 8, no. 1 (2014); Walterfang, personal communication. See also Jürgen Kremb, "Fund Am Schwarzen Felsen," *Der Spiegel*, 2004; TMC News, "Nelson-Based Treasure Hunter Pleased with Indonesian Crackdown." *TMC News*. Last updated April 9, 2006. Accessed July 8, 2021. http://www.tmcnet.com/usubmit/2006/04/09/1554954.htm.

53. Walterfang says, "I learned later that the Japanese initiator of this transaction sued his Japanese partners for stealing those artefacts." Walterfang, personal communication; Tilman Walterfang, "About Seabed Explorations." *Seabed Explorations*. Last updated 2012. Accessed July 8, 2021. https://tilmanwalterfang.org/Tilman-Walterfang-Seabed-Explorations-3.html.

54. Walterfang, personal communication.

55. Walterfang sought and won an injunction against the German magazine that had published the news for thirteen counts of false reporting. The article has been stricken from the archives, its contents becoming just another of the many claims and allegations made about the management of the *Belitung* objects. My efforts to obtain a copy of this *Der Spiegel* article from 2003 were not successful.

56. Walterfang, personal communication; Barclay Crawford, "Jakarta Targets Jebsen Chief over Role in Treasure Deal," *South China Morning Post*, February 28, 2006.

57. Walterfang's website states that it took "six years at a cost of several million dollars" to desalinate and conserve "53,000 Tang Dynasty relics." Tilman Walterfang, "The Wrecks > Tang Wreck > Conservation > Overview." *Seabed Explorations*. Last updated 2012. Accessed July 8, 2021. http://seabedexplorations.com/discoveries/.

58. Currency not provided in original source, but assumed to be US dollars. Zhu, "Treasure Hunter Seeks More Riches."

59. Andreas Rettel, "The Concept of the Conservation of Seawater Finds," in *The Belitung Shipwreck: Sunken Treasures from Tang China*, ed. Jayne Ward and Zoi Kotitsa (New Zealand: Seabed Explorations, 2004), 105–108.

60. Walterfang, personal communication.

61. Ibid. Some media reports suggest that "under-the table 'gifts'" were also made to high-ranking officials. See Robin McDowell, "Indonesia's Shipwrecks Means Riches and Headaches," *San Diego Union Tribune*, March 31, 2012. Any competitive advantage Indonesia had, for example through republishing, was lost in 2010 with the publication of *Shipwrecked: Tang Treasures and Monsoon Winds*.

62. Walterfang, personal communication.

63. Abdul Khalik, "Bribery Ensures Spoils Go to the Treasure Hunters," *The Jakarta Post*, 20 March 2006; McDowell, "Indonesia's Shipwrecks Means Riches and Headaches."

64. Khalik, "Bribery Ensures Spoils."

65. Walterfang, personal communication.

66. Flecker, "Wrecked Twice," 24–29.

67. Crawford, "Jakarta Targets Jebsen."

68. Walterfang, personal communication.

69. Ridwan, "The Belitung Shipwreck."

70. Mai Lin Tjoa-Bonatz, "Struggles over Historic Shipwrecks in Indonesia: Economic Versus Preservation Interests," in *Cultural Property and Contested Ownership: The Trafficking of Artefacts and the Quest for Restitution*, ed. Brigitta Hauser-Schäublin and Lyndel V. Prott (Abingdon and New York: Routledge, 2016).

71. TMC News, "Treasure Hunter Pleased."

72. Jeffrey Lee Adams, "New Directions in International Heritage Management Research" (PhD dissertation, University of Minnesota, 2010).

73. Tjoa-Bonatz, "Struggles over Historic Shipwrecks," 88.

74. Walterfang, personal communication.

75. Walterfang, "About Seabed Explorations."

76. An attempt by the Indonesian government to auction an entire shipwreck assemblage as a single collection was spectacularly unsuccessful: the 2010 auction of the *Cirebon* cargo received not a single bid. Horst Hubertus Liebner, "The Siren of Cirebon: A 10th Century Trading Vessel Lost in the Java Sea" (PhD dissertation, University of Leeds, 2014).

77. Kremb, "Schwarzen Felsen."

78. Guy, "Arab Dhows and the Persian Gulf-China Connection in the 8th and 9th Centuries"; Da, "Sunken Chinese Treasures."

79. Kremb, "Schwarzen Felsen."

80. Anonymous, "Sentosa Bids on Tang Artifacts." *United Press International.* Last updated 2004. Accessed July 8, 2021. https://www.upi.com/Sentosa-bids-on-Tang-artifacts/10701098655638/.

81. Melissa Wansin Wong, "Negotiating Class, Taste and Culture via the Arts Scene in Singapore," *Asian Theatre Journal* 29, no. 1 (2012): 250.

82. Peggy Levitt, "Arabia and the East: How Singapore and Doha Display the Nation and the World," in *Artifacts and Allegiances: How Museums Put the Nation and the World on Display*, ed. Peggy Levitt (Oakland University of California Press, 2015), 132.

83. George Yeo, "Shipwrecked: Tang Treasures and Monsoon Winds—Opening Address," in *Marine Archaeology in Southeast Asia: Innovation and Adaptation*, ed. Heidi Tan and Alan Chong (Singapore: Asian Civilisations Museum, 2011), 185.

84. William Campbell, "Of Matters Maritime: Lively Display Centre of Sea-Going Activities," *The Straits Times*, September 15, 1974.

85. Yeo, "Opening Address," 184.

86. Ibid., 185.

87. Singapore Law Reports, "Rickshaw Investments Ltd and Another v Nicolai Baron von Uexkull: Case number CA 30/2006, SUM 2929/2006," Court of Appeal Judgement. Last updated 2006. Accessed April 7, 2022. https://www.singaporelawwatch.sg/Portals/0/Docs/Judgments/%5b2006%5d%20SGCA%2039.pdf.

88. Walterfang, personal communication.

89. *Rickshaw Investments Ltd and Another v Nicolai Baron von Uexküll.*

90. Ibid.

91. Ibid.

92. Yeo, "Opening Address," 186.

93. Ibid.; Sentosa, "Sentosa Proceeds to Buy 9th Century Treasure: New Maritime Heritage Foundation Set Up," press release, April 8, 2005, https://archive.is/NXdL3.

94. Rachel Leow, "Curating the Oceans: The Future of Singapore's Past." *A Historian's Craft*. Last updated July 14, 2009. Accessed July 8, 2021. https://idlethink.wordpress.com/2009/07/14/curating-the-oceans-the-future-of-singapores-past/.

95. Roberto Gardellin and Aileen Lau, "Exhibition Review: The Belitung Wreck: A Tang Dynasty (618–906) Cargo," *Oriental Arts* LV, no. 1 (2005).

96. Yeo, "Opening Address," 185. See also Hugh Chow, "Khoo Teck Puat's Grip on 3 Firms Bigger Than Declared," *The Straits Times*, March 19, 2004; L. S. Siow and V. Chong, "Khoo Teck Puat's Secret Stakes Come to Light," *The Business Times*, March 19, 2004.

97. Han Shih Lee, "Not So Khoo Kids." *The Asia Mag*. Last updated March 3, 2009. Accessed 1 June 2017. http://www.theasiamag.com/cheat-sheet/not-so-khoo-kids.

98. Yeo, "Opening Address," 185. One report from 2012 states it was as high as US$28 million—see Deepika Shetty, "Tang Treasures at Hotel," *The Straits Times*, February 9, 2012.

99. Michelle Quah, "Khoo Sisters Fined $500,000, Escape Jail," *The Business Times*, June 21, 2005.

100. George Yeo, "Transcript of Speech Made at Jewel of Muscat Gala Dinner, July 5, 2010, Asian Civilisations Museum." *Facebook*. Last updated July 11, 2010. Accessed May 7, 2016. https://www.facebook.com/note.php?note_id=407550843615. See also Yeo, "Opening Address," 185–186.

101. Sentosa, "Sentosa Proceeds to Buy 9th Century Treasure."

102. Tilman Walterfang, "Discoveries > The Wrecks > Tang Wreck > Exhibitions." *Seabed Explorations*. Last updated 2012. Accessed July 8, 2021. https://seabedexplorations.com/discoveries/.

103. Natali Pearson, "Shipwrecked? The Ethics of Underwater Cultural Heritage in Indonesia," *TAASA Review* 25, no. 2 (2016).

104. Sentosa, "Sentosa Proceeds to Buy 9th Century Treasure."

105. Ibid.

106. *Museum Kabupaten Belitung*; Walterfang, personal communication.

107. Klaus Brinkbäumer et al., "Pyramiden der Tiefsee," *Spiegel Special*, March 31, 2006.

108. Anonymous, "Tongguanyao Museum Opens in Changsha." *China Daily.* Last updated May 16, 2018. Accessed July 8, 2021. http://www.chinadaily.com.cn/a/201805/16/WS5afbf392 a3103f6866ee8c1f.html; Yang Zheng Li Xing, "Hunan Bank of China Successfully Opened the Country's First Beneficiary's Personal Heritage Import Letter of Credit." *Changsha Evening News.* Last updated November 1, 2017. Accessed October 23, 2018. https://m.rednet.cn/mip /detail.asp?id=4462104.

109. Levitt, "Arabia and the East," 91.

110. The *Cirebon*'s pearls warranted scrutiny from Swiss gem experts—see, for example, Michael S. Krzemnicki, "Dating of 1000 year old Pearls from an Archeological Ship Wreck," *Facette Magazine,* February 2016. But the ceramic portion of Qatar's *Cirebon* cargo has suffered a devastating fate by being stored in a hot, dry shipping container in the desert.

111. Lingchao Xu, "Shipwreck 'Treasures' Trace Maritime History." *Shine.* Last updated May 18, 2018. Accessed July 8, 2021. https://www.shine.cn/news/metro/1805184788/; Anony-mous, "Tongguanyao Museum Opens in Changsha."

112. Bruce D. Doar, "China Maritime Silk Road Museum." *China Heritage Quarterly.* Last updated 2005. Accessed July 8, 2021. http://www.chinaheritagequarterly.org/articles.php ?searchterm=001_maritimesilk.inc&issue=001.

113. Kennie Ting, "One Year at the Job—Maritime Silk Route and 'Ilm علم." *Dream of a City.* Last updated September 28, 2017. Accessed July 8, 2021. https://tinyurl.com/Kenny Maritime.

114. Green, "Book Review: Shipwreck," 452.

115. Ibid.

116. Ibid.

117. Michael McCarthy, "Museums and Maritime Archaeology," in *The Oxford Handbook of Maritime Archaeology,* ed. Ben Ford, Donny L. Hamilton, and Alexis Catsambis (Oxford: Oxford University Press, 2011), 1047.

118. Meg Lambert, "In Response." *Things You Can't Take Back: The Illicit Antiquities Trade and Other Cultural Heritage Issues. By a Mouthy Youth. For the Mouthy Youth.* Last updated October 30, 2011. Accessed July 8, 2021. http://mouthyheritage.blogspot.com.au/2011/10/in -response.html.

Chapter 4. Contested

1. Meg Lambert, "I'm Back. I Hope." *Things You Can't Take Back: The Illicit Antiquities Trade and Other Cultural Heritage Issues. By a Mouthy Youth. For the Mouthy Youth.* Last up-dated October 20, 2011. Accessed July 8, 2021. http://mouthyheritage.blogspot.com.au/2011/10 /im-back-i-hope.html.

2. Sean McGrail, "Models, Replicas and Experiments in Nautical Archaeology," *The Mari-ner's Mirror* 61, no. 1 (1975).

3. Alan Chong and Stephen Murphy, eds., *The Tang Shipwreck: Art and Exchange in the 9th Century* (Singapore: Asian Civilisations Museum, 2017), 19.

4. Sentosa, "Sentosa Proceeds to Buy 9th Century Treasure: New Maritime Heritage Foun-dation Set Up," press release, April 8, 2005, https://archive.is/NXdL3; Imtiaz Muqbil, "Pamelia Lee, Senior Director, Tourism Development, Singapore Tourism Board." *Travel Impact News-wire.* Last updated February 2, 2017. Accessed July 8, 2021. https://www.travel-impact-newswire .com/2017/02/pamelia-lee-senior-director-tourism-development-singapore-tourism-board/.

5. Anonymous, "Unearthed Treasure Waits in Singapore," *The Jakarta Globe*, September 22, 2009.

6. Deepika Shetty, "Tang Treasures at Hotel," *The Straits Times*, February 9, 2012.

7. Rachel Leow, "Curating the Oceans: The Future of Singapore's Past." *A Historian's Craft*. Last updated July 14, 2009. Accessed July 8, 2021. https://idlethink.wordpress.com/2009/07/14/curating-the-oceans-the-future-of-singapores-past/; Pamelia Lee, *Singapore, Tourism & Me* (Singapore: Pamelia Lee Pte Ltd., 2004).

8. Lee, *Singapore, Tourism & Me*; Pamelia Lee, "50 Years of Urban Planning and Tourism," in *50 Years of Urban Planning in Singapore*, ed. Chye Kiang Heng (Singapore and Hackensack, NJ: World Scientific Publishing, 2017).

9. Anonymous, "Unearthed Treasure."

10. Nien Yuan Cheng, "'This Is My Doodle': Non-Participation, Performance, and the Singapore Memory Project," *Performance Paradigm* 14 (2018).

11. Sentosa, "Sentosa Proceeds to Buy 9th Century Treasure."

12. Anonymous, "Unearthed Treasure."

13. John Miksic, "Shipwrecked," *IIAS–The Newsletter* 64 (Summer 2013).

14. Kwok recalled that when the museum had opened on nearby Armenian Street in 1997, museum-going culture in Singapore had been "limited." At that time, museums in Singapore had "a rather dusty image . . . the visitors were mainly schoolchildren going to see whalebones. In those days, many people would say that Singapore was a cultural desert." Kenson Kwok, "A Nation Forges Ahead 1985–1994: Hard Slog Building up an Art Collection," in *Living the Singapore Story: Celebrating Our 50 Years, 1965–2015*, ed. Suk Wai Cheong (Singapore: National Library Board, 2015), 105.

15. Anonymous, "Asian Civilisation Museum's Founding Director to Retire," *The Straits Times*, 2008.

16. Kwok, "A Nation Forges Ahead," 105.

17. Krishnasamy Kesavapany and Geoff Wade, "Background Paper on Potential Singapore Maritime Museum" (Singapore: ISEAS, 2009).

18. The Hua Song Museum closed permanently in 2012 and its collection was installed at the Asian Civilisations Museum.

19. Leow, "Curating the Oceans."

20. Ibid.

21. George Yeo, "Transcript of Speech Made at Jewel of Muscat Gala Dinner, July 5, 2010, Asian Civilisations Museum." *Facebook*. Last updated July 11, 2010. Accessed May 7, 2016. https://www.facebook.com/note.php?note_id=407550843615.

22. Kesavapany and Wade, "Background Paper." Advocates included then-director of the Institute of South East Asian Studies, K. Kesavapany; Geoff Wade; historian Tansen Sen; archaeologist John Miksic; influential scholar Kwa Chong Guan; founding director of the ACM Kenson Kwok; Pamelia Lee and Alvin Chia, both of whom were involved in managing the Tang Shipwreck Collection; David Chin; and Chung Chee Kit.

23. Ibid.

24. Stephen Davies, *Maritime Museums: Who Needs Them?*

25. Shetty, "Treasures at Hotel."

26. Ibid.

27. Site visit, June 9, 2016.

28. Shetty, "Treasures at Hotel."

29. The items displayed at NUS Museum were not loaned free of charge; NUS Museum had to pay the Singapore Tourism Board a fee per item per year. Since the ownership of the collection shifted to the National Heritage Board, more *Belitung* items have gone on display in the NUS Museum and no fee is charged.

30. John Miksic, ed. *Southeast Asian Ceramics: New Light on Old Pottery* (Singapore: Southeast Asian Ceramic Society of Singapore, 2010).

31. Pei Jun Jermaine Chua and Tse Siang Lim, "UCV2208 Sinbad, Shipwrecks and Singapore." *National University of Singapore.* Last updated 2009/2010. Accessed July 8, 2021. https:// tinyurl.com/Sinbadand-Singapore. This module was adapted for two other undergraduate modules: one focusing on Singapore's maritime history and identity, and the other on Southeast Asia's maritime history and culture. See John Miksic, "GES1030 Singapore and the Sea." *National University of Singapore.* Last updated 2016/2017. Accessed July 8, 2021. https://tinyurl .com/SingaporeandtheSea; John Miksic, "SE3227 Maritime History and Culture of Southeast Asia." *National University of Singapore.* Last updated 2017/2018. Accessed July 8, 2021. https:// tinyurl.com/MaritimeSEA.

32. Michael Flecker, "A 9th-Century Arab or Indian Shipwreck in Indonesian Waters: Addendum," *International Journal of Nautical Archaeology* 37, no. 2 (2008): 386.

33. As discussed in chapter 1, the timber used for the hull and most of the frames was determined to be *Afzelia africana* from Africa. The through-beams—transverse timbers that lock the two sides of the ship together, their ends protruding outside the hull—were teak (*Tectona grandis*), probably from India. The ceiling timbers were a species of juniper (*Juniperus spp.*), "which grows in Arabia, among other areas." Tom Vosmer et al., "The 'Jewel of Muscat' Project: Reconstructing an Early Ninth-Century CE Shipwreck," *Proceedings of the Seminar for Arabian Studies* 41 (2011): 412. Note, however, that these findings are contested. See Stephen Haw, "The Genus Afzelia and the Belitung Ship," *Journal of the Royal Asiatic Society* 29, no. 3 (2019).

34. Vosmer et al., "Reconstructing an Early Ninth-Century Shipwreck," 414.

35. Ibid.

36. Flecker, "Addendum," 386.

37. Eric Staples, "Sewn-Plank Reconstructions of Oman: Construction and Documentation," *International Journal of Nautical Archaeology* 48, no. 2 (2019).

38. Singapore's proposal, with which Pamelia Lee was involved, was originally sent to the Oman Ministry of Foreign Affairs, which referred it to His Excellency Abdul Aziz al-Rowas, Cultural Affairs Advisor to the Sultan. He sought advice from Tom Vosmer, who was at the time undertaking postgraduate research on maritime technologies of the western Indian Ocean and acting as an archaeological and museum adviser. Due to the size of the project it was subsequently returned to the Ministry of Foreign Affairs, which saw it as an opportunity to enhance relations with Singapore. Vosmer remained involved in the project and played an important role in assembling the international team of archaeologists, many of whom had previously worked together on the *Magan* reed boat project. Tom Vosmer, Personal communication, *Omani Involvement with Belitung*, July 6, 2021.

39. Robert Jackson, "Sailing through Time: The Jewel of Muscat," *Saudi Aramco World: Arab and Islamic Cultures and Connections*, May/June 2012; Vosmer, personal communication.

40. Linda Pappas Funsch, *Oman Reborn: Balancing Tradition and Modernization* (New York: Palgrave Macmillan, 2015).

41. Staples, "Sewn-Plank Reconstructions," 315. See also George Hourani, *Arab Seafaring in the Indian Ocean in Ancient and Early Medieval Times*, 2nd ed. (Princeton, NJ: Princeton

University Press, 1995); *The Periplus Maris Erythraei: Text with Introduction, Translation, and Commentary*, trans. Lionel Casson (Princeton, NJ: Princeton University Press, 1989).

42. Tim Severin, *The Sindbad Voyage* (New York: Putnam, 1983).

43. Staples, "Sewn-Plank Reconstructions," 328.

44. Ibid.

45. Funsch, *Oman Reborn*.

46. Staples, "Sewn-Plank Reconstructions."

47. Vosmer et al., "Reconstructing an Early Ninth-Century Shipwreck," 414.

48. Ibid., 416.

49. The team also conducted tank tests using a model and wind tunnel tests of a model of the rig, both of which led to some minor modifications. In the end, the *Jewel of Muscat* performed even better than these tests had suggested. Tom Vosmer, personal communication, *Belitung Afterlives*, June 10, 2021; Vosmer et al., "Reconstructing an Early Ninth-Century Shipwreck."

50. Vosmer et al., "Reconstructing an Early Ninth-Century Shipwreck," 416.

51. Michael Flecker, "A 9th-Century Arab or Indian Shipwreck in Indonesian Waters," *International Journal of Nautical Archaeology* 29, no. 2 (2000): 209.

52. Vosmer et al., "Reconstructing an Early Ninth-Century Shipwreck," 414.

53. Ibid., 416.

54. Steaming was found to be the most effective method for the project team to fit a hot softened plank to the right bend and twist, as they had neither the skills nor the experience for the soaking/fork-bending or fire-bending techniques. Vosmer, personal communication.

55. Staples, "Sewn-Plank Reconstructions."

56. Vosmer et al., "Reconstructing an Early Ninth-Century Shipwreck," 417.

57. Such stitched-hull construction techniques are still used by some boatbuilding communities in the Middle East.

58. Tom Vosmer, "The Jewel of Muscat: Reconstructing a Ninth-Century Sewn-Plank Boat," in *Shipwrecked: Tang Treasures and Monsoon Winds*, ed. Regina Krahl et al. (Singapore: Arthur M. Sackler Gallery, Smithsonian Institution, Washington D.C.; National Heritage Board, Singapore; Singapore Tourism Board, 2010), 131.

59. Vosmer et al., "Reconstructing an Early Ninth-Century Shipwreck."

60. Ibid.; Megan Furman, *Jewel of Muscat: On the High Seas in a 9th Century Sailing Ship* (Oman: Lingua Franca Television Limited, 2015); Eric Staples and Lucy Blue, "Archaeological, Historical, and Ethnographic Approaches to the Study of Sewn Boats: Past, Present, and Future," *International Journal of Nautical Archaeology* 48, no. 2 (2019); Eric Staples, "An Experiment in Arab Navigation: The Jewel of Muscat Passage," in *The Principles of Arab Navigation*, ed. Anthony R. Constable and William Facey (London: Arabian Publishing, 2013); Vosmer et al., "Reconstructing an Early Ninth-Century Shipwreck"; Staples, "Sewn-Plank Reconstructions"; Anonymous, "Jewel of Muscat." Last updated 2010. Accessed July 8, 2021. http://jewelofmuscat.tv/.

61. Staples, "Sewn-Plank Reconstructions." See also Vosmer et al., "Reconstructing an Early Ninth-Century Shipwreck."

62. Staples, "An Experiment in Arab Navigation," 49; Noel Hidalgo Tan, "Aboard the Jewel of Muscat." *The Southeast Asian Archaeology Newsblog*. Last updated June 16, 2010. Accessed July 8, 2021. https://www.southeastasianarchaeology.com/2010/06/16/aboard-jewel-muscat/.

63. Staples, "An Experiment in Arab Navigation," 49.

64. Vosmer et al., "Reconstructing an Early Ninth-Century Shipwreck," 422.

65. Anonymous, "Jewel of Muscat—Timeline." Last updated 2010. Accessed July 8, 2021. http://jewelofmuscat.tv/the-timeline/.

66. Vosmer et al., "Reconstructing an Early Ninth-Century Shipwreck," 416. Furthermore, it had survived the edge of a cyclone in the Bay of Bengal, winds of over fifty knots, seas of five to six meters, and boat speeds of up to eleven knots. Vosmer, personal communication.

67. Site visit, June 11, 2016.

68. Yeo, "Gala Dinner Speech."

69. Ibid.

70. Resorts World Sentosa, *Maritime Experiential Museum & Aquarium Grand Opening*, distributed by YouTube, October 19, 2011. Accessed October 19, 2017. https://www.youtube.com/watch?v=55cf-YaW3xU.

71. Resorts World Sentosa, "Presenting the World's Largest Oceanarium, the Marine Life Park." *Resorts World Sentosa*. Last updated September 25, 2011. Accessed October 19, 2017. http://www.rwsentosablog.com/so%E2%80%A6-why-should-i-visit-mema/.

The Maritime Experiential Museum closed in March 2020 as part of a major redevelopment of Resorts World Sentosa. The adjacent S.E.A. Aquarium will be expanded, taking over the museum to become a much larger aquarium. The fate of the *Jewel of Muscat* as part of this refurbishment is unknown.

72. Nicholas Dejiki, "Maritime Experiential Museum and Aquarium." *Dejiki*. Last updated October 8, 2011. Accessed July 8, 2021. https://dejiki.com/2011/10/mema/.

73. Resorts World Sentosa, "So . . . Why Should I Visit Maritime Experiential Museum?" *Resorts World Sentosa*. Last updated October 3, 2011. Accessed October 19, 2017. http://www.rwsentosablog.com/so%E2%80%A6-why-should-i-visit-mema/.

74. Dejiki, *Maritime Experiential Museum*.

75. Resorts World Sentosa, "Discovering Southeast Asia's Maritime History." *Resorts World Sentosa*. Last updated September 6, 2011. Accessed October 19, 2017. http://www.rwsentosablog.com/discovering-southeast-asias-maritime-history/.

76. Ibid. There were "a Chinese junk, an Indian dhow, a Javanese jong, an Indonesian borobudur, and a South China Seas trading vessel." Note that the "borobudur" terminology betrays a fundamental mistake. This is a replica of an Indonesian (probably Javanese) ship modeled on one shown in a relief at Borobudur temple in central Java, Indonesia. It would be more accurate to describe it as a tentative reconstruction of an eighth-century Indonesian ship. This Indonesian ship is one of a pair, the other being housed at the Samudra Raksa Museum, located near Borobudur temple.

77. Site visit, June 11, 2016.

78. Electrosonic, "Typhoon Theatre at the Maritime Experiential Museum." *Electrosonic*. Last updated 2015. Accessed July 8, 2021. https://www.electrosonic.com/projects/typhoon-theatre-at-the-maritime-experiential-museum.

79. Pierre Balloffet, François H. Courvoisier, and Joëlle Lagier, "From Museum to Amusement Park: The Opportunities and Risks of Edutainment," *International Journal of Arts Management* 16, no. 2 (2014): 4.

80. Kai Ling Ng, "Sail through a Typhoon at Maritime Museum: Typhoon Theatre among Main Attractions," *The Straits Times*, October 7, 2011.

81. Ibid.

82. Ibid. Walterfang had initially intended for the *Bakau* wreck objects to go on display at the maritime museum he had committed to building in Bali as part of the *Intan/Belitung* deal.

Reuters, "US$50m Plan Is in Place to Salvage Asian Wrecks," *New Zealand Herald,* August 3, 2006. The *Bakau* objects have not been on display since at least 2018, and their current whereabouts are unknown.

83. *Shipwrecked* was initially scheduled to be exhibited at the ArtScience Museum until July 31, 2011. However, on July 28, 2011, three days before it was due to close, the exhibition was extended until October 2, 2011. Marina Bay Sands and Singapore Tourism Board, "Shipwrecked: Tang Treasures and Monsoon Winds Exhibition Extended till 2 October 2011 at ArtScience Museum: Complimentary Entry to Exhibition during the Week of National Day," press release, July 28, 2011, https://tinyurl.com/ShipwreckedExtension.

84. Meg Lambert, "Belitung Shipwreck." *Trafficking Culture.* Last updated August 8, 2012. Accessed July 8, 2021. http://traffickingculture.org/encyclopedia/case-studies/biletung-shipwreck/.

85. Smithsonian Institution, "Shipwrecked: Tang Treasures and Monsoon Winds—About the Organizers." *Smithsonian Institution.* Last updated 2011. Accessed October 11, 2017. https://www.asia.si.edu/Shipwrecked/about.asp.

86. Jacqueline Trescott, "Sackler Gallery Postpones Controversial 'Shipwreck' Show," *Washington Post,* June 28, 2011; Office of Public Affairs and Marketing, Freer Gallery of Art and the Arthur M. Sackler Gallery, "Smithsonian and Singapore Organize World Tour of Shipwreck Treasure: Exhibition Highlights One of the Most Important Marine Archaeological Finds of the Late 20th Century," press release, September 27, 2010, https://web.archive.org/web/20100927094716/http://www.asia.si.edu/press/prShipwreck.htm.

87. Smithsonian Institution, "Shipwrecked: Tang Treasures and Monsoon Winds—Venues." *Smithsonian Institution.* Last updated 2011. Accessed October 11, 2017. https://www.asia.si.edu/Shipwrecked/venues.asp.

88. Rachel Leow, "The Oceans Curated: A Review of 'Shipwrecked' at the Singapore ArtScience Museum." *A Historian's Craft.* Last updated June 6, 2011. Accessed July 8, 2021. https://idlethink.wordpress.com/2011/06/06/the-oceans-curated/.

89. Nicholas Dejiki, "The ArtScience Museum." *Dejiki.* Last updated April 30, 2011. Accessed July 8, 2021. https://dejiki.com/2011/04/.

90. Leow, *The Oceans Curated.*

91. Duncan Macleod, "Shipwrecked Tang Treasures and Monsoon Winds." *The Inspiration Room.* Last updated 2011. Accessed July 8, 2021. http://theinspirationroom.com/daily/2011/shipwrecked-tang-treasures-and-monsoon-winds/.

92. Campaign Brief Asia, "BBH Uncovers Treasures of the Deep." *Campaign Brief Asia.* Last updated March 14, 2011. Accessed July 8, 2021. http://www.campaignbriefasia.com/2011/03/bbh-uncovers-treasures-of-the.html.

93. Marina Bay Sands, "Titanic: The Artifact Exhibition Sails to New Record-Breaking Attendance," press release, May 4, 2012, https://tinyurl.com/MarinaBayTitanic.

94. Sonia Kolesnikov-Jessop, "Ancient Arab Shipwreck Yields Secrets of Ninth-Century Trade," *New York Times,* March 7, 2011.

95. Heather Pringle, "Worries Mount over Smithsonian Shipwreck Exhibit," *Science* (website). Last updated April 29, 2011. Accessed April 7, 2022. https://www.science.org/content/article/worries-mount-over-smithsonian-shipwreck-exhibit.

96. When it first opened, entrance fees to the ArtScience Museum were significantly higher than for the Maritime Experiential Museum or Singapore's national museums: SGD$30 to en-

ter the ArtScience Museum, compared with national museums such as the Asian Civilisations Museum (SGD\$8) or the National Museum of Singapore (SGD\$10).

97. International Council of Museums, *ICOM Definition of a Museum* (Austria: International Council of Museums, 2007).

98. The other two temporary exhibitions were from overseas. *Genghis Khan: The Exhibition* featured over two hundred "rare authentic treasures" loaned by private collectors, and was organized and curated by Don Lessem, a dinosaur expert and president of commercial exhibition company Exhibits Rex. Marina Bay Sands, "Genghis Khan 'Invades' Singapore: Largest Collection of Genghis Khan Artifacts Makes Exclusive Asian Appearance in Singapore," press release, January 10, 2011, https://tinyurl.com/MarinaBayGenghisKhan. Meanwhile, *Traveling the Silk Road: Ancient Pathway To the Modern World* was organized by the American Museum of Natural History, and subsequently traveled to national museums in the Asia Pacific and Europe, including the National Museum of Australia. Marina Bay Sands, "Travel the Ancient Silk Road for the First Time in Asia," Press Release, February 1, 2011, https://tinyurl.com/MarinaBaySilkRoad.

The long-term exhibition, *A Journey Through Creativity,* centered on three thematic galleries: Curiosity, Inspiration, and Expression. This exhibition was, as Zaller explained, designed to "explore the relationships between art and science in the creative process." Dejiki, *The ArtScience Museum*; Enilyn Eng, "ArtScience: A Journey through Creativity." *Fresh Grads: Dreams of Life.* Last updated March 20, 2011. Accessed October 23, 2017. http://freshgrads.sg/index.php/articles/lifestyle/upcoming-events/1195-artscience-a-journey-through-creativity; Iliyas Ong, "In New Museum, Art and Science Collide." *Design Taxi.* Last updated February 25, 2011. Accessed October 23, 2017. http://designtaxi.com/article/101536/In-New-Museum-Art-and-Science-Collide/.

99. Deepika Shetty, "Treasure Trails: Three Mega Exhibitions Opening at the ArtScience Museum Take Viewers Back into the Past," *The Straits Times,* 2011.

100. Following the closure of *Titanic: The Artifact Exhibition* at the ArtScience Museum in April 2012, another Titanic exhibition, *Titanic: The Exhibition,* opened just a few months later at the Venetian Macao Resort Hotel (October 25, 2012–February 24, 2013). This new exhibition was owned by Imagine Exhibitions—which, as noted, had a close connection with the ArtScience Museum through Thomas Zaller—and was near-identical to the original *Titanic: The Artifact Exhibition.* The owners of *Titanic: The Artifact Exhibition,* RMS Titanic Inc. and Premier Exhibitions, responded to the new exhibition by commencing legal proceedings. They alleged that Zaller had used his role, as a promoter and as a former executive of Premier Exhibitions, to facilitate the placement of *Titanic: The Artifact Exhibition* at the ArtScience Museum in 2011. They also claimed he had used confidential material to create "a striking copy" of the original exhibition, and that he had used underwater videos and photographs from the original exhibition to promote his own exhibition. These events led legal observers to describe the ArtScience Museum as the site of "a compelling story of corporate intrigue and systematic piracy of an entire Titanic exhibition by a former employee." Kirk W. Watkins, "Titanic Intellectual Lawsuit Launched to Sink Competing Enterprise." *The National Law Review.* Last updated March 9, 2013. Accessed October 23, 2017. https://www.natlawreview.com/article/titanic-intellectual-property-lawsuit-launched-to-sink-competing-enterprise. To this day, *Titanic: The Artifact Exhibition* and *Titanic: The Exhibition* continue to tour the world.

101. Marina Bay Sands, "Record-Breaking Attendance"; Akshita Nanda, "Moored in Controversy: The Excavation of Tang Relics from a Shipwreck in Indonesia puts Museums in a Quandary," *The Straits Times,* June 30, 2011.

102. Ross Anderson, "From the President's Desk: Advisory Council for Underwater Archaeology," *AIMA Newsletter: Australasian Institute for Maritime Archaeology* 30, no. 1 (2011).

103. Kate Taylor, "Treasure Poses Ethics Issues for Smithsonian," *New York Times*, April 24, 2011; Heather Pringle, "Smithsonian Shipwreck Exhibit Draws Fire from Archaeologists," *Science*. Last updated March 10, 2011. Accessed April 7, 2022. https://www.science.org/content /article/smithsonian-shipwreck-exhibit-draws-fire-archaeologists.

104. Nanda, "Moored in Controversy."

105. Pringle, "Shipwreck Exhibit Draws Fire."

106. Heather Pringle, "Flap over Shipwreck Exhibit," *Science* 331, no. 6023 (2011).

107. They included the Society for American Archaeology, ACUA, SHA, CAMM (of which the Smithsonian Institution was a member), the ICOMOS International Committee on the Underwater Cultural Heritage, and representatives from the National Academy of Sciences. The controversy was widely covered in blogs and media outlets and has also been the focus of at least four research theses: Natali Pearson, "Salvaging a Wreck: The Afterlife of the *Belitung* Shipwreck" (PhD dissertation, University of Sydney, 2018); Pelin Rohde, "Sunken Treasures, Worldly Pleasures: The Smithsonian's Shipwrecked Exhibition and the Museum's Role in the Preservation of Underwater Cultural Heritage" (Master's thesis, Harvard University, 2013); Laura Gongaware, "Finding a Middle Ground in the Protection of the Underwater Cultural Heritage" (Master's thesis, Texas A&M, 2013); and Meg Lambert, "'Shipwrecked': Private Feuds and Public Consequences" (Bachelor's thesis, Bennington College, 2012).

108. Laura Allsop, "Shipwreck Exhibit Stirs Up Storm at Smithsonian." *CNN*. Last updated 2011. Accessed July 8, 2021. http://edition.cnn.com/2011/WORLD/asiapcf/03/19/indonesia .wreck.smithsonian.row/index.html; Taylor, "Treasure Poses Ethics Issues"; Ira Mellman, "Treasure Hunting Complicates Exhibit of Important Shipwreck Find." *Voice of America*. Last updated 2011. Accessed July 8, 2021. https://www.voanews.com/a/treasure-hunting-complicates -important-shipwreck-find-120730039/167373.html; Jacqueline Trescott, "Another Smithsonian Debate: Should the Sackler Gallery Show Artifacts from a Commercially Excavated Shipwreck?," *Washington Post*, April 28, 2011; Elizabeth Blair, *From Beneath, A Smithsonian Shipwreck Controversy*, NPR, 2011.

109. Smithsonian Institution, "Archives Accession 15–174: Office of the Secretary, Administrative Records" (Washington D.C.: Smithsonian Institution, 2011).

110. Archaeological Institute of America, "AIA Statement on Belitung Shipwreck," press release, June 8, 2011, http:// www.archaeological.org/statement-on-belitung-shipwreck/.

111. Rohde, "Sunken Treasures, Worldly Pleasures."

112. Lambert, "Belitung Shipwreck."

113. Julian Raby, "Why Exhibit This Material?" *Freer Sackler*. Last updated 2011. Accessed August 25, 2017. http://www.asia.si.edu/exhibitions/SW-CulturalHeritage/why.asp.

114. Ibid.

115. Miksic, "Shipwrecked," 43.

116. Jeremy Green, "Book Review: Shipwreck [*sic*]: Tang Treasures and Monsoon Winds," *International Journal of Nautical Archaeology* 40, no. 2 (2011).

117. Ibid.

118. Nancy Micklewright and Cheryl Sobas, *Shipwrecked: Tang Treasures and Monsoon Winds*, distributed by YouTube, June 18, 2011. Accessed July 13, 2021. https://www.youtube.com /watch?v=6gQbvUVWSto.

119. Ibid.

120. Blair, *From Beneath, A Smithsonian Shipwreck Controversy*, 2011.

121. Smithsonian Institution, *Smithsonian Directive 604: Misconduct in Research* (Washington D.C.: Smithsonian Institution, 2009).

122. Trescott, "Another Smithsonian Debate"; Caixia Lu, "The Belitung Shipwreck Controversy," *The Newsletter—Institute for Southeast Asian Studies, Nalanda-Sriwijaya Centre*, no. 58 (Autumn/Winter 2011).

123. Taylor, "Treasure Poses Ethics Issues."

124. Derek Fincham, "The Smithsonian Postpones Dhow Exhibition." *Illicit Cultural Property*. Last updated June 29, 2011. Accessed July 8, 2021. http://illicitculturalproperty.com/the-smithsonian-postpones-dhow-exhibition/.

125. Richard Hodges (director of the University of Pennsylvania Museum of Archeology and Anthropology) quoted in Trescott, "Another Smithsonian Debate."

126. Thijs Maarleveld (president of the International Committee on the Underwater Cultural Heritage) quoted in Trescott, "Another Smithsonian Debate."

127. I have chosen not to identify this individual, or the details of when and where this statement was made, due to the inflammatory nature of the debate.

128. June 18–19, 2011, Asian Civilisations Museum, Singapore. See: Heidi Tan, ed., *Marine Archaeology in Southeast Asia: Innovation and Adaptation* (Singapore: Asian Civilisations Museum, 2012).

129. Micklewright and Sobas, *Shipwrecked: Tang Treasures and Monsoon Winds.*

130. Ibid.

131. Ibid.

132. Ibid.

133. The only other paper not published was that presented by the SEAMEO-SPAFA representative. Tan, *Marine Archaeology in Southeast Asia.*

134. Micklewright and Sobas, *Shipwrecked: Tang Treasures and Monsoon Winds.*

135. Again, I have chosen not to identify this individual, or the details of when and where this statement was made.

136. The suddenness was significant. Exhibitions are often planned up to five years in advance, so this announcement, coming as it did in late June 2011, gave curators at the Sackler Gallery just nine months' notice.

137. Trescott, "Sackler Gallery Postpones."

138. Chuck Meide, "Smithsonian Postpones Controversial Treasure Hunting Shipwreck Exhibit." *The Keeper's Blog*. Last updated July 6, 2011. Accessed April 7, 2022. http://www.blogstaugustinelighthouse.org/blog/lamposts/smithsonian_postpones_controve.php.

139. Quoted in ibid.

140. Nanda, "Moored in Controversy."

141. Ibid.

142. Marina Bay Sands, "ArtScience Museum at Marina Bay Sands Launches New Ticketing Structure Benefiting Singaporeans," press release, July 29, 2011, https://tinyurl.com/MarinaBayTickets.

143. Nanda, "Moored in Controversy."

144. Marina Bay Sands and Singapore Tourism Board, "Exhibition Extended."

145. Ibid.

146. Nanda, "Moored in Controversy."

147. Robyn Woodward, "The Belitung Shipwreck: To Exhibit or Not: A Question of Ethics," *INA Quarterly* 39 (2012).

148. Akshita Nanda, "Salvaging a Wrecked Opportunity," *The Straits Times*, December 28, 2011; Jacqueline Trescott, "Sackler Gallery Cancels Controversial Exhibit of Tang Dynasty Treasures from Shipwreck," *Washington Post*, December 15, 2011. See also Heather Pringle, "Smithsonian Scuppers Shipwreck Exhibit, Plans to Re-Excavate," *Science*. Last updated December 16, 2011. Accessed April 7, 2022. https://www.science.org/content/article/smithsonian -scuppers-shipwreck-exhibit-plans-re-excavate.

149. Woodward, "A Question of Ethics."

150. Ibid.

151. Agus Sudaryadi, "The Belitung Wreck Site after Commercial Salvage in 1998" (paper presented at *Asia/Pacific Regional Conference on Underwater Cultural Heritage, Manila, The Philippines, November 8–11, 2011*).

152. The divers, one of whom had worked on the first season of the *Belitung* salvage, were subsequently released without charge. Underwater Times News Service, "German, French Diver Accused of Looting Shipwreck in Indonesia Freed on Bond; '100% Innocent'." *Underwater Times News Service*. Last updated April 13, 2006. Accessed July 8, 2021. http://www.underwa-tertimes.com/news.php?article_id=17561090324; "French Diver Condemns Detention by Indonesia over Salvaging Treasure." *Do Fundo Do Mar*. Last updated March 27, 2006. Accessed July 8, 2021. http://dofundodomar.blogspot.com.au/2006_03_01_dofundodomar_archive.html; Abdul Khalik, "Police Arrest Two Foreigners for Taking Ancient Ceramics," *Jakarta Post*, March 10, 2006; Semy Havid, "Harta Karun di Dasar Laut Perairan Indonesia, Menunggu Diangkat!" *Indonesia Waters*. Last updated March 24, 2011. Accessed July 8, 2021. https://semyhavid.blogspot.com.au/2011/03/harta-karun-di-dasar-laut-perairan.html.

153. Sudaryadi, "The Belitung Wreck Site after Commercial Salvage in 1998."

154. Krishnasamy Kesavapany, "Vital to Spread Knowledge about South-East Asia's Past," *The Straits Times*, January 13, 2012.

155. Akshita Nanda, "Salvaging a Wrecked Opportunity," *The Straits Times*, December 28, 2011.

156. Andy Ho, "Academe's Exhibition of Parochialism," *The Straits Times*, December 23, 2011.

157. Nanda, "Salvaging a Wrecked Opportunity."

158. Derek Fincham, "Looting Shipwrecks, Archaeology and the Smithsonian." *Illicit Cultural Property*. Last updated May 6, 2011. Accessed July 8, 2021. http://illicitculturalproperty. com/looting-shipwrecks-archaeology-and-the-smithsonian/.

159. Rohde, "Sunken Treasures, Worldly Pleasures," 56–57.

160. Aw Kah Peng, "Foreword," in *Shipwrecked: Tang Treasures and Monsoon Winds*, ed. Regina Krahl et al. (Singapore: Arthur M. Sackler Gallery, Smithsonian Institution, Washington, D.C.; National Heritage Board, Singapore; Singapore Tourism Board, 2010).

161. Yeo, "Gala Dinner Speech."

Chapter 5. Reimagined

1. Refer to Appendix: Exhibition List for details.

2. Deepika Shetty, "Tang Treasures at Hotel," *The Straits Times*, February 9, 2012.

3. Akshita Nanda, "Moored in Controversy: The Excavation of Tang Relics from a Shipwreck in Indonesia puts Museums in a Quandary," *The Straits Times*, June 30, 2011.

4. Akshita Nanda, "Salvaging a Wrecked Opportunity," *The Straits Times*, December 28, 2011.

5. Peggy Levitt, "Arabia and the East: How Singapore and Doha Display the Nation and the World," in *Artifacts and Allegiances: How Museums Put the Nation and the World on Display*, ed. Peggy Levitt (Oakland: University of California Press, 2015), 95.

6. Sharon See, "ACM Showcases Tang Dynasty Artefacts from 9th Century Shipwreck." *Archaeology News Network*. Last updated January 31, 2012. Accessed July 8, 2021. https://archaeologynewsnetwork.blogspot.com.au/2012/01/acm-showcases-tang-dynasty-artefacts.html#CVH4I1MFVXFdLop8.97.

7. Sandra H. Dudley, "Materiality Matters: Experiencing the Displayed Object," *University of Michigan Working Papers in Museum Studies* 8 (2012): 1.

8. See "ACM Showcases Tang Dynasty Artefacts."

9. Ibid.

10. Dudley, "Materiality Matters."

11. Ibid., 2. See also: Sandra H. Dudley, ed., *Museum Materialities: Objects, Engagements, Interpretations* (Abingdon: Routledge, 2010).

12. Dudley, "Materiality Matters," 2.

13. Stephen Greenblatt, "Resonance and Wonder," in *Exhibiting Cultures: The Poetics and Politics of Museum Display*, ed. Ivan Karp and Steven D. Levine (Washington and London: Smithsonian Institution Press, 1991), 45.

14. National Heritage Board. *National Heritage Board Annual Report 2014/2015—Financial Statements*.

15. Lisa Rochon, "Maki's Aga Khan Museum Makes Its Debut." *Architectural Record*. Last updated September 19, 2014. Accessed July 8, 2021. https://www.architecturalrecord.com/articles/3233-makis-aga-khan-museum-makes-its-debut?

16. Aga Khan Museum, "Mission." *Aga Khan Museum*. Last updated 2018. Accessed July 8, 2021. https://www.agakhanmuseum.org/about/mission.

17. Kate Taylor, "Why Toronto's Aga Khan Park Risks Becoming a White Elephant," *The Globe and Mail*, May 28, 2015.

18. Dionisius A. Agius, *In the Wake of the Dhow: The Arabian Gulf and Oman* (Reading, UK: Garnet Publishing, 2002); Abdul Sheriff, *Dhow Cultures of the Indian Ocean: Cosmopolitanism, Commerce, and Islam* (London: Hurst, 2010).

19. Aga Khan Museum, "North American Exclusive Premiere Showcases Ancient Cargo Lost at Sea: The Lost Dhow Exhibition Opens December 13 at the Aga Khan Museum," press release, December 8, 2014, https://www.agakhanmuseum.org/about/pdf/LostDhow_Press%20release2014.12.08.pdf.

20. Canada Art Channel, *Interview with Alan Chong, Director, Asian Civilisations Museum*, distributed by YouTube, December 11, 2014. Accessed April 10, 2017. https://www.youtube.com/watch?v=jfI5pnTn-1U.

21. Simon Worrall, *The Lost Dhow: A Discovery from the Maritime Silk Route* (Toronto: Aga Khan Museum, 2015). Worrall had previously written about the *Belitung* cargo for *National Geographic*. See: Simon Worrall, "Made in China: A 1,200-year-old Shipwreck Opens a Window on Ancient Global Trade," *National Geographic Magazine*, June 2009.

22. Origin Studios, "Aga Khan Museum The Lost Dhow: A Discovery from the Maritime Silk Route." Last updated 2015. Accessed July 8, 2021. http://www.originstudios.com/aga -khan-lost-dhow/.

23. The instructions to the model-makers were that they were to proceed at the same pace as the construction of the *Jewel of Muscat*, copying each feature to scale. In reality, they did not match the speed of the *Jewel of Muscat* construction. I am grateful to Tom Vosmer for this point.

24. Footage of the exhibition from Christian de Caermichael, *The Book of 25—The Aga Khan Museum—The Lost Dhow Part 1*, distributed by YouTube, January 19, 2015. Accessed April 10, 2017. https://www.youtube.com/watch?v=YIgE1Yg1DT8.

25. Footage of the exhibition. Ibid.

26. Alan Chong and Stephen Murphy, eds., *The Tang Shipwreck: Art and Exchange in the 9th Century* (Singapore: Asian Civilisations Museum, 2017), 118.

27. Ibid., 107.

28. James Wiener, "Treasures of the Lost Dhow." *Ancient History et cetera*. Last updated 2015. Accessed July 8, 2021. http://etc.ancient.eu/interviews/treasures-of-the-lost-dhow/.

29. Aga Khan Museum, "Shipwrecked at the Aga Khan: Position Paper" (Toronto: Aga Khan Museum, 2014), 2.

30. Ibid.

31. Ibid., 11.

32. Stephen Murphy, interview by Natali Pearson, June 10, 2016, Singapore.

33. Aga Khan Museum, "North American Exclusive."

34. Ibid.

35. Aga Khan Museum, "Symposium: The Belitung Shipwreck and the Maritime Silk Route," (Toronto: Aga Khan Museum, 2015).

36. Ibid.

37. Ibid. The roundtable was moderated by Dan Rahimi (Executive Director of Galleries, University of Pennsylvania Museum of Archaeology and Anthropology). Speakers were James Delgado (Director of Maritime Heritage, National Marine Sanctuaries, National Oceanic and Atmospheric Administration), Bobby Orillaneda (Underwater Archaeology Section, National Museum of the Philippines), and Chen Shen (Vice President, World Cultures, Senior Curator, Bishop White Chair of East Asian Archaeology, Royal Ontario Museum).

38. Aga Khan Museum, "Position Paper." There was an entrance fee for the symposium (CAD$50 for the general public, CAD$45 for members, and CAD$25 for seniors and students), which, while typical for a symposium, does seem to work against the goal of increased public engagement. Aga Khan Museum, "Symposium."

39. Kate Taylor, "Treasure Poses Ethics Issues for Smithsonian," *New York Times*, April 24, 2011.

40. Murphy, "Interview: Murphy/Pearson."

41. Chen Shen, "The Lost Dhow: Cultural Heritage and Museum Engagement" (paper presented at *Lost Dhow Symposium, Aga Khan Museum, Toronto, February 28, 2015*).

42. Murphy, "Interview: Murphy/Pearson."

43. Channel News Asia, "Asian Civilisations Museum to House Tang Shipwreck Collection." *Channel News Asia*. Last updated April 28, 2015. Accessed October 20, 2017. http://www .channelnewsasia.com/news/singapore/asian-civilisations/1813022.html.

44. National Heritage Board, "Our Treasures." *National Heritage Board*. Last updated August 29, 2017. Accessed July 8, 2021. https://oursgheritage.sg/what-is-the-heritage-plan-for -singapore/our-treasures/.

45. National Heritage Board. *National Heritage Board Annual Report 2014/2015–Financial Statements.*

46. Huang Lijie, "Welcoming Wings: Asian Civilisations Museum Opens Two New Wings and Has a 24-hour Celebration of Its First Phase of Revamp," *The Straits Times,* November 10, 2015.

47. Levitt, "Arabia and the East," 95.

48. Lijie, "Welcoming Wings."

49. Murphy, "Interview: Murphy/Pearson."

50. Ibid.

51. Site visits, June 10, 2016, January 17, 2018, and December 11, 2019.

52. Of the 53,227 objects in the Tang Shipwreck Collection, 50,589 are ceramics from Changsha. Chong and Murphy, *Art and Exchange,* 19.

53. Charles Saumarez-Smith, "Museums, Artefacts, and Meanings," in *The New Museology,* ed. Peter Vergo (London: Reaktion Books, 1989).

54. John Guy, "Arab Dhows and the Persian Gulf-China Connection in the 8th and 9th Centuries" (paper presented at *Exhibition Symposium 'Secrets of the Sea: A Tang Shipwreck and Early Trade in Asia,'* Tang Center for Early China, New York, April 22, 2017).

55. Elizabeth S. Greene and Justin Leidwanger, "Museum Review: Damien Hirst's Tale of Shipwreck and Salvaged Treasure," *American Journal of Archaeology* 122, no. 1 (2018): 3.

56. Lijie, "Welcoming Wings."

57. *Aventuriers des Mers* is not to be confused with the *Oman and the Sea (Oman et la Mer)* exhibition, which ran at the National Navy Museum (Musée National de la Marine) in Paris from October 16, 2013, to January 5, 2014, and featured a traditional Omani boat, the *Badan,* which was docked in the Trocadero foundation. A ship's model of the *Jewel of Muscat* was displayed in the *Oman et la Mer* exhibition.

58. Site visit, August 2017.

59. The *Nizwa* was built in the Omani shipyards of Sur in 1992. Embassy of France in Muscat, "An Omani Dhow in Paris!" *Embassy of France in Muscat.* Last updated November 27, 2016. Accessed July 8, 2021. https://om.ambafrance.org/An-omani-dhow-in-Paris.

60. Caroline Delabroy, "Marseille Museum a Bridge between Mediterranean Cultures," *France 24,* June 7, 2013.

61. Ethnographic Museum of the Trocadero (Musée d'Ethnographie du Trocadéro) (1878–1936) and the two museums that succeeded it—the Museum of Man (Musée de l'Homme) and the National Museum of Popular Arts and Traditions (Musée National des Arts et Traditions Populaires).

62. Site visit, August 2017.

63. Heather Pringle, "Worries Mount over Smithsonian Shipwreck Exhibit," *Science* (website). Last updated April 29, 2011. Accessed April 7, 2022. https://www.science.org/content/article/worries-mount-over-smithsonian-shipwreck-exhibit.

64. Asia Society, "Asia Society–Frequently Asked Questions." *Asia Society.* Last updated 2018. Accessed July 8, 2021. http://asiasociety.org/about/faqs.

65. The collection has subsequently been enlarged through gifts and acquisitions, and its focus now includes both premodern Asia as well as contemporary Asian art. Natali Pearson, "Museums, Masterpieces and Morals." *New Mandala: Perspectives on the Past.* Last updated March 24, 2017. Accessed July 8, 2021. https://www.newmandala.org/museums-masterpieces-and-morals/.

66. Asia Society, "Boon Hui Tan appointed VP for Global Arts and Cultural Programs, Director of Asia Society Museum," press release, August 24, 2015, https://asiasociety.org/media /museum/tan-boon-hui-appointed-asia-society-vice-president-global-arts-and-cultural -programs-an.

67. Ivan Karp and Steven D. Levine, eds., *Exhibiting Cultures: The Poetics and Politics of Museum Display* (Washington and London: Smithsonian Institution Press, 1991).

68. Traci Watson, "Salvaged Treasures Trouble Scientists," *Nature* 542, no. 7640 (2017); Robin Pogrebin, "A Sunken Treasure Will Appear in New York Despite Its Controversial Excavation," *New York Times*, February 23, 2017; Victoria Stapley-Brown, "Controversial Trove from Imperial Chinese Shipwreck Lands in New York." Last updated March 7, 2017. Accessed April 7, 2022. https://www.theartnewspaper.com/2017/03/07/controversial-trove-from-imperial -chinese-shipwreck-lands-in-new-york.

69. Pogrebin, "A Sunken Treasure."

70. Kristin Nord, "Secrets of the Sea: A Tang Shipwreck & Early Trade in Asia." *Antiques and the Arts*. Last updated May 9, 2017. Accessed July 8, 2021. https://www.antiquesandthearts .com/secrets-of-the-sea-a-tang-shipwreck-early-trade-in-asia/.

71. Asia Society, *Secrets of the Sea: A Tang Shipwreck and Early Trade in Asia—A Conversation between Asia Society Vice President Tom Nagorski and Boon Hui Tan, Vice President of Global Arts and Cultural Programs*, distributed by YouTube, February 23, 2017. Accessed March 21, 2018. https://www.youtube.com/watch?v=gCyQx2BMmOk.

72. Stapley-Brown, "Controversial Trove Lands in NY."

73. Wall panel, *Secrets of the Sea*.

74. Aga Khan Museum, "Position Paper."

75. These articles were as follows, in the order presented:
Paul Forsythe Johnston, "Treasure Salvage, Archaeological Ethics and Maritime Museums," *International Journal of Nautical Archaeology* 22, no. 1 (1993); Julian Raby, "Why Exhibit This Material?" *Freer Sackler*. Last updated 2011. Accessed August 25, 2017. http://www. asia.si.edu/exhibitions/SW-CulturalHeritage/why.asp; Smithsonian Institution. *Tang Cargo Exhibit: Briefing Paper*; Sonia Kolesnikov-Jessop, "Ancient Arab Shipwreck Yields Secrets of Ninth-Century Trade," *New York Times*, March 7, 2011; Sean Kingsley, "Editorial: Tang Treasures, Monsoon Winds and a Storm in a Teacup." *Wreck Watch International: The Undertow*. Last updated March 13, 2011. Accessed July 8, 2021. http://wreckwatch.org/2011/03/13/ editorial-tang-treasures-monsoon-winds-and-a-storm-in-a-teacup/; Taylor, "Treasure Poses Ethics Issues"; Archaeological Institute of America, "AIA Statement on Belitung Shipwreck," press release, June 8, 2011, http:// www.archaeological.org/statement-on-belitung-shipwreck/; Jacqueline Trescott, "Sackler Gallery Cancels Controversial Exhibit of Tang Dynasty Treasures from Shipwreck," *Washington Post*, December 15, 2011; Meg Lambert, "Belitung Shipwreck." *Trafficking Culture*. Last updated August 8, 2012. Accessed July 8, 2021. http:// traffickingculture.org/encyclopedia/case-studies/biletung-shipwreck/; Wiener, "Treasures of the Lost Dhow."

76. Michael Flecker, "Rake and Pillage: The Fate of Shipwrecks in Southeast Asia," in *Marine Archaeology in Southeast Asia: Innovation and Adaptation*, ed. Heidi Tan (Singapore: Asian Civilisations Museum, 2012); Michael Flecker, "The Ethics, Politics, and Realities of Maritime Archaeology in Southeast Asia," *International Journal of Nautical Archaeology* 31, no. 1 (2002).

77. Pogrebin, "A Sunken Treasure."

78. New York University, "The Belitung Shipwreck Symposium: Intersections of History, Archaeology, and Capitalism." *New York University*. Last updated March 2017. Accessed July 8, 2021. https://wp.nyu.edu/belitung/symposium-schedule/.

79. Marco Meniketti, "Letter from Marco Meniketti, Chair of Advisory Council on Underwater Archaeology, to David Ludden, Professor of History, New York University" (February 20, 2017).

80. Principle 2, which requires taking into account the long-term interests of a site, and avoiding or protecting a site *in situ* when possible; Principle 3, which requires publishing the findings from the site as it is excavated; and Principle 6, which states that archaeologists should not assign a commercial value to artifacts unless required to do so to meet regulatory or legal obligations. Society for Historical Archaeology, *Committee: Ethics Toolbox*, Annapolis, MD: Society for Historical Archaeology (2015–2021).

81. Meniketti, "Letter from Marco Meniketti."

82. Kimberly Faulk, "Letter from Kimberly Faulk, Advisory Council on Underwater Archaeology, to Dr. Wayne Clough, Secretary Smithsonian Institution" (2011).

83. artsdecoantique, "A Sunken 9th C. Tang Dynasty Treasure (Belitung wreck) Price US$289.90." *eBay >decoartsantique*. Last updated February 2, 2011. Accessed October 23, 2017.

84. Presenters included Hsueh-man Shen (New York University), Pierre-Yves Manguin (L'École française d'Extrême-Orient), Tansen Sen (NYU Shanghai), Kenneth Hall (Ball State University), Edward A. Alpers (University of California, Los Angeles), and Roxani Margariti (Emory University).

85. Tang Center for Early China, "Exhibition Symposium 'Secrets of the Sea: A Tang Shipwreck and Early Trade in Asia'." *Tang Center for Early China*. Last updated 2017. Accessed July 8, 2021. http://tangcenter-columbia.org/exhibition-symposium-secrets-of-the-sea-a-tang-ship wreck-and-early-trade-in-asia/; Tang Center for Early China, "Exhibition Symposium: 'Secrets of the Sea: A Tang Shipwreck and Early Trade in Asia'." *Tang Center for Early China*. Last updated May 22, 2017. Accessed July 8, 2021. http://tangcenter-columbia.org/april-22–2017/.

86. Regina Krahl, "Keynote: Precious Metals, Precious Earths: Luxury Goods in Ninth-Century China" (paper presented at *Exhibition Symposium "Secrets of the Sea: A Tang Shipwreck and Early Trade in Asia,"* Tang Center for Early China, New York, April 21, 2017).

87. The morning panel included Arab Dhows and the Persian Gulf–China connection in the 8th and 9th Centuries, John Guy; The Tang Shipwreck and the Nature of China's Maritime Trade during the Late Tang Period, Derek Heng (who had recently moved from Ohio State University to Northern Arizona University); Frankincense and Camphor in Canton: Islamic Merchant-Seafarers and Indo-Pacific Trade, 8th–11th Centuries C.E., Bryan Averbuch (City University of New York). The afternoon panel included: The *Belitung* Shipwreck and Its Implications for the History of Tea, Victor Mair (University of Pennsylvania); Decorative Motifs on Changsha Bowls from the Belitung Wreck, Liu Yang (Minneapolis Institute of Art); Networks of Wealth: Tang Gold and Silverware in the Ninth Century, François Louis (the Bard Graduate Center).

88. Tang Center for Early China, "Exhibition Symposium"; Tang Center for Early China, "Exhibition Symposium: 'Secrets of the Sea'."

89. Wade, Geoff. "China's 'One Belt, One Road' Initiative." *Parliament of Australia* (website). Last updated 2016. Accessed April 7, 2022. https://www.aph.gov.au/about_parliament /parliamentary_departments/parliamentary_library/pubs/briefingbook45p/chinasroad. Tim

Winter, *Geocultural Power: China's Quest to Revive the Silk Roads for the Twenty-First Century* (Chicago: University of Chicago Press, 2019); Tim Winter, "Geocultural Power: China's Belt and Road Initiative," *Geopolitics* (2020), doi: 10.1080/14650045.2020.1718656.

90. Kennie Ting, "One Year at the Job—Maritime Silk Route and 'Ilm عِلْم." *Dream of a City.* Last updated September 28, 2017. Accessed July 8, 2021. https://tinyurl.com/KennyMaritime.

91. Yang Zheng Li Xing, "Hunan Bank of China Successfully Opened the Country's First Beneficiary's Personal Heritage Import Letter of Credit." *Changsha Evening News.* Last updated November 1, 2017. Accessed October 23, 2018. https://m.rednet.cn/mip/detail.asp?id=4462104.

92. At Nanjing Museum in Jiangsu province (September 28–December 28, 2017) and at Ningbo Museum in Zhejiang province (January 19–April 8, 2018). Lingchao Xu, "Shipwreck 'Treasures' Trace Maritime History." *Shine.* Last updated May 18, 2018. Accessed July 8, 2021. https://www.shine.cn/news/metro/1805184788/; Kun Zhang, "Sunken Ceramic Treasures Star in Maritime Exhibition." *China Daily.* Last updated May 29, 2018. Accessed July 8, 2021. http://www.chinadaily.com.cn/a/201805/29/WS5b0ca30ca31001b82571ccbd.html.

93. Simon Sinaga Boyke, "Marine Heritage Gallery." Last updated June 17, 2017. Accessed July 8, 2021. https://marineheritagegallery.wordpress.com/2017/06/17/pos-blog-pertama/.

94. A number of ceramic vessels, as well as the gold leaf, are also in the collection of the National Museum in Jakarta.

95. Korea–Singapore International Exchange Exhibition, *Secret of the Sea: The Tang Shipwreck* (Korea: National Research Institute of Maritime Cultural Heritage, 2018).

96. The *Sinan* was a ship from Ningbo (Mingzhou) in China's eastern province of Zhejiang. It sank off the coast of Korea in the fourteenth century and was discovered in 1976.

97. Igor Kopytoff, "The Cultural Biography of Things: Commoditization as Process," in *The Social Life of Things: Commodities in Cultural Perspective*, ed. A. Appadurai (Cambridge: Cambridge University Press, 1986).

Conclusion

1. Euan Graham, "Singapore at 50: Time's Up on the 'Fishing Village' Narrative." *Lowy Institute.* Last updated August 10, 2015. Accessed July 8, 2021. https://www.lowyinstitute.org/the-interpreter/singapore-50-times-fishing-village-narrative.

2. Chong Guan Kwa et al., eds., *Seven Hundred Years: A History of Singapore* (Singapore: National Library Board, 2019). In 2021, Singapore announced two wrecks had been discovered and excavated in its waters—a first for the nation. The wrecks, which date to the 14th and 18th centuries, were excavated by Michael Flecker. Ng Keng Gene, "How the Centuries-old Shipwrecks in Singapore Waters Were Discovered," *The Straits Times*, June 17, 2021.

3. John Miksic, *Singapore & the Silk Road of the Sea, 1300–1800* (Singapore: NUS Press, 2014), 444.

4. Tim Winter, "Geocultural Power: China's Belt and Road Initiative," *Geopolitics* (2020). doi: 10.1080/14650045.2020.1718656.

5. Ibid., 10.

6. Kate Hill, "Introduction: Museums and Biographies—Telling Stories about People, Things and Relationships," in *Museums and Biographies: Stories, Objects, Identities*, ed. Kate Hill (Boydell & Brewer, 2012), 8.

7. At the time of writing, Indonesia was again reviewing its moratorium on commercial salvage. See Natali Pearson, "At What Cost: The Impact of Indonesia's Omnibus Law on

Underwater Cultural Heritage." *New Mandala: Perspectives on the Past*. Last updated March 12, 2021. Accessed July 8, 2021. https://www.newmandala.org/museums-masterpieces-and-morals/; Natali Pearson, "An Ocean Sewn with Islands—and Shipwrecks," *The Jakarta Post*, July 2, 2021.

8. International Congress of Maritime Museums, "Open Letter to International Press and Cultural Heritage Networks re: RMS Titanic." *International Congress of Maritime Museums*. Last updated May 20, 2020. Accessed July 8, 2021. https://icmm-maritime.org/2020/06/01/open -letter-re-rms-titanic/.

9. International Congress of Maritime Museums, *The Åland Accord—Statement of Code of Ethics for Maritime Museums* (Mariehamn, Åland Islands: ICMM, 2019).

10. Ibid., Article 5.

11. ICOM, *Code of Ethics for Museums*, Article 3.4 (Paris: International Council of Museums, 2004).

12. Janet Marstine, Jocelyn Dodd, and Ceri Jones, "Reconceptualizing Museum Ethics for the Twenty-First Century: A View from the Field," in *The International Handbooks of Museum Studies*, ed. S. Macdonald and H. Rees Leahy (2015).

13. Ibid.

14. Christina Kreps, "Appropriate Museology and the "New Museum Ethics": Honoring Diversity," *Nordisk Museologi* 2 (2015).

15. Elizabeth S. Greene and Justin Leidwanger, "Museum Review: Damien Hirst's Tale of Shipwreck and Salvaged Treasure," *American Journal of Archaeology* 122, no. 1 (2018): 2.

16. Janet Marstine, "The Contingent Nature of the New Museum Ethics," in *The Routledge Companion to Museum Ethics: Redefining Ethics for the Twenty-First Century Museum*, ed. Janet Marstine (London and New York: Routledge, 2011), 7.

17. Ibid., 6.

18. Witcomb cited in Sandra H. Dudley, ed., *Museum Materialities: Objects, Engagements, Interpretations* (Abingdon: Routledge, 2010).

19. Igor Kopytoff, "The Cultural Biography of Things: Commoditization as Process," in *The Social Life of Things: Commodities in Cultural Perspective*, ed. A. Appadurai (Cambridge: Cambridge University Press, 1986).

20. Rodney Harrison, *Heritage: Critical Approaches* (London and New York: Routledge, 2013), 14.

21. Association of Critical Heritage Studies, "Association of Critical Heritage Studies Manifesto." Last updated 2012. Accessed July 8, 2021. https://www.criticalheritagestudies.org /history.

22. Tim Winter, "Clarifying the Critical in Critical Heritage Studies," *International Journal of Heritage Studies* 19, no. 6 (2013).

Bibliography

Adams, Jeffrey Lee. "New Directions in International Heritage Management Research." PhD dissertation. University of Minnesota. 2010.

Aga Khan Museum. "Mission." *Aga Khan Museum* (website). Last updated 2018. Accessed July 8, 2021. https://www.agakhanmuseum.org/about/mission.

———. "North American Exclusive Premiere Showcases Ancient Cargo Lost at Sea: The Lost Dhow Exhibition Opens December 13 at the Aga Khan Museum." Press release, December 8, 2014, https://www.agakhanmuseum.org/about/pdf/LostDhow_Press%20release2014.12.08.pdf.

———. "Shipwrecked at the Aga Khan: Position Paper." Toronto: Aga Khan Museum, 2014.

———. "Symposium: The Belitung Shipwreck and the Maritime Silk Route." Toronto: Aga Khan Museum, 2015.

Agius, Dionisius A. *In the Wake of the Dhow: The Arabian Gulf and Oman.* Reading, UK: Garnet Publishing, 2002.

Alisjahbana, Tamalia. "Indonesia Is Not Signing UNESCO's Convention for the Protection of Underwater Cultural Heritage." *Independent Observer* (website). Last updated November 28, 2019. Accessed April 6, 2020. https://observerid.com/indonesia-declines-to-sign-unesco-convention-for-protection-of-underwater-cultural-heritage/.

Allsop, Laura. "Shipwreck Exhibit Stirs Up Storm at Smithsonian." *CNN* (website). Last updated 2011. Accessed July 8, 2021. http://edition.cnn.com/2011/WORLD/asiapcf/03/19/indonesia.wreck.smithsonian.row/index.html.

Andaya, Leonard Y. *Leaves of the Same Tree: Trade and Ethnicity in the Straits of Melaka.* Honolulu: University of Hawai'i Press, 2008.

Anderson, Ross. "From the President's Desk: Advisory Council for Underwater Archaeology." *AIMA Newsletter: Australasian Institute for Maritime Archaeology* 30, no. 1 (March 2011).

Anonymous. "Asian Civilisation Museum's Founding Director to Retire." *The Straits Times*, 2008.

———. "Jewel of Muscat" (website). Last updated 2010. Accessed July 8, 2021. http://jewelofmuscat.tv/.

———. "Jewel of Muscat—Timeline" (website). Last updated 2010. Accessed July 8, 2021. http://jewelofmuscat.tv/the-timeline/.

———. "Sentosa Bids on Tang Artifacts." *United Press International* (website). Last updated 2004. Accessed July 8, 2021. https://www.upi.com/Sentosa-bids-on-Tang -artifacts/10701098655638/.

———. "Tongguanyao Museum Opens in Changsha." *China Daily* (website). Last updated May 16, 2018. Accessed July 8, 2021. http://www.chinadaily.com.cn/a/201805/16/ WS5afbf392a3103f6866ee8c1f.html.

———. "Unearthed Treasure Waits in Singapore." *The Jakarta Globe*, September 22, 2009.

———. "Unpublished Report: Discovery of the Shipwreck "BATU HITAM" of the Tang Period in 1998." 2002.

Archaeological Institute of America. "AIA Statement on Belitung Shipwreck." Press release, June 8, 2011, http:// www.archaeological.org/statement-on-belitung-shipwreck/.

artsdecoantique. "A Sunken 9th C. Tang Dynasty Treasure (Belitung wreck) Price US$289.90." *eBay >decoartsantique* (website). Last updated February 2, 2011. Accessed October 23, 2017.

Asia Society. "Asia Society—Frequently Asked Questions." *Asia Society* (website). Last updated 2018. Accessed July 8, 2021. http://asiasociety.org/about/faqs.

———. "Boon Hui Tan appointed VP for Global Arts and Cultural Programs, Director of Asia Society Museum." Press release, August 24, 2015, https://asiasociety.org/media /museum/tan-boon-hui-appointed-asia-society-vice-president-global-arts-and -cultural-programs-an.

———. "Photos: Asia Society Members Celebrate and Discover 'Secrets of the Sea'." *Asia Society* (website). Last updated March 8, 2017. Accessed July 8, 2021. http:// asiasociety.org/new-york/photos-asia-society-members-celebrate-and-discover -secrets-sea.

———. *Secrets of the Sea: A Tang Shipwreck and Early Trade in Asia—A Conversation between Asia Society Vice President Tom Nagorski and Boon Hui Tan, Vice President of Global Arts and Cultural Programs.* Distributed by YouTube, February 23, 2017. Accessed March 21, 2018. https://www.youtube.com/watch?v=gCyQx2BMmOk.

Aspinall, Edward. *Opposing Suharto: Compromise, Resistance, and Regime Change in Indonesia.* Stanford, CA: Stanford University Press, 2005.

Aspinall, Edward, and Greg Fealy, eds. *Soeharto's New Order and Its Legacy: Essays in Honour of Harold Crouch.* Canberra: ANU ePress, 2010.

Association of Critical Heritage Studies. "Association of Critical Heritage Studies Manifesto" (website). Last updated 2012. Accessed July 8, 2021. https://www.criticalheri tagestudies.org/history.

Austin, John. "Our New Dinner Service Is 235 years Old and Has Never Been Used." *Colonial Williamsburg News* 39, no. 8 (1986): 3.

Australian Museum. "Tektites." *Australian Museum* (website). Last updated November 12, 2018. Accessed April 2, 2020. https://australianmuseum.net.au/learn/minerals /shaping-earth/tektites/.

Balloffet, Pierre, François H. Courvoisier, and Joëlle Lagier. "From Museum to Amusement Park: The Opportunities and Risks of Edutainment." *International Journal of Arts Management* 16, no. 2 (2014): 4–18.

Bass, George, and Peter Throckmorton. *Cape Gelidonya: A Bronze Age Shipwreck*. Transactions of the American Philosophical Society. Philadelphia: American Philosophical Society, 1967.

Beaujard, Philippe. "Tang China and the Rise of the Silk Roads." In *The Worlds of the Indian Ocean: A Global History*, 18–41. Cambridge: Cambridge University Press, 2019.

Blair, Elizabeth. *From Beneath, A Smithsonian Shipwreck Controversy*. Radio Broadcast. Distributed by NPR. 2011.

Blake, Janet. "From Traditional Culture and Folklore to Intangible Cultural Heritage: Evolution of a Treaty." *Santander Art Culture Law Review* 2, no. 3 (2017): 41–60.

Blake, Janet, and Lucas Lixinski, eds. *The 2003 UNESCO Intangible Heritage Convention: A Commentary*. Series edited by Francesco Francioni and Ana Filipa Vrdoljak, Oxford Commentaries on International Cultural Heritage Law. Oxford: Oxford University Press, 2020.

Bloembergen, Marieke. *Colonial Spectacles: The Netherlands and the Dutch East Indies at the World Exhibitions, 1880–1931*. Translated by Beverly Jackson. Singapore: Singapore University Press, 2006.

Bloembergen, Marieke, and Martijn Eickhoff. "Conserving the Past, Mobilizing the Indonesian Future: Archaeological Sites, Regime Change and Heritage Politics in Indonesia in the 1950s." *Bijdragen tot de Taal-, Land- en Volkenkunde* 167, no. 4 (2011): 405–436.

———. "Critical Heritage Studies and the Importance of Studying Histories of Heritage Formation." *International Institute for Asian Studies* 70 (Spring 2015).

———. "Decolonizing Borobudur: Moral Engagements and the Fear of Loss. The Netherlands, Japan and (Post)Colonial Heritage Politics in Indonesia." In *Sites, Bodies and Stories: Imagining Indonesian History*, edited by Susan Legêne, Bambang Purwanto and Henk Schulte Nordholt, 33–66. Singapore: NUS Press, 2015.

———. "Exchange and the Protection of Java's Antiquities: A Transnational Approach to the Problem of Heritage in Colonial Java." *The Journal of Asian Studies* 72, no. 4 (November 2013): 893–916.

———. *The Politics of Heritage in Indonesia: A Cultural History*. Asian Connections. Edited by Sunil Amrith, Tim Harper, and Engseng Ho. Cambridge: Cambridge University Press, 2020.

———. "Save Borobudur! The Moral Dynamics of Heritage Formation in Indonesia across Orders and Borders, 1930s–1980s." In *Cultural Heritage as Civilizing Mission: From Decay to Recovery*, edited by Michael Falser, 83–119. Switzerland: Springer International Publishing, 2015.

Boyke, Simon Sinaga. "Marine Heritage Gallery" (website). Last updated June 17, 2017. Accessed July 8, 2021. https://marineheritagegallery.wordpress.com/2017/06/17/pos-blog-pertama/.

Brinkbäumer, Klaus, Clemens Höges, Jürgen Kremb, and Erich Wiedemann. "Pyramiden der Tiefsee." *Spiegel Special*, March 31, 2006, 8–15.

Brown, Roxanna M., and Sten Sjostrand. *Turiang: A Fourteenth-Century Shipwreck in Southeast Asian Waters*. Edited by David Kamansky. Pasadena, CA: Pacific Asia Museum, 2000.

Burger, Pauline, Armelle Charrié-duhaut, Jacques Connan, Pierre Albrecht, and Michael Flecker. "The 9th-Century-AD Belitung Wreck, Indonesia: Analysis of a Resin Lump." *International Journal of Nautical Archaeology* 39, no. 2 (2010): 383–386.

Butcher, John G., and R. E. Elson. *Sovereignty and the Sea: How Indonesia Became an Archipelagic State.* Singapore: NUS Press, 2017.

Campaign Brief Asia. "BBH Uncovers Treasures of the Deep." *Campaign Brief Asia* (website). Last updated March 14, 2011. Accessed July 8, 2021. http://www.campaignbriefasia .com/2011/03/bbh-uncovers-treasures-of-the.html.

Campbell, William. "Of Matters Maritime: Lively Display Centre of Sea-Going Activities." *The Straits Times*, September 15, 1974.

Canada Art Channel. *Interview with Alan Chong, Director, Asian Civilisations Museum.* Distributed by YouTube, December 12, 2014. Accessed April 10, 2017. https://www .youtube.com/watch?v=jfI5pnTn-1U.

Channel News Asia. "Asian Civilisations Museum to House Tang Shipwreck Collection." *Channel News Asia* (website). Last updated April 28, 2015. Accessed October 20, 2017. http://www.channelnewsasia.com/news/singapore/asian-civilisations/1813022.html.

Charlotte Minh-Hà L. Pham. "Asian Shipbuilding Technology." In *Training Manual for the UNESCO Foundation Course on the Protection and Management of Underwater Cultural Heritage in Asia and the Pacific.* Bangkok: UNESCO Bangkok, 2012.

Cheng, Nien Yuan. "'This Is My Doodle': Non-Participation, Performance, and the Singapore Memory Project." *Performance Paradigm* 14 (2018): 64–86.

Cherry, Deborah. "The Afterlives of Monuments." *South Asian Studies* 29, no. 1 (2013): 1–14.

Chittick, Andrew. "Maritime Trade and the Transformation of the Chinese Ceramics Industry." 2020. Paper presented at *China and the Maritime Silk Road: Shipwrecks, Ports and Products, Asian Civilisations Museum, Singapore, August 21–23, 2020.*

Chong, Alan, and Stephen Murphy, eds. *The Tang Shipwreck: Art and Exchange in the 9th Century.* Singapore: Asian Civilisations Museum, 2017.

———. "As Green as Jade: Celadons." In *The Tang Shipwreck: Art and Exchange in the 9th Century,* edited by Alan Chong and Stephen Murphy, 106–113. Singapore: Asian Civilisations Museum, 2017.

———. "Chinese on Board." In *The Tang Shipwreck: Art and Exchange in the 9th Century,* edited by Alan Chong and Stephen Murphy, 256–259. Singapore: Asian Civilisations Museum, 2017.

———. "Green-Splashed Ceramics for the Middle East." In *The Tang Shipwreck: Art and Exchange in the 9th Century,* edited by Alan Chong and Stephen Murphy, 118–135. Singapore: Asian Civilisations Museum, 2017.

Chow, Hugh. "Khoo Teck Puat's Grip on 3 Firms Bigger than Declared." *The Straits Times*, March 19, 2004.

Chua, Pei Jun Jermaine, and Tse Siang Lim. "UCV2208 Sinbad, Shipwrecks and Singapore." *National University of Singapore* (website). Last updated 2009/2010. Accessed July 8, 2021. https://tinyurl.com/Sinbadand-Singapore.

Clément, Etienne. "The Elaboration of the UNESCO 2001 Convention on the Protection of the Underwater Cultural Heritage." 2017. Paper presented at *Asia/Pacific Re-*

gional Conference on Underwater Cultural Heritage, Hong Kong SAR, Novem-ber 27–December 2, 2017.

Clifford, James. *Routes: Travel and Translation in the Late Twentieth Century.* Cambridge, MA: Harvard University Press, 1997.

Coleman, Patrick. "UNESCO and the Belitung Shipwreck: The Need for a Permissive Definition of 'Commercial Exploitation'." *The George Washington International Law Review* 45, no. 4 (2013): 847–874.

Counts, C. M. "Spectacular Design in Museum Exhibitions." *Curator* 52, no. 3 (2009): 273–288.

Crawford, Barclay. "Jakarta Targets Jebsen Chief over Role in Treasure Deal." *South China Morning Post*, February 28, 2006.

Curtis, Neil G. W. "Universal Museums, Museum Objects and Repatriation: The Tangled Stories of Things." *Museum Management and Curatorship* 21, no. 2 (2006): 117–127.

Da, Shao. "Sunken Chinese Treasures Rewrite History." *China through a Lens* (website). Last updated May 27, 2004. Accessed July 8, 2021. http://www.china.org.cn/english /2004/May/96658.htm.

Davies, Stephen. "Maritime Museums: Who Needs Them?" In *Nalanda-Sriwijaya Centre Working Paper Series*, edited by Geoff Wade and Joyce Zaide. Singapore: ISEAS, 2012.

de Caermichael, Christian. *The Book of 25—The Aga Khan Museum—The Lost Dhow Part 1.* Distributed by YouTube, January 19, 2015. Accessed April 10, 2017. https://www .youtube.com/watch?v=YIgE1Yg1DT8.

Dejiki, Nicholas. "The ArtScience Museum." *Dejiki* (blog). Last updated April 30, 2011. Accessed July 8, 2021. https://dejiki.com/2011/04/.

———. "Maritime Experiential Museum and Aquarium." *Dejiki* (blog). Last updated October 8, 2011. Accessed July 8, 2021. https://dejiki.com/2011/10/mema/.

Delabroy, Caroline. "Marseille Museum a Bridge between Mediterranean Cultures." *France 24* (website). Last updated June 7, 2013. Accessed April 7, 2022. https://www.france24 .com/en/20130604-marseille%E2%80%99-mucem-offers-bridge-between-mediter ranean-europe.

Doar, Bruce D. "China Maritime Silk Road Museum." *China Heritage Quarterly* (website). Last updated 2005. Accessed July 8, 2021. http://www.chinaheritagequarterly.org /articles.php?searchterm=001_maritimesilk.inc&issue=001.

Dongfang, Qi. "Gold and Silver on the Tang Shipwreck." In *The Tang Shipwreck: Art and Exchange in the 9th Century*, edited by Alan Chong and Stephen Murphy, 184–194. Singapore: Asian Civilisations Museum, 2017.

Dragojlovic, Ana, Marieke Bloembergen, and Henk Schulte Nordholt. "Colonial Re-Collections: Memories, Objects, and Performances." *Bijdragen tot de Taal-, Land- en Volkenkunde* 170, no. 4 (2014): 435–441.

Dudley, Sandra H., ed. "Materiality Matters: Experiencing the Displayed Object." *University of Michigan Working Papers in Museum Studies* 8 (2012): 1–9.

———. *Museum Materialities: Objects, Engagements, Interpretations.* Abingdon: Routledge, 2010.

Dyson, John. "Captain Hatcher's Richest Find." *Reader's Digest* 129, no.10 (1986), 111–115.

Electrosonic. "Typhoon Theatre at the Maritime Experiential Museum." *Electrosonic* (website). Last updated 2015. Accessed July 8, 2021. https://www.electrosonic.com /projects/typhoon-theatre-at-the-maritime-experiential-museum.

Embassy of France in Muscat. "An Omani Dhow in Paris!" *Embassy of France in Muscat* (website). Last updated November 27, 2016. Accessed July 8, 2021. https://om .ambafrance.org/An-omani-dhow-in-Paris.

Eng, Enilyn. "ArtScience: A Journey through Creativity." *Fresh Grads: Dreams of Life* (website). Last updated March 20, 2011. Accessed October 23, 2017. http://freshgrads .sg/index.php/articles/lifestyle/upcoming-events/1195-artscience-a-journey-through -creativity.

Farid, Hilmar. "The Backward Current of Culture—History as Critique." 2014. Paper presented at *Cultural Lecture, Arts Council of Jakarta, November 10, 2014.*

Faulk, Kimberly. "Letter from Kimberly Faulk, Advisory Council on Underwater Archaeology, to Dr. Wayne Clough, Secretary Smithsonian Institution." 2011.

Fincham, Derek. "Looting Shipwrecks, Archaeology and the Smithsonian." *Illicit Cultural Property* (blog). Last updated May 6, 2011. Accessed July 8, 2021. http://illicitcultural property.com/looting-shipwrecks-archaeology-and-the-smithsonian/.

———. "The Smithsonian Postpones Dhow Exhibition." *Illicit Cultural Property* (blog). Last updated June 29, 2011. Accessed July 8, 2021. http://illicitculturalproperty.com/ the-smithsonian-postpones-dhow-exhibition/.

Flecker, Michael. *The Archaeological Excavation of the 10th Century Intan Wreck.* BAR International Series 1047. Oxford: Archaeopress, 2002.

———. "The Bakau Wreck: An Early Example of Chinese Shipping in Southeast Asia." *International Journal of Nautical Archaeology* 30, no. 2 (2001): 221–230.

———. "The Ethics, Politics, and Realities of Maritime Archaeology in Southeast Asia." *International Journal of Nautical Archaeology* 31, no. 1 (2002): 12–24.

———. *Legislation on Underwater Cultural Heritage in Southeast Asia: Evolution and Outcomes.* Trends in Southeast Asia. Singapore: ISEAS-Yusof Ishak Institute, 2017.

———. "Maritime Archaeology in Southeast Asia." In *Southeast Asian Ceramics: New Light on Old Pottery*, edited by John Miksic, 34–47. Singapore: Southeast Asian Ceramic Society of Singapore, 2010.

———. "A Ninth-Century AD Arab or Indian Shipwreck in Indonesia: First Evidence for Direct Trade with China." *World Archaeology* 32, no. 3 (2001): 335–354.

———. "A 9th-Century Arab or Indian Shipwreck in Indonesian Waters." *International Journal of Nautical Archaeology* 29, no. 2 (2000): 199–217.

———. "A 9th-Century Arab or Indian Shipwreck in Indonesian Waters: Addendum." *International Journal of Nautical Archaeology* 37, no. 2 (2008): 384–386.

———. "The Origin of the Tang Shipwreck: A Look at Its Archaeology and History." In *The Tang Shipwreck: Art and Exchange in the 9th Century*, edited by Alan Chong and Stephen Murphy, 22–39. Singapore: Asian Civilisations Museum, 2017.

———. Personal Communication. September 19, 2020.

———. "Rake and Pillage: The Fate of Shipwrecks in Southeast Asia." In *Marine Archaeology in Southeast Asia: Innovation and Adaptation*, edited by Heidi Tan, 70–85. Singapore: Asian Civilisations Museum, 2012.

———. "Treasures from the Java Sea: The 10th Century Intan Shipwreck." *Heritage Asia Magazine*, December 2004.

———. "Wrecked Twice: Shipwrecks as a Cultural Resource in Southeast Asia." In *Rethinking Cultural Resource Management in Southeast Asia: Preservation, Development and Neglect*, edited by John Miksic, Geok Yian Goh, and Sue O'Connor, 15–35. London and New York: Anthem Press, 2011.

Forrest, Craig. *International Law and the Protection of Cultural Heritage*. Abingdon: Routledge, 2010.

"French Diver Condemns Detention by Indonesia over Salvaging Treasure." *Do Fundo Do Mar* (blog). Last updated March 27, 2006. Accessed July 8, 2021. http://dofundodomar.blogspot.com.au/2006_03_01_dofundodomar_archive.html.

Funsch, Linda Pappas. *Oman Reborn: Balancing Tradition and Modernization*. New York: Palgrave Macmillan, 2015.

Furman, Megan. *Jewel of Muscat: On the High Seas in a 9th Century Sailing Ship*. Oman: Lingua Franca Television Limited, 2015.

Gardellin, Roberto, and Aileen Lau. "Exhibition Review: The Belitung Wreck: A Tang Dynasty (618–906) Cargo." *Oriental Arts* LV, no. 1 (2005): 64–79.

Gautama, Gatot. "Underwater Archaeology in Indonesia: Experiences and Prospects." In *Marine Archaeology in Southeast Asia: Innovation and Adaptation*, edited by Heidi Tan, 114–119. Singapore: Asian Civilisations Museum, 2012.

Gibbins, David, and Jonathan Adams. "Shipwrecks and Maritime Archaeology." *World Archaeology* 32, no. 3 (2001): 279–291.

Gongaware, Laura. "To Exhibit or Not to Exhibit?: Establishing a Middle Ground for Commercially Exploited Underwater Cultural Heritage under the 2001 UNESCO Convention." *Tulane Maritime Law Journal* 37, no. 1 (2012): 203–229.

———. "Finding a Middle Ground in the Protection of the Underwater Cultural Heritage." Master's thesis. Texas A&M. 2013.

Gosden, Christopher, and Yvonne Marshall. "The Cultural Biography of Objects." *World Archaeology* 31, no. 2 (1999): 169–178.

Graham, Euan. "Singapore at 50: Time's Up on the 'Fishing Village' Narrative." *Lowy Institute* (website). Last updated August 10, 2015. Accessed July 8, 2021. https://www.lowyinstitute.org/the-interpreter/singapore-50-times-fishing-village-narrative.

Green, Jeremy. "Book Review: The Nanking Cargo by Michael Hatcher with Max de Rham and Other Books on the Geldermalsen." *International Journal of Nautical Archaeology* 17, no. 4 (1988): 357–359.

———. "Book Review: Shipwreck [*sic*]: Tang Treasures and Monsoon Winds." *International Journal of Nautical Archaeology* 40, no. 2 (2011): 449–452.

Greenblatt, Stephen. "Resonance and Wonder." In *Exhibiting Cultures: The Poetics and Politics of Museum Display*, edited by Ivan Karp and Steven D. Levine, 42–56. Washington and London: Smithsonian Institution Press, 1991.

Greene, Elizabeth S. "What Is Underwater Cultural Heritage and Why Does It Matter?" 2011. Paper presented at *Keeping the Lid on Davy Jones' Locker: The Protection of Underwater Cultural Heritage from Titanic to Today*, Washington, D.C., November 3, 2011.

Greene, Elizabeth S., and Justin Leidwanger. "Museum Review: Damien Hirst's Tale of Shipwreck and Salvaged Treasure." *American Journal of Archaeology* 122, no. 1 (2018).

Gurian, Elaine Heumann. *Civilizing the Museum: The Collected Writings of Elaine Heumann Gurian*. London and New York: Routledge, 2006.

Guy, John. "Arab Dhows and the Persian Gulf-China Connection in the 8th and 9th Centuries." 2017. Paper presented at *Exhibition Symposium 'Secrets of the Sea: A Tang Shipwreck and Early Trade in Asia', Tang Center for Early China, New York, April 22, 2017.*

———. "Hollow and Useless Luxuries: The Tang Shipwreck and the Emerging Role of Arab Traders in the Late First Millennium Indian Ocean." In *The Tang Shipwreck: Art and Exchange in the 9th Century*, edited by Alan Chong and Stephen Murphy, 160–176. Singapore: Asian Civilisations Museum, 2017.

———. "Late Tang Ceramics and Asia's International Trade." In *The Belitung Wreck: Sunken Treasures from Tang China*, edited by Jayne Ward, Zoi Kotitsa, and Alessandra D'Angelo, 57–73. New Zealand: Seabed Explorations, 2004.

———. "Rare and Strange Goods: International Trade in Ninth-Century Asia." In *Shipwrecked: Tang Treasures and Monsoon Winds*, edited by Regina Krahl, John Guy, J. Keith Wilson, and Julian Raby, 19–29. Singapore: Arthur M. Sackler Gallery, Smithsonian Institution, Washington D.C.; National Heritage Board, Singapore; Singapore Tourism Board, 2010.

Habermehl, Nick. "Shipwrecks and Lost Treasures of the Seven Seas—Famous Wrecks—VOC Geldermalsen: Porcelain and Gold Bullion from Asia." *Shipwrecks and Lost Treasures of the Seven Seas* (website). Last updated 2011. Accessed July 8, 2021. http:// www.oceantreasures.org/pages/content/famous-wrecks/old-treasures-and-shipwreck -news-voc-geldermalsen.html.

Hall, Jerome Lynn. "The Fig and the Spade: Countering the Deceptions of Treasure Hunters." *AIA Archaeology Watch* (website). Last updated August 15, 2007. Accessed April 7, 2022. https://www.archaeological.org/pdfs/archaeologywatch/figandspade.pdf.

Harpster, Matthew. "Shipwreck Identity, Methodology, and Nautical Archaeology." *Journal of Archaeological Method and Theory* 20, no. 4 (2013): 588–622.

Harrison, Rodney. *Heritage: Critical Approaches*. London and New York: Routledge, 2013.

Havid, Semy. "Harta Karun di Dasar Laut Perairan Indonesia, Menunggu Diangkat!" *Indonesia Waters* (blog). Last updated March 24, 2011. Accessed July 8, 2021. https:// semyhavid.blogspot.com.au/2011/03/harta-karun-di-dasar-laut-perairan.html.

Haw, Stephen. "The Genus Afzelia and the Belitung Ship." *Journal of the Royal Asiatic Society* 29, no. 3 (2019): 505–518.

———. "The Maritime Routes between China and the Indian Ocean during the Second to Ninth Centuries C.E." *Royal Asiatic Society* 27, no. 1 (2017): 53–81.

Heng, Derek. "The Tang Shipwreck and the Nature of China's Maritime Trade during the Late Tang Period." In *The Tang Shipwreck: Art and Exchange in the 9th Century*, edited by Alan Chong and Stephen Murphy, 142–159. Singapore: Asian Civilisations Museum, 2017.

Heng, Geraldine. "An Ordinary Ship and Its Stories of Early Globalism: World Travel, Mass Production, and Art in the Global Middle Ages." *Journal of Medieval Worlds* 1, no. 1 (2019): 11–54.

Hidalgo Tan, Noel. "Aboard the Jewel of Muscat." *The Southeast Asian Archaeology Newsblog* (blog). Last updated June 16, 2010. Accessed July 8, 2021. https://www.southeastasianarchaeology.com/2010/06/16/aboard-jewel-muscat/.

———. "The Belitung Shipwreck." *The Southeast Asian Archaeology Newsblog* (blog). Last updated June 28, 2007. Accessed July 8, 2021. http://www.southeastasianarchaeology.com/2007/06/28/the-belitung-shipwreck/.

———. "Whose Treasure Is It Anyway?" *The Southeast Asian Archaeology Newsblog* (blog). Last updated September 11, 2007. Accessed July 8, 2021. http://www.southeastasianarchaeology.com/2007/09/11/whose-treasure-is-it-anyway/.

Hill, Kate. "Introduction: Museums and Biographies—Telling Stories about People, Things and Relationships." In *Museums and Biographies: Stories, Objects, Identities*, edited by Kate Hill, 1–10. Boydell & Brewer, 2012.

Ho, Andy. "Academe's Exhibition of Parochialism." *The Straits Times*, December 23, 2011.

Holtorf, Cornelius. "Averting Loss Aversion in Cultural Heritage." *International Journal of Heritage Studies* 21, no. 4 (2015): 405–421.

Hosty, Kieran. "A Matter of Ethics: Shipwrecks, Salvage, Archaeology and Museums." *Bulletin of the Australasian Institute for Maritime Archaeology* 19, no. 1 (1995): 33–36.

Hourani, George. *Arab Seafaring in the Indian Ocean in Ancient and Early Medieval Times.* 2nd ed. Princeton, NJ: Princeton University Press, 1995.

ICMM. *The Åland Accord—Statement of Code of Ethics for Maritime Museums.* Mariehamn, Åland Islands: International Congress of Maritime Museums, 2019.

———. "Open Letter to International Press and Cultural Heritage Networks re: RMS Titanic." *International Congress of Maritime Museums* (website). Last updated May 20, 2020. Accessed July 8, 2021. https://icmm-maritime.org/2020/06/01/open-letter-re-rms-titanic/.

ICOM. *Code of Ethics for Museums.* Paris: International Council of Museums, 2004.

———. *ICOM Definition of a Museum.* Austria: International Council of Museums, 2007.

Jackson, Robert. "Sailing through Time: The Jewel of Muscat." *Saudi Aramco World: Arab and Islamic Cultures and Connections*, May/June 2012, 25–33.

Johnston, Paul Forsythe. "Treasure Salvage, Archaeological Ethics and Maritime Museums." *International Journal of Nautical Archaeology* 22, no. 1 (1993): 53–60.

Junaedy, Cahyo. "Arkeologi Bawah Air Nusantara." *Arkaeologi Bawah Air* (blog). Last updated 2011. Accessed March 3, 2018. http://arkeologibawahair.blogspot.com.au/2011/03/arkeologi-bawah-laut-nusantara.html.

Karp, Ivan, and Steven D. Levine, eds. *Exhibiting Cultures: The Poetics and Politics of Museum Display.* Washington and London: Smithsonian Institution Press, 1991.

Kesavapany, Krishnasamy. "Vital to Spread Knowledge about South-East Asia's Past." *The Straits Times*, January 13, 2012.

Kesavapany, Krishnasamy, and Geoff Wade. "Background Paper on Potential Singapore Maritime Museum." Singapore: ISEAS, 2009.

Khalik, Abdul. "Bribery Ensures Spoils Go to the Treasure Hunters." *The Jakarta Post*, March 20, 2006.

———. "Police Arrest Two Foreigners for Taking Ancient Ceramics." *The Jakarta Post*, March 10, 2006.

Kingsley, Sean. "Editorial: Tang Treasures, Monsoon Winds and a Storm in a Teacup." *Wreck Watch International: The Undertow* (blog). Last updated March 13, 2011. Accessed July 8, 2021. http://wreckwatch.org/2011/03/13/editorial-tang-treasures -monsoon-winds-and-a-storm-in-a-teacup/.

Kitchener, Darrel J., and Heny Kustiarsih, eds. *Ceramics from the Musi River, Palembang, Indonesia: Based on a Private Collection*. Vol. 22. Australian National Centre of Excellence for Maritime Archaeology, 2019.

KKP. "FAQ Barang Muatan Kapal Tenggelam (BMKT)." *Kementerian Kelautan dan Perikanan Republik Indonesia* (website). Last updated September 1, 2017. Accessed January 1, 2018. http://kkp.go.id/2017/09/01/faq-barang-muatan-kapal-tenggelam -bmkt/.

Kolesnikov-Jessop, Sonia. "Ancient Arab Shipwreck Yields Secrets of Ninth-Century Trade." *New York Times*, March 7, 2011.

Kopytoff, Igor. "The Cultural Biography of Things: Commoditization as Process." In *The Social Life of Things: Commodities in Cultural Perspective*, edited by A. Appadurai, 64–91. Cambridge: Cambridge University Press, 1986.

Korea–Singapore International Exchange Exhibition. *Secret of the Sea: The Tang Shipwreck*. Korea: National Research Institute of Maritime Cultural Heritage, 2018.

Krahl, Regina. "Green, White, and Blue-and-White Stonewares." In *The Tang Shipwreck: Art and Exchange in the 9th Century*, edited by Alan Chong and Stephen Murphy, 80–104. Singapore: Asian Civilisations Museum, 2017.

———. "Keynote: Precious Metals, Precious Earths: Luxury Goods in Ninth-Century China." 2017. Paper presented at *Exhibition Symposium 'Secrets of the Sea: A Tang Shipwreck and Early Trade in Asia,' Tang Center for Early China, New York, April 21, 2017*.

Krahl, Regina, John Guy, J. Keith Wilson, and Julian Raby. *Shipwrecked: Tang Treasures and Monsoon Winds*. Singapore: Arthur M. Sackler Gallery, Smithsonian Institution, Washington, D.C.; National Heritage Board, Singapore; Singapore Tourism Board, 2010.

———. *Shipwrecked: Tang Treasures and Monsoon Winds (Special Souvenir Edition)*. Special Souvenir Edition. Singapore: Arthur M. Sackler Gallery, Smithsonian Institution, Washington D.C.; National Heritage Board, Singapore; Singapore Tourism Board, 2011.

Kremb, Jürgen. "Fund Am Schwarzen Felsen." *Der Spiegel* 2004, 166–175.

Kreps, Christina. "Appropriate Museology and the 'New Museum Ethics': Honoring Diversity." *Nordisk Museologi* 2 (2015): 4–16.

Krzemnicki, Michael S. "Dating of 1000 year old Pearls from an Archeological Ship Wreck." *Facette Magazine*, February 2016, 29.

Kwa, Chong Guan, Derek Thiam Soon Heng, Peter Borschberg, and Tai Yong Tan, eds. *Seven Hundred Years: A History of Singapore*. Singapore: National Library Board, 2019.

Kwok, Kenson. "A Nation Forges Ahead 1985–1994: Hard Slog Building Up an Art Collection." In *Living the Singapore Story: Celebrating Our 50 Years, 1965–2015*, edited by Suk Wai Cheong. Singapore: National Library Board, 2015.

Lambert, Meg. "I'm Back. I Hope." *Things You Can't Take Back: The Illicit Antiquities Trade and Other Cultural Heritage Issues. By a Mouthy Youth. For the Mouthy Youth.* (blog). Last updated October 20, 2011. Accessed July 8, 2021. http://mouthyheritage.blogspot .com.au/2011/10/im-back-i-hope.html.

———. "Belitung Shipwreck." *Trafficking Culture* (website). Last updated August 8, 2012. Accessed July 8, 2021. http://traffickingculture.org/encyclopedia/case-studies /biletung-shipwreck/.

———. "In Response." *Things You Can't Take Back: The Illicit Antiquities Trade and Other Cultural Heritage Issues. By a Mouthy Youth. For the Mouthy Youth.* (blog). Last updated October 30, 2011. Accessed July 8, 2021. http://mouthyheritage.blogspot.com .au/2011/10/in-response.html.

———. "'Shipwrecked': Private Feuds and Public Consequences." Bachelor's thesis. Bennington College. 2012.

Lapian, Adrian B. *Orang Laut, Bajak Laut, Raja Laut: Sejarah Kawasan Laut Sulawesi Abad XIX.* Jakarta: Komunitas Baru, 2009.

Leadbetter, Michael. "Beyond the Temple Trail: The Sacred Landscapes of Southeast Asia." *TAASA Review* 25, no. 4 (2016): 24–26.

Lee, Han Shih. "Not So Khoo Kids." *The Asia Mag* (website). Last updated March 3, 2009. Accessed June 1, 2017. http://www.theasiamag.com/cheat-sheet/not-so-khoo-kids.

Lee, Pamelia. "50 Years of Urban Planning and Tourism." In *50 Years of Urban Planning in Singapore*, edited by Chye Kiang Heng, 197–210. Singapore and Hackensack, NJ: World Scientific Publishing Co. Pte. Ltd., 2017.

———. *Singapore, Tourism & Me.* Singapore: Pamelia Lee Pte. Ltd., 2004.

Legêne, Susan, Bambang Purwanto, and Henk Schulte Nordholt, eds. *Sites, Bodies and Stories: Imagining Indonesian History.* Singapore: NUS Press, 2015.

Leidwanger, Justin. "From Time Capsules to Networks: New Light on Roman Shipwrecks in the Maritime Economy." *American Journal of Archaeology* 121, no. 4 (2017): 595–619.

Leow, Rachel. "Curating the Oceans: The Future of Singapore's Past." *A Historian's Craft* (blog). Last updated July 14, 2009. Accessed July 8, 2021. https://idlethink.wordpress .com/2009/07/14/curating-the-oceans-the-future-of-singapores-past/.

———. "The Oceans Curated: A Review of 'Shipwrecked' at the Singapore ArtScience Museum." *A Historian's Craft* (blog). Last updated June 6, 2011. Accessed July 8, 2021. https://idlethink.wordpress.com/2011/06/06/the-oceans-curated/.

Levitt, Peggy. "Arabia and the East: How Singapore and Doha Display the Nation and the World." In *Artifacts and Allegiances: How Museums Put the Nation and the World on Display*, edited by Peggy Levitt, 91–132. Oakland: University of California Press, 2015.

Li, Baoping. "The Origin of Blue and White: Research Progress, Latest Finds and Their Significance." *The Oriental Ceramic Society Newsletter*, 16 (2008), 9–11.

Liebner, Horst Hubertus. "The Siren of Cirebon: A 10th Century Trading Vessel Lost in the Java Sea." PhD dissertation. University of Leeds. 2014.

Lijie, Huang. "Welcoming Wings: Asian Civilisations Museum Opens Two New Wings and Has a 24-hour Celebration of Its First Phase of Revamp." *The Straits Times*, November 10, 2015.

Louis, François. "Bronze Mirrors." In *Shipwrecked: Tang Treasures and Monsoon Winds*, edited by Regina Krahl, John Guy, J. Keith Wilson, and Julian Raby, 213–219. Singapore: Arthur M. Sackler Gallery, Smithsonian Institution, Washington D.C.; National Heritage Board, Singapore; Singapore Tourism Board, 2010.

———. "Gold and Silver." In *The Belitung Shipwreck: Sunken Treasures from Tang China*, edited by Jayne Ward, Zoi Kotitsa, and Alessandra D'Angelo, 135–153. New Zealand: Seabed Explorations, 2004.

———. "Metal Objects on the Tang Shipwreck." In *The Tang Shipwreck: Art and Exchange in the 9th Century*, edited by Alan Chong and Stephen Murphy, 204–219. Singapore: Asian Civilisations Museum, 2017.

———. "Mirrors." In *Shipwrecked: Tang Treasures and Monsoon Winds*, edited by Regina Krahl, John Guy, J. Keith Wilson, and Julian Raby, 82–83. Singapore: Arthur M. Sackler Gallery, Smithsonian Institution, Washington D.C.; National Heritage Board, Singapore; Singapore Tourism Board, 2010.

Lowry, Glenn. "Keynote." In *Making a Museum in the 21st Century*, edited by Melissa Chiu. New York: Asia Society, 2014.

Lu, Caixia. "The Belitung Shipwreck Controversy." *The Newsletter–Institute for Southeast Asian Studies, Nalanda-Sriwijaya Centre* no. 58 (Autumn/Winter 2011): 41–42.

Macleod, Duncan. "Shipwrecked Tang Treasures and Monsoon Winds." *The Inspiration Room* (website). Last updated 2011. Accessed July 8, 2021. http://theinspirationroom.com/daily/2011/shipwrecked-tang-treasures-and-monsoon-winds/.

Mair, Victor, and Erling Hoh. *The True History of Tea*. London: Thames & Hudson, 2009.

Manders, Martijn. "*In Situ* Preservation: The Preferred Option." *Museum International* 60, no. 4 (2008): 31–41.

Manguin, Pierre-Yves. "Austronesian Shipping in the Indian Ocean: From Outrigger Boats to Trading Ships." In *Early Exchange between Africa and the Wider Indian Ocean World*, edited by Gwyn Campbell. Palgrave Series in Indian Ocean World Studies, 51–76. Montreal: Palgrave Macmillan, 2016.

———. "Southeast Asian and Other Shipwrecks, Cosmopolitan Cargoes: A Distorted View of the Maritime Scene in the Java Sea." 2017. Paper presented at *Belitung Shipwreck Symposium: Intersections of History, Archaeology, and Capitalism, New York University, March 4, 2017*.

Marbun, Jhohannes. "An Advocacy Approach on Underwater Heritage in Indonesia, Case Study: An Auction on Underwater Heritage from Cirebon Waters in 2010." Yogyakarta: Masyarakat Advokasi Warisan Budaya (MADYA), 2011.

Marina Bay Sands. "ArtScience Museum at Marina Bay Sands Launches New Ticketing Structure Benefiting Singaporeans." Press release, July 29, 2011, https://tinyurl.com/MarinaBayTickets.

———. "Genghis Khan 'Invades' Singapore: Largest Collection of Genghis Khan Artifacts Makes Exclusive Asian Appearance in Singapore." Press release, January 10, 2011, https://tinyurl.com/MarinaBayGenghisKhan.

———. "Titanic: The Artifact Exhibition Sails to New Record-Breaking Attendance." Press release, May 4, 2012, https://tinyurl.com/MarinaBayTitanic.

———. "Travel the Ancient Silk Road for the First Time in Asia." Press release, February 1, 2011, https://tinyurl.com/MarinaBaySilkRoad.

Marina Bay Sands and Singapore Tourism Board. "Shipwrecked: Tang Treasures and Monsoon Winds Exhibition Extended till 2 October 2011 at ArtScience Museum: Complimentary Entry to Exhibition during the Week of National Day." Press release, July 28, 2011, https://tinyurl.com/ShipwreckedExtension.

Marstine, Janet. "The Contingent Nature of the New Museum Ethics." In *The Routledge Companion to Museum Ethics: Redefining Ethics for the Twenty-First Century Museum*, edited by Janet Marstine, 3–25. London and New York: Routledge, 2011.

Marstine, Janet, Jocelyn Dodd, and Ceri Jones. "Reconceptualizing Museum Ethics for the Twenty-First Century: A View from the Field." In *The International Handbooks of Museum Studies*, edited by Sharon Macdonald and Helen Rees Leahy, 69–96, 2015.

Marx, Robert F., and Jenifer Marx. *The Search for Sunken Treasure: Exploring the World's Great Shipwrecks*. Toronto: Key-Porter Books, 1993.

Mathers, William M., and Michael Flecker. *Archaeological Recovery of the Java Sea Wreck*. Annapolis, Maryland MD: Pacific Sea Resources, 1997.

McCann, Ian Kenneth. "The Binh Chau Anchors: A 7th–8th CE Composite Conundrum." Master's thesis. University of New England. 2019.

McCarthy, Michael. "Museums and Maritime Archaeology." In *The Oxford Handbook of Maritime Archaeology*, edited by Ben Ford, Donny L. Hamilton, and Alexis Catsambis, 1032–1054. Oxford: Oxford University Press, 2011.

McDowell, Robin. "Indonesia's Shipwrecks Means Riches and Headaches." *San Diego Union Tribune*, March 31, 2012.

McGrail, Sean. "Models, Replicas and Experiments in Nautical Archaeology." *The Mariner's Mirror* 61, no. 1 (1975): 3–8.

Meide, Chuck. "Smithsonian Postpones Controversial Treasure Hunting Shipwreck Exhibit." *The Keeper's Blog* (blog). Last updated July 6, 2011. Accessed April 7, 2022. https://www.staugustinelighthouse.org/2011/07/06/smithsonian-postpones-controversial-treasure-hunting-shipwreck-exhibit/.

Mellefont, Jeffrey. "UNESCO Heritage-lists Indonesian Wooden Boat Building." *Perspectives on the Past at New Mandala* (website). Last updated 2018. Accessed June 7, 2021. https://www.newmandala.org/unesco-heritage-lists-indonesian-wooden-boat-building/.

Mellman, Ira. "Treasure Hunting Complicates Exhibit of Important Shipwreck Find." *Voice of America* (website). Last updated 2011. Accessed July 8, 2021. https://www.voanews.com/a/treasure-hunting-complicates-important-shipwreck-find-120730039/167373.html.

Meniketti, Marco. "Letter from Marco Meniketti, Chair of Advisory Council on Underwater Archaeology, to David Ludden, Professor of History, New York University." February 20, 2017.

Message, Kylie. "Contentious Politics and Museums as Contact Zones." In *Museum Theory*, edited by Andrea Witcomb and Kylie Message, 253–281. Hoboken, NJ: John Wiley & Sons, 2020.

———. *The Disobedient Museum: Writing at the Edge.* Oxford and New York: Routledge, 2018.

Micklewright, Nancy, and Cheryl Sobas, *Shipwrecked: Tang Treasures and Monsoon Winds.* Distributed by YouTube, June 18, 2011. Accessed July 13, 2021. https://www.youtube.com/watch?v=6gQbvUVWSto.

Miksic, John, ed. "GES1030 Singapore and the Sea." *National University of Singapore* (website). Last updated 2016/2017. Accessed July 8, 2021. https://tinyurl.com/SingaporeandtheSea.

———. "SE3227 Maritime History and Culture of Southeast Asia." *National University of Singapore* (website). Last updated 2017/2018. Accessed July 8, 2021. https://tinyurl.com/MaritimeSEA.

———. "Shipwrecked." *IIAS–The Newsletter* 64, no. Summer (2013): 43.

———. "Sinbad, Shipwrecks and Singapore." In *The Tang Shipwreck: Art and Exchange in the 9th Century*, edited by Alan Chong and Stephen Murphy, 222–232. Singapore: Asian Civilisations Museum, 2017.

———. *Singapore & the Silk Road of the Sea, 1300–1800.* Singapore: NUS Press, 2014.

———. *Southeast Asian Ceramics: New Light on Old Pottery.* Singapore: Southeast Asian Ceramic Society of Singapore, 2010. Miksic, John, and Geok Yian Goh. *Ancient Southeast Asia.* Abingdon and New York: Routledge, 2017.

Miller, George L. "The Second Destruction of the Geldermalsen." *Historical Archaeology* 26, no. 4 (1992): 124–131.

Ming-liang, Hsieh. "The Navigational Route of the Belitung Wreck and Late Tang Ceramic Trade." In *The Belitung Wreck: Sunken Treasures from Tang China*, edited by Jayne Ward, Zoi Kotitsa, and Alessandra D'Angelo, 74–91. New Zealand: Seabed Explorations, 2004.

Muqbil, Imtiaz. "Pamelia Lee, Senior Director, Tourism Development, Singapore Tourism Board." *Travel Impact Newswire* (website). Last updated February 2, 2017. Accessed July 8, 2021. https://www.travel-impact-newswire.com/2017/02/pamelia-lee-senior-director-tourism-development-singapore-tourism-board/.

Murphy, Stephen. "Asia in the Ninth Century: The Context of the Tang Shipwreck." In *The Tang Shipwreck: Art and Exchange in the 9th Century*, edited by Alan Chong and Stephen Murphy, 12–20. Singapore: Asian Civilisations Museum, 2017.

Nanda, Akshita. "Moored in Controversy: The Excavation of Tang Relics from a Shipwreck in Indonesia Puts Museums in a Quandary." *The Straits Times*, June 30, 2011.

———. "Our Treasures." *National Heritage Board* (website). Last updated August 29, 2017. Accessed July 8, 2021. https://oursgheritage.sg/what-is-the-heritage-plan-for-singapore/our-treasures/.

———. "Salvaging a Wrecked Opportunity." *The Straits Times*, December 28, 2011.

National Heritage Board. *National Heritage Board Annual Report 2014 / 2015–Financial Statements.* Singapore: National Heritage Board, 2015.

Nayati, Pudak. "Ownership Rights over Archaeological / Historical Objects Found in Indonesian Waters: Republic of Indonesia Act No. 5 of 1992 on Cultural Heritage Objects and Its Related Regulations." *Singapore Journal of International and Comparative Law* 2 (1998): 142–174.

———. "Ownership Rights over Archaeological / Historical Objects Found at Sea: A Study of the Republic of Indonesia's Act No. 5 of 1992." Master's thesis. Dalhousie University. 1995.

New York University. "The Belitung Shipwreck Symposium: Intersections of History, Archaeology, and Capitalism." *New York University* (website). Last updated March 2017. Accessed July 8, 2021. https://wp.nyu.edu/belitung/symposium-schedule/.

Ng, Kai Ling. "Sail through a Typhoon at Maritime Museum: Typhoon Theatre among Main Attractions." *The Straits Times*, October 7, 2011.

Ng, Keng Gene. "How the Centuries-old Shipwrecks in Singapore Waters Were Discovered." *The Straits Times*, June 17, 2021.

Nord, Kristin. "Secrets of the Sea: A Tang Shipwreck & Early Trade in Asia." *Antiques and the Arts* (website). Last updated May 9, 2017. Accessed July 8, 2021. https://www.antiquesandthearts.com/secrets-of-the-sea-a-tang-shipwreck-early-trade-in-asia/.

O'Keefe, Patrick J. "Protecting the Underwater Cultural Heritage: The International Law Association Draft Convention." *Marine Policy* 20, no. 4 (1996): 297–307.

Oegroseno, Arif Havas. "Indonesia's Maritime Boundaries." In *Indonesia beyond the Water's Edge: Managing an Archipelagic State*, edited by Robert Cribb and Michele Ford. Singapore: ISEAS Publishing, 2009.

Office of Public Affairs and Marketing, Freer Gallery of Art and the Arthur M. Sackler Gallery. "Smithsonian and Singapore Organize World Tour of Shipwreck Treasure: Exhibition Highlights One of the Most Important Marine Archaeological Finds of the Late 20th Century." Press release, September 27, 2010, https://web.archive.org/web/20100927094716/http://www.asia.si.edu/press/prShipwreck.htm.

Ong, Iliyas. "In New Museum, Art and Science Collide." *Design Taxi* (website). Last updated February 25, 2011. Accessed October 23, 2017. http://designtaxi.com/article/101536/In-New-Museum-Art-and-Science-Collide/.

Origin Studios. "Aga Khan Museum The Lost Dhow: A Discovery from the Maritime Silk Route." (website). Last updated 2015. Accessed July 8, 2021. http://www.originstudios.com/aga-khan-lost-dhow/.

Paterson, Tony. "The 1,200-year-old Sunken Treasure That Revealed an Undiscovered China." *The Independent*, April 13, 2004.

Pearson, Natali. "At What Cost: The Impact of Indonesia's Omnibus Law on Underwater Cultural Heritage." *New Mandala: Perspectives on the Past* (blog). Last updated March 12, 2021. Accessed July 8, 2021. https://www.newmandala.org/museums-masterpieces-and-morals/.

———. "Heritage Adrift." *Inside Indonesia* (website). Last updated July 5, 2016. Accessed July 8, 2021. http://www.insideindonesia.org/heritage-adrift.

———. "Interview with Michael Flecker (Director, Maritime Explorations)." June 15, 2016.

———. "Interview with Stephen Murphy (Curator, Asian Civilisations Museum)." June 10, 2016.

———. "Maritime Archaeology in Vietnam: Australian Involvement." *TAASA Review* 25, no. 4 (2016): 14–15.

———. "Museums, Masterpieces and Morals." *New Mandala: Perspectives on the Past* (blog). Last updated March 24, 2017. Accessed July 8, 2021. https://www.newmandala .org/museums-masterpieces-and-morals/.

———. "Naval Shipwrecks in Indonesia." 2017. Paper presented at *Asia/Pacific Regional Conference on Underwater Cultural Heritage, Hong Kong SAR, November 27–December 2, 2017.*

———. "An Ocean Sewn with Islands—and Shipwrecks." *The Jakarta Post*, July 2, 2021, 7.

———. "Salvaging a Wreck: The Afterlife of the *Belitung* Shipwreck." PhD dissertation. University of Sydney. 2018.

———. "Shipwrecked? The Ethics of Underwater Cultural Heritage in Indonesia." *TAASA Review* 25, no. 2 (2016): 10–11.

Peng, Aw Kah. "Foreword." In *Shipwrecked: Tang Treasures and Monsoon Winds*, edited by Regina Krahl, John Guy, J. Keith Wilson, and Julian Raby. Singapore: Arthur M. Sackler Gallery, Smithsonian Institution, Washington D.C.; National Heritage Board, Singapore; Singapore Tourism Board, 2010.

The Periplus Maris Erythraei: Text with Introduction, Translation, and Commentary. Translated by Lionel Casson. Princeton: Princeton University Press, 1989.

Pogrebin, Robin. "A Sunken Treasure Will Appear in New York Despite Its Controversial Excavation." *New York Times*, February 23, 2017.

Preeyanuch Jumprom. "The Phanom Surin Shipwreck: New Discovery of an Arab-style Shipwreck in Central Thailand." *Southeast Asian Ceramics Museum Newsletter* VIII, no. 1 (June–September 2014): 1–4.

Pringle, Heather. "Flap over Shipwreck Exhibit." *Science*, 331, no. 6023 (2011): 1370–1371.

———. "Smithsonian Scuppers Shipwreck Exhibit, Plans to Re-Excavate." *Science* (website). Last updated December 16, 2011. Accessed April 7, 2022. https://www.science .org/content/article/smithsonian-scuppers-shipwreck-exhibit-plans-re-excavate.

———. "Smithsonian Shipwreck Exhibit Draws Fire from Archaeologists." *Science* (website). Last updated March 10, 2011. Accessed April 7, 2022. https://www.science.org /content/article/smithsonian-shipwreck-exhibit-draws-fire-archaeologists.

———. "Worries Mount over Smithsonian Shipwreck Exhibit." *Science* (website). Last updated April 29, 2011. Accessed April 7, 2022. https://www.science.org/content /article/worries-mount-over-smithsonian-shipwreck-exhibit.

Prott, Lyndel V. "The Significance of World-Wide Ratification of the 2001 UNESCO Convention on the Protection of the Underwater Cultural Heritage." In *Towards Ratification: Papers from the 2013 AIMA Conference Workshop*, edited by Graeme Henderson and Andrew Viduka, 5–6. Fremantle: Australasian Institute for Maritime Archaeology, 2014.

Qin, Dashu. "Sri Vijaya—The Entrepôt for Circum-Indian Ocean Trade—The Evidence from Chinese Documentary Records and Materials from Shipwrecks of the 9th–10th Centuries." 2014. Paper presented at *ST Lee Annual Lecture in Asian Art and Archaeology, The University of Sydney, September 2, 2014.*

Qin, Dashu, and Kunpeng Xiang. "Sri Vijaya as the Entrepôt for Circum-Indian Ocean Trade." *Études Océan Indien* 46–47 (2011): 308–336.

Quah, Michelle. "Khoo Sisters Fined $500,000, Escape Jail." *The Business Times*, 21 June 2005.

Raby, Julian. "Why Exhibit This Material?" *Freer Sackler* (website). Last updated 2011. Accessed August 25, 2017. http://www.asia.si.edu/exhibitions/SW-CulturalHeritage/why. asp.

Ray, Himanshu Prabha. *Coastal Shrines and Transnational Maritime Networks across India and Southeast Asia*. London: Routledge India, 2021. doi:10.4324/9780429285233.

Resorts World Sentosa. "Discovering Southeast Asia's Maritime History." *Resorts World Sentosa* (blog). Last updated September 6, 2011. Accessed October 19, 2017. http:// www.rwsentosablog.com/discovering-southeast-asias-maritime-history/.

———. *Maritime Experiential Museum & Aquarium Grand Opening*. Distributed by YouTube, October 19, 2011. Accessed October 19, 2017. https://www.youtube.com/watch ?v=55cf-YaW3xU.

———. "Presenting the World's Largest Oceanarium, the Marine Life Park." *Resorts World Sentosa* (blog). Last updated September 25, 2011. Accessed October 19, 2017. http://www.rwsentosablog.com/so%E2%80%A6-why-should-i-visit-mema/.

———. "Sentosa Proceeds to Buy 9th Century Treasure: New Maritime Heritage Foundation Set Up." Press release, April 8, 2005, https://archive.is/NXdL3.

———. "So . . . Why Should I Visit Maritime Experiential Museum?" *Resorts World Sentosa* (blog). Last updated October 3, 2011. Accessed October 19, 2017. http://www .rwsentosablog.com/so%E2%80%A6-why-should-i-visit-mema/.

Respess, Amanda. "The Abode of Water: Shipwreck Evidence and the Maritime Circulation of Medicine between Iran and China in the 9th through 14th Centuries." PhD dissertation. University of Michigan. 2020.

———. "Islamic Inscriptions on the Belitung Bowls: Ninth-century Changsha Designs for the Abbasid Market." 2020. Paper presented at *China and the Maritime Silk Road: Shipwrecks, Ports and Products, Asian Civilisations Museum, Singapore, August 21–23, 2020*.

Rettel, Andreas. "The Concept of the Conservation of Seawater Finds." In *The Belitung Shipwreck: Sunken Treasures from Tang China*, edited by Jayne Ward and Zoi Kotitsa, 93–115. New Zealand: Seabed Explorations Ltd., 2004.

Reuters. "US$50m Plan Is in Place to Salvage Asian Wrecks." *New Zealand Herald*, August 3, 2006.

Ridwan, Nia Naelul Hasanah. "The Belitung Shipwreck and Its Ceramic Cargo." *Southeast Asian Ceramics Museum Newsletter* 8, no. 1 (June–September 2014): 4–8.

———. "Maritime Archaeology in Indonesia: Resources, Threats, and Current Integrated Research." *Journal of Indo-Pacific Archaeology* 36 (2015): 16–24.

Rochon, Lisa. "Maki's Aga Khan Museum Makes Its Debut." *Architectural Record* (website). Last updated September 19, 2014. Accessed July 8, 2021. https://www.archite cturalrecord.com/articles/3233-makis-aga-khan-museum-makes-its-debut?

Rodley, Edward. "The Ethics of Exhibiting Salvaged Shipwrecks." *Curator* 55, no. 4 (2012): 383–391.

Rodrigues, Jennifer, Lyndel V. Prott, Patrick J. O'Keefe, Aleks Seglenieks, Graeme Henderson, Vicki Richards, Jeremy Green, and Myra Stanbury. "The UNESCO Convention on the Protection of the Underwater Cultural Heritage: A One-Day Workshop held on 23 May 2004." *Department of Maritime Archaeology, WA Maritime Museum* (website). Last updated 2005. Accessed May 2, 2015. http://museum.wa.gov.au/maritime -archaeology-db/sites/default/files/no._189_uneco_report.pdf.

Rohde, Pelin. "Sunken Treasures, Worldly Pleasures: The Smithsonian's Shipwrecked Exhibition and the Museum's Role in the Preservation of Underwater Cultural Heritage." Master's thesis. Harvard University. 2013.

Sandell, Richard. *Museums, Prejudice and the Reframing of Difference.* London and New York: Routledge, 2007.

Sarr, Felwine, and Bénédicte Savoy. *The Restitution of African Cultural Heritage: Toward a New Relational Ethics.* Paris: 2018.

Sasongko, Mahirta, Geok Yian Goh, Widya Nayati, and John Miksic. *Dieng Temple Complex Excavation Report.* Singapore: NUS Press, 2010.

Saumarez-Smith, Charles. "Museums, Artefacts, and Meanings." In *The New Museology*, edited by Peter Vergo, 6–21. London: Reaktion Books, 1989.

Scriven, Guy. "Interview with Tilman Walterfang." *Seabed Explorations* (website). Last updated February 24, 2013. Accessed July 8, 2021. https://tilmanwalterfang.org/news /index.html.

Secrets of the Tang Treasure Ship. Documentary. Distributed by National Geographic. 2010.

See, Sharon. "ACM Showcases Tang Dynasty Artefacts from 9th Century Shipwreck." *Archaeology News Network* (website). Last updated January 31, 2012. Accessed July 8, 2021. https://archaeologynewsnetwork.blogspot.com.au/2012/01/acm-showcases -tang-dynasty-artefacts.html#CVH411MFVXFdLop8.97.

Severin, Tim. *The Sindbad Voyage.* New York: Putnam, 1983.

Shefi, Debra. "The 'First Option' in Underwater Cultural Heritage Management: A Plea for the Establishment and Application of Universal Terminology and Best Practices." *The Journal of the Australasian Institute for Maritime Archaeology* 37 (2013): 20–25.

Shen, Chen. "The Lost Dhow: Cultural Heritage and Museum Engagement." 2015. Paper presented at *Lost Dhow Symposium, Aga Khan Museum, Toronto, February 28, 2015.*

Sheriff, Abdul. *Dhow Cultures of the Indian Ocean: Cosmopolitanism, Commerce, and Islam.* London: Hurst, 2010.

Shetty, Deepika. "Tang Treasures at Hotel." *The Straits Times*, February 9, 2012.

———. "Treasure Trails: Three Mega Exhibitions Opening at the ArtScience Museum Take Viewers Back into the Past." *The Straits Times*, 2011.

Shuyi, Kan. "Ceramics from Changsha: A World Commodity." In *The Tang Shipwreck: Art and Exchange in the 9th Century*, edited by Alan Chong and Stephen Murphy, 44–60. Singapore: Asian Civilisations Museum, 2017.

Singapore Law Reports, "Rickshaw Investments Ltd and Another v Nicolai Baron von Uexkull: Case number CA 30/2006, SUM 2929/2006," Court of Appeal Judgement. Last updated 2006. Accessed April 7, 2022. https://www.singaporelawwatch.sg/Portals /0/Docs/Judgments/%5b2006%5d%20SGCA%2039.pdf.

Siow, L. S., and V. Chong. "Khoo Teck Puat's Secret Stakes Come to Light." *The Business Times*, March 19, 2004.

Smith, Laurajane. "A Pilgrimage of Masculinity: The Stockman's Hall of Fame and Outback Heritage Centre." *Australian Historical Studies* 43, no. 3 (2012): 472–482.

———. *Uses of Heritage*. London: Routledge, 2006.

Smithsonian Institution. *Archives Accession 15–174: Office of the Secretary, Administrative Records*. Washington D.C.: Smithsonian Institution, 2011.

———. "Media Backgrounder: Discovery, Recovery, Conservation and Exhibition of the Belitung Cargo." Press release, March 16, 2011, http://www.asia.si.edu/press/2011/prShipwreckedBackgrounder.asp.

———. "Shipwrecked: Tang Treasures and Monsoon Winds–About the Organizers." *Smithsonian Institution* (website). Last updated 2011. Accessed October 11, 2017. https://www.asia.si.edu/Shipwrecked/about.asp.

———. "Shipwrecked: Tang Treasures and Monsoon Winds–Venues." *Smithsonian Institution* (website). Last updated 2011. Accessed October 11, 2017. https://www.asia.si.edu/Shipwrecked/venues.asp.

———. *Smithsonian Directive 604: Misconduct in Research*. Washington D.C.: Smithsonian Institution, 2009.

———. *Tang Cargo Exhibit: Briefing Paper*. Washington D.C.: 2012.

Society for Historical Archaeology *Committee: Ethics Toolbox*. Maryland: Society for Historical Archaeology 2015–2021.

Staniforth, Mark. "Factors Affecting the Ratification of the UNESCO Convention 2001 in the Asia and the Pacific Region." 2017. Paper presented at *ICLAFI—ICUCH Symposium, Amersfoort, The Netherlands, July 1, 2017*.

Staples, Eric. "An Experiment in Arab Navigation: The Jewel of Muscat Passage." In *The Principles of Arab Navigation*, edited by Anthony R. Constable and William Facey. London: Arabian Publishing, 2013.

———. "Sewn-Plank Reconstructions of Oman: Construction and Documentation." *International Journal of Nautical Archaeology* 48, no. 2 (2019): 314–334.

Staples, Eric, and Lucy Blue. "Archaeological, Historical, and Ethnographic Approaches to the Study of Sewn Boats: Past, Present, and Future." *International Journal of Nautical Archaeology* 48, no. 2 (2019).

Stapley-Brown, Victoria. "Controversial Trove from Imperial Chinese Shipwreck Lands in New York." (website). Last updated March 7, 2017. Accessed April 7, 2022. https://www.theartnewspaper.com/2017/03/07/controversial-trove-from-imperial-chinese-shipwreck-lands-in-new-york.

Stargardt, Janice. "Indian Ocean Trade in the Ninth and Tenth Centuries: Demand, Distance, and Profit." *South Asian Studies* 30, no. 1 (2014): 35–55.

Strati, Anastasia. *Draft Convention on the Protection of Underwater Cultural Heritage: A Commentary Prepared for UNESCO by Dr. Anastasia Strati*. 1999.

Sudaryadi, Agus. "The Belitung Wreck Site after Commercial Salvage in 1998." 2011. Paper presented at *Asia/Pacific Regional Conference on Underwater Cultural Heritage, Manila, The Philippines, November 8–11, 2011*.

Tahir, Zainab. "Cultural Attitude and Values towards Underwater Cultural Heritage and Its Influences on the Management Actions in Indonesia." 2014. Paper presented at

Asia/Pacific Regional Conference on Underwater Cultural Heritage, Honolulu, Hawaii, May 14, 2014.

Tan, Heidi, ed. *Marine Archaeology in Southeast Asia: Innovation and Adaptation.* Singapore: Asian Civilisations Museum, 2012.

Tang Center for Early China. "Exhibition Symposium 'Secrets of the Sea: A Tang Shipwreck and Early Trade in Asia'." *Tang Center for Early China* (website). Last updated 2017. Accessed July 8, 2021. http://tangcenter-columbia.org/exhibition-symposium-secrets-of-the-sea-a-tang-shipwreck-and-early-trade-in-asia/.

———. "Exhibition Symposium: 'Secrets of the Sea: A Tang Shipwreck and Early Trade in Asia'." *Tang Center for Early China* (website). Last updated May 22, 2017. Accessed July 8, 2021. http://tangcenter-columbia.org/april-22-2017/.

Taylor, Jean Gelman. *Indonesia: Peoples and Histories.* New Haven, CT and London: Yale University Press, 2003.

Taylor, Kate. "Treasure Poses Ethics Issues for Smithsonian." *New York Times*, April 24, 2011.

———. "Why Toronto's Aga Khan Park Risks Becoming a White Elephant." *The Globe and Mail*, May 28, 2015.

The Mary Rose. *Mary Rose Museum* (website). Last updated 2021. Accessed July 8, 2021. https://maryrose.org/.

Ting, Kennie. "One Year at the Job—Maritime Silk Route and 'Ilm علم." *Dream of a City* (blog). Last updated September 28, 2017. Accessed July 8, 2021. https://tinyurl.com/KennyMaritime.

Tjoa-Bonatz, Mai Lin. "Struggles over Historic Shipwrecks in Indonesia: Economic Versus Preservation Interests." In *Cultural Property and Contested Ownership: The Trafficking of Artefacts and the Quest for Restitution*, edited by Brigitta Hauser-Schäublin and Lyndel V. Prott, 85–107. Abingdon and New York: Routledge, 2016.

TMC News. "Nelson-Based Treasure Hunter Pleased with Indonesian Crackdown." *TMC News* (website). Last updated April 9, 2006. Accessed July 8, 2021. http://www.tmcnet.com/usubmit/2006/04/09/1554954.htm.

Trescott, Jacqueline. "Another Smithsonian Debate: Should the Sackler Gallery Show Artifacts from a Commercially Excavated Shipwreck?" *Washington Post*, April 28, 2011.

———. "Sackler Gallery Cancels Controversial Exhibit of Tang Dynasty Treasures from Shipwreck." *Washington Post*, December 15, 2011.

———. "Sackler Gallery Postpones Controversial 'Shipwreck' Show." *Washington Post*, June 28, 2011.

Underwater Times News Service. "German, French Diver Accused of Looting Shipwreck In Indonesia Freed on Bond; '100% Innocent'." *Underwater Times News Service* (website). Last updated April 13, 2006. Accessed July 8, 2021. http://www.underwatertimes.com/news.php?article_id=17561090324.

UNESCO. *Convention on the Protection of the Underwater Cultural Heritage.* Paris: United Nations Educational, Scientific and Cultural Organization, 2001.

———. "In Situ Protection." *United Nations Educational, Scientific and Cultural Organization* (website). Last updated 2017. Accessed April 3, 2018. http://www.unesco.org/new/en/culture/themes/underwater-cultural-heritage/protection/protection/in-situ-protection/.

Viganò, Marco. "The Lost Wood: African Seamasters across the Indian Ocean." 2013. Paper presented at *Anno Domini 1000, Finale Ligure, Italy, August 31–September 1, 2013.*

Vosmer, Tom. "The Jewel of Muscat: Reconstructing a Ninth-Century Sewn-Plank Boat." In *Shipwrecked: Tang Treasures and Monsoon Winds*, edited by Regina Krahl, John Guy, J. Keith Wilson, and Julian Raby, 120–135. Singapore: Arthur M. Sackler Gallery, Smithsonian Institution, Washington D.C.; National Heritage Board, Singapore; Singapore Tourism Board, 2010.

———. Personal communication. June 10, 2021.

———. Personal communication. July 6, 2021.

Vosmer, Tom, Luca Belfioretti, Eric Staples, and Alessandro Ghidoni. "The 'Jewel of Muscat' Project: Reconstructing an Early Ninth-Century CE Shipwreck." *Proceedings of the Seminar for Arabian Studies* 41 (2011): 411–424.

Wade, Geoff. "China's 'One Belt, One Road' Initiative." *Parliament of Australia* (website). Last updated 2016. Accessed April 7, 2022. https://www.aph.gov.au/about_parliament /parliamentary_departments/parliamentary_library/pubs/briefingbook45p/china sroad.

Wahjudin, Judi. "Human Resources Development in Indonesia's Underwater Archaeology." 2011. Paper presented at *Asia/Pacific Regional Conference on Underwater Cultural Heritage, Manila, The Philippines, November 8–12, 2011.*

Waller, Daniel James. "Curious Characters, Invented Scripts, and . . . Charlatans? " 'Pseudo-Scripts' " in the Mesopotamian Magic Bowls." *Journal of Near Eastern Studies* 78, no. 1 (2019): 119–139.

Walterfang, Tilman. "About Seabed Explorations." *Seabed Explorations* (website). Last updated 2012. Accessed July 8, 2021. https://tilmanwalterfang.org/Tilman-Walterfang -Seabed-Explorations-3.html.

———. "Discoveries > The Wrecks > Tang Wreck > Exhibitions." *Seabed Explorations* (website). Last updated 2012. Accessed July 8, 2021. https://seabedexplorations.com /discoveries/.

———. Personal communication. March 14–April 16, 2018.

———. "The Wrecks > Tang Wreck > Conservation > Overview." *Seabed Explorations* (website). Last updated 2012. Accessed July 8, 2021. http://seabedexplorations.com /discoveries/.

Watkins, Kirk W. "Titanic Intellectual Lawsuit Launched to Sink Competing Enterprise." *The National Law Review* (blog). Last updated March 9, 2013. Accessed October 23, 2017. https://www.natlawreview.com/article/titanic-intellectual-property-lawsuit -launched-to-sink-competing-enterprise.

Watson, Traci. "Salvaged Treasures Trouble Scientists." *Nature* 542, no. 7640 (February 9, 2017): 150.

Wiener, James. "Treasures of the Lost Dhow." *Ancient History et cetera* (website). Last updated 2015. Accessed July 8, 2021. http://etc.ancient.eu/interviews/treasures-of -the-lost-dhow/.

Wilson, J. Keith, and Michael Flecker. "Dating the Belitung Shipwreck." In *Shipwrecked: Tang Treasures and Monsoon Winds*, edited by Regina Krahl, John Guy, J. Keith

Wilson, and Julian Raby, 35–37. Singapore: Arthur M. Sackler Gallery, Smithsonian Institution, Washington D.C.; National Heritage Board, Singapore; Singapore Tourism Board, 2010.

Winter, Tim. "Clarifying the Critical in Critical Heritage Studies." *International Journal of Heritage Studies* 19, no. 6 (2013): 532–545.

———. "Geocultural Power: China's Belt and Road Initiative." *Geopolitics* (2020). Published electronically January 28, 2020. doi: 10.1080/14650045.2020.1718656.

———. *Geocultural Power: China's Quest to Revive the Silk Roads for the Twenty-First Century.* Chicago: University of Chicago Press, 2019.

———. "Heritage and the Politics of Cooperation." In *The Oxford Handbook of Public Heritage Theory and Practice*, edited by Angela Labrador and Neil Silberman, 1–15. Oxford: Oxford University Press, 2018.

Witcomb, Andrea. "Book Review: Civilizing the Museum: The Collected Writings of Elaine Heumann Gurian." *reCollections* 1, no. 2 (2006).

———. "Exhibition Review: *Titanic: The Artefact Exhibition.*" *reCollections* 5, no. 2 (2010).

Wong, Melissa Wansin. "Negotiating Class, Taste and Culture via the Arts Scene in Singapore." *Asian Theatre Journal* 29, no. 1 (2012): 233–254.

Woodward, Robyn. "The Belitung Shipwreck: To Exhibit or Not: A Question of Ethics." *INA Quarterly* 39 (2012): 22–24.

Worrall, Simon. *The Lost Dhow: A Discovery from the Maritime Silk Route.* Toronto: Aga Khan Museum, 2015.

———. "Made in China: A 1,200-year-old Shipwreck Opens a Window on Ancient Global Trade." *National Geographic Magazine*, June 2009.

Xing, Yang Zheng Li. "Hunan Bank of China Successfully Opened the Country's First Beneficiary's Personal Heritage Import Letter of Credit." *Changsha Evening News* (website). Last updated November 1, 2017. Accessed October 23, 2018. https://m.rednet.cn/mip/detail.asp?id=4462104.

Xu, Lingchao. "Shipwreck 'Treasures' Trace Maritime History." *Shine* (website). Last updated May 18, 2018. Accessed July 8, 2021. https://www.shine.cn/news/metro/1805184788/.

Yeo, George. "Shipwrecked: Tang Treasures and Monsoon Winds—Opening Address." In *Marine Archaeology in Southeast Asia: Innovation and Adaptation*, edited by Heidi Tan and Alan Chong, 184–188. Singapore: Asian Civilisations Museum, 2011.

———. "Transcript of Speech Made at Jewel of Muscat Gala Dinner, July 5, 2010, Asian Civilisations Museum." *Facebook* (website). Last updated July 11, 2010. Accessed May 7, 2016. https://www.facebook.com/note.php?note_id=407550843615.

Yurnaldi. "Melacak Kapal Karam." *Arkeologi Bawah Air* (website). Last updated April 28, 2010. Accessed April 7, 2022. https://arkeologibawahair.wordpress.com/2010/12/16/arkeologi-bawah-air-melacak-kapal-karam/.

Zhang, Kun. "Sunken Ceramic Treasures Star in Maritime Exhibition." *China Daily* (website). Last updated May 29, 2018. Accessed July 8, 2021. http://www.chinadaily.com.cn/a/201805/29/WS5b0ca30ca31001b82571ccbd.html.

Zhu, Charlie. "Treasure Hunter Seeks More Shipwreck Riches in Asia." *TreasureNet* (website). Last updated August 20, 2006. Accessed April 7, 2022. https://www.treasurenet.com/threads/indonesia-and-the-far-east.25153/.

Index

Page numbers in boldface type refer to illustrations.

shipwrecks (cont.)
169n82; *Batavia*, 161n40; *Binh Thuan*,
155n48; *Buaya*, 127; *Cirebon*, **42**, 81, 103,
127, 159n5, 163n76, 165n110;
Geldermalsen, 45–46, 52, 56, 62, 70,
154n32, 154n41, 155n52; HMAS *Perth*
(I), 155n52; *Intan*, 14, **42**, 57, 60, 62, 64,
71, 73–77, 81, 127, 134; *Maranei*, 57; *Mary
Rose*, 5–6, 55, 161n40; *Nanhai One*, 6, 81,
161n40; *Nanking*, 46; *Phanom Surin*,
21–22, 23, 68, **91**, 133; *Sinan*, 128–129,
180n96; *Titanic*, 8–9, 52, 97, 144n31,
171n100; *Turiang*, 57; USS *Houston*,
155n52; *Vasa*, 161n40
Silk Road. *See* Belt and Road Initiative
Singapore Tourism Board, 77–79, 102, 113
Sriwijaya, 41, 43, 45, 78, 127, 132

standards, international, 6, 9, 49, 130,
134–136, 144n20, 145n33, 181n9;
conventions, 4, 50–51, 54; UNCLOS,
51–52, 154n42, 156n64; UNESCO, 2, 4,
5, 6, 50–55, 112, 143n1–2, 156n62,
156n70, 157n72–73, 157n77, 157n79

timber. *See* construction
Tongguanyao Museum, 80, 81, 127, 141
tourism, 96; benefits for local communities,
60–61, 69; economic development, 55, 77,
106; sustainable, 15, 61. *See also* heritage

UNCLOS. *See* standards, international
UNESCO. *See* standards, international

wadding. *See* construction

About the Author

NATALI PEARSON teaches and researches at the Sydney Southeast Asia Centre at the University of Sydney, Australia. Her research focuses on the protection, management, and interpretation of underwater cultural heritage. She is coeditor of *Perspectives on the Past* at New Mandala and a regular contributor to *The Conversation* and *Inside Indonesia*. Natali holds a PhD in Museum Studies. She has worked at the Asia Society's galleries in New York and Hong Kong, and as a consultant to the Asia Society Arts & Museum Summit. She is an alumna of the Australian Consortium for In-Country Indonesian Studies and the Asialink Leaders Program. Prior to joining the university, she worked in Asia-focused defense and anti–money laundering/counterterrorism financing roles in the Australian federal government.